CHINESE

A ROUGH GUIDE DICTIONARY PHRASEBOOK

Compiled by

LEXUS

Credits

Compiled by Lexus with Julian Ward and Xu Yinong
Lexus Series Editor: Sally Davies
Rough Guides Phrase Book Editor: Jonathan Buckley
Rough Guides Series Editor: Mark Ellingham

First edition published in 1997 by Rough Guides Ltd,
62–70 Shorts Gardens, London WC2H 9AB.
Revised in 1999.

Distributed by the Penguin Group.

Penguin Books Ltd, 27 Wrights Lane, London W8 5TZ
Penguin Books USA Inc., 375 Hudson Street, New York 10014, USA
Penguin Books Australia Ltd, 487 Maroondah Highway,
PO Box 257, Ringwood, Victoria 3134, Australia
Penguin Books Canada Ltd, Alcorn Avenue,
Toronto, Ontario, Canada M4V 1E4
Penguin Books (NZ) Ltd, 182–190 Wairau Road,
Auckland 10, New Zealand

Typeset in Bembo and Helvetica to an original design by Henry Iles.
Printed in Spain by Graphy Cems.

No part of this book may be reproduced in any form without permission from
the publisher except for the quotation of brief passages in reviews.

© Lexus Ltd 1999
288pp.

British Library Cataloguing in Publication Data
A catalogue for this book is available from the British Library.

ISBN 1-85828-607-7

HELP US GET IT RIGHT

Lexus and Rough Guides have made great efforts to be accurate and
informative in this Rough Guide Mandarin Chinese phrasebook. However,
if you feel we have overlooked a useful word or phrase, or have any other
comments to make about the book, please let us know. All contributors
will be acknowledged and the best letters will be rewarded with a free
Rough Guide phrasebook of your choice. Please write to 'Mandarin
Chinese Phrasebook Update', at either Shorts Gardens (London) or Hudson
Street (New York) – for full addresses see above. Alternatively you can email
us at mail@roughguides.co.uk

Online information about Rough Guides can be found at our website
www.roughguides.com

CONTENTS

Introduction

The Rough Guide Mandarin Chinese dictionary phrasebook is a highly practical introduction to the contemporary language. Laid out in clear A-Z style, it uses key-word referencing to lead you straight to the words and phrases you want – so if you need to book a room, just look up 'room'. The Rough Guide gets straight to the point in every situation, in bars and shops, on trains and buses, and in hotels and banks.

The first part of the Rough Guide is a section called **The Basics**, which sets out the fundamental rules of the language and its pronunciation, with plenty of practical examples. You'll also find here other essentials like numbers, dates, telling the time and basic phrases.

Forming the heart of the guide, the **English-Chinese** section gives easy-to-use transliterations of the Chinese words plus the text in Chinese script, so that if the pronunciation proves too tricky, you can simply indicate what you want to say. To get you involved quickly in two-way communication, the Rough Guide also includes dialogues featuring typical responses on key topics – such as renting a room and asking directions. Feature boxes fill you in on cultural pitfalls as well as the simple mechanics of how to make a phone call, what to do in an emergency, where to change money, and more. Throughout this section, cross-references enable you to pinpoint key facts and phrases, while asterisked words indicate where further information can be found in the Basics.

The **Chinese-English** section is in two parts: a dictionary, arranged phonetically, of all the words and phrases you're likely to hear (starting with a section of slang and colloquialisms); then a compilation, arranged by subject, of various signs, labels, instructions and other basic words you may come across in print or in public places.

Finally the Rough Guide rounds off with an extensive **Menu Reader**. Consisting of food and drink sections arranged by subject (each starting with a list of essential terms), it's indispensable whether you're eating out, stopping for a quick drink or browsing through a local food market.

一路顺风
yílù shùnfēng!
have a good trip!

Basics

Pronunciation

Throughout this book Chinese words have been written in the standard romanized system known as pinyin (see below). Pinyin, which was introduced in China in the 1950s, can for the most part be used as a guide to pronunciation. However, some of the syllables are not pronounced in an immediately obvious way. For this reason, a simplified transliteration is also provided in almost all instances. This transliteration should be read as though it were English, bearing in mind the notes on pronunciation below:

Vowels

ah	long 'a' as in **a**rt		eh	'e' as in b**e**d
ai	'i' as in **I**, **eye** .		oh	'o' as in g**o**, **oh**
ay	as in h**ay**		ow	as in c**ow**

Consonants

ch	as in **Ch**inese		ts	as in **ts**ar
dz	like the 'ds' in hea**ds**		y	as in **y**es
g	hard 'g' as in **g**et			

Pinyin

Chinese words are made up of one or more syllables, each of which is represented in the written language by a character. These syllables can be divided into initials (consonants) and finals (vowels or vowels followed by either n or ng). In spoken Chinese, the consonant finals are often not fully sounded. A full list of initials and finals, along with the closest equivalent sound in English appears below. There are, however, some sounds that are unlike anything in English. In this pronunciation guide, words containing these sounds are given in Chinese characters as well; ask a Chinese person to pronounce them for you.

Initials

f, l, m, n, s, w and y	are all similar to English
b, d, g	similar to English, but a shorter sound
p, t, k	a more emphatic pronunciation as in **p**op, **t**ap and **c**ap (more strongly pronounced than b, d and g above)
h	slightly harsher than an **h** in English, closer to the **ch** sound in lo**ch** or Ba**ch**
j, q, x	pronounced with the lips positioned as if you were smiling:
j	'j' as in **j**eer
q	'ch' as in **ch**eer
x	'sh' as in **sh**eer
c	'ts' as in **ts**ar 菜
z	'ds' as in hea**ds** 自
ch, sh, zh, r	the last group of initials is the most difficult for a non-Chinese to perfect; they are all pronounced with the tip of the tongue curled back till it touches the palate:
ch	as ch in bir**ch** 茶
sh	as sh in **sh**ower 少
zh	as ge in bud**ge** 中
r	as r in **r**ung 人

Finals

a	as in **a**rt
ai	as in **ai**sle
an	as in r**an**, but with a longer 'a' as in **a**rt
ang	as in h**ang**, but with a longer 'a' as in **a**rt
ao	'ow' as in c**ow**
e	like the 'e' in th**e** or the 'u' in f**u**r

ei	as in w**ei**ght
en	as in shak**en**
eng	like 'en' followed by a softly spoken 'g'
er	similar to **err**, pronounced with the tongue curled back so that it touches the palate
i	usually pronounced as in margar**i**ne; however, after the initials c, ch, r, s, sh, z and zh it is pronounced like the 'i' in sh**i**rt or f**i**rst
ia	'ya' as in **ya**rn
ian	similar to **yen**
iang	**yang** ('i' plus 'ang', but with shorter 'a' sound)
iao	'yow' as in **yow**l
ie	'ye' as in **ye**ti
in	as in d**in**
ing	as in br**ing**
iong	**yoong** ('i' plus 'ong')
iu	'yo' as in **yo-yo**
o	as in l**o**re
ou	like **oh**
ong	**oong** ('ung' as in l**ung**, with the vowel given a longer, more rounded sound)
u	as in r**u**le; or like French **u**ne or German **ü**ber
ua	**wah** ('wa' plus 'a' as in **a**rt)
uai	similar to **why**
uan	**wahn** in most cases ('w' plus 'an'); after 'y', the second pronunciation of 'u' plus 'an'
uang	**wahng** ('w' plus 'ang')
ue	the second pronunciation of 'u' plus 'e' as in b**e**t
ui	'wai' as in **wai**t
un	as in f**u**ngi
uo	similar to **war**
ü	like French **u**ne or German **ü**ber
üe	'ü' followed by 'e' as in b**e**t

Northern Chinese

In Northern Chinese, the suffix **r** is often placed at the end of a syllable, producing a sound reminiscent of the burr of southwest England. This is represented in pinyin by the addition of an **r** to the syllable so that **men** (door), for example, becomes **menr**, with the 'n' barely pronounced. Such pronunciation is most apparent in Beijing.

Tones

The Chinese language only uses about four hundred different sounds. The number of sounds available is increased by the use of tones: the particular pitch at which a word is pronounced determines its meaning. The same combination of letters pronounced with a different tone will produce different words. There are four tones: first tone (ˉ), second tone (ˊ), third tone (ˇ) and fourth tone (ˋ).

Not all syllables are pronounced with tones; where there is no tone, the syllable is written without a tone mark. Often when you have a word consisting of two syllables, the second syllable, for example, **xuésheng** (student), is written without a tone.

In Chinese, the tone is as important a part of the word as the consonant and vowel sounds. Context usually makes the meaning clear, but it is still important whenever possible to use the correct tone in order to reduce the chance of misunderstanding. The character **ma** [mah] has five meanings, differentiated by the tones:

mā	妈	mother
má	麻	hemp
mǎ	马	horse
mà	骂	abuse, scold
ma	吗	(added to the end of a sentence to turn it into a question)

To help you get a clearer idea of how the tones sound,

Chinese character equivalents are given for the words in this section. Ask a Chinese speaker to read the words for you so that you can hear the tonal differences.

First tone (ˉ). High, level tone, with unchanging volume, held briefly:

gū [goo]	孤	solitary
guān [gwahn]	观	look at
kāi	开	open (verb)
yān [yahn]	烟	cigarette

Second tone (ˊ). Starting about mid-range, rising quickly and becoming louder; a shorter sound than the first tone, similar to a question showing surprise such as 'eh?':

héng [hung]	衡	balance (verb)
rén [run]	人	person
shí [shur]	十	ten
yán [yahn]	言	speech

Third tone (ˇ). Starts low and falls before rising again to slightly above the starting point; starts quietly then increases in volume; slightly longer than first tone:

běn [bun]	本	book
fǎ [fah]	法	law
qǐ [chee]	起	rise (verb)
yǎn [yahn]	掩	cover (verb)

Fourth tone (ˋ). Starts high, falling abruptly in pitch and volume; shorter than the second tone:

bèn [bun]	笨	stupid
dà [dah]	大	big
pà [pah]	怕	fear (verb)
yàn [yahn]	雁	wild goose

The tones can be illustrated in diagram form like this:

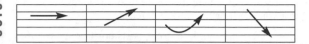

In speech, a third tone which precedes another third tone becomes a second tone. Where instances of this occur in the pinyin text of this phrasebook, the adjustment has been made.

Abbreviations

adj	adjective
pl	plural
pol	polite
sing	singular

General

The Chinese language has a number of characteristics which are very different from European languages, the most important of these being that there are no inflections for case, number or gender and that verbs do not decline. References to past, present or future are identified by context and the addition of various time words such as **míngtian** [ming-tyen] (tomorrow), **jântian** [jin-tyen] (today), or **qùnián** [chew-nyen] (last year). In both the written and spoken language, statements are kept short and the repetition of what has already been expressed is avoided. Pronouns, both personal and impersonal, are often omitted.

Nouns

Singular and plural forms of nouns are nearly always the same. For example, **shū** can mean either 'book' or 'books' depending on the context:

wó mǎile yíběn shū
wor mai-lur yee-bun shoo
I bought one book

wó mǎile liángběn shū
wor mai-lur lyang-bun shoo
I bought two books

The few exceptions tend to be nouns used in addressing groups of people, in which case the suffix **-men** is added to the end of the noun:

péngyoumen
pung-yoh-mun
friends

háizimen
hai-dzur-mun
children

However, **-men** is not used for the plural when numbers are involved as the plural is obvious from the context:

sìge péngyou
sur-gur pung-yoh
four friends

Articles

There is no equivalent in Chinese for either the definite article 'the' or the indefinite articles 'a' and 'an'. The exact meaning will be clear from the context or word order. Therefore, **zázhì** (magazine) can mean 'a magazine' or 'the magazine' depending on the context.

If you want to be more precise, you can use **nèi** (that) or **zhèi** (this) with the appropriate measure word (see page 22).

The number **yī** (one), along with the appropriate measure word (see page 22) can also be used to translate 'a/an'. But often in such sentences **yi** is either unstressed or omitted altogether, leaving just the measure word:

> **wó xiáng mǎi yìběn zázhì**
> wor hsyang mai yee-bun dzah-jur
> I am going to buy a magazine

or:

> **wó xiáng mái běn zázhì**
> I am going to buy a magazine

Adjectives

Adjectives are placed before the noun and usually the word **de** is added between the adjective and the noun:

piányi de shū	**hěn suān de sùcài**
pyen-yee dur shoo	hun swahn dur soo-tsai
cheap book(s)	very sour vegetable dish(es)

The **de** is frequently omitted if the adjective is monosyllabic:

gǔ huà	**hǎo bànfǎ**
goo hwah	how bahn-fah
ancient paintings	a good method

Some nouns can be used adjectivally:

lìshǐ	**lìshǐ xiǎoshuō**
lee-shur	lee-shur hsyow-shwor
history	historical novel(s)

shùxué	**shùxué jiàokēshū**
shoo-hsyew-eh	shoo-hsyew-eh jyow-kur-shoo
mathematics	maths textbook

Adjectival Verbs

Some verbs also function as adjectives and are known as adjectival verbs. In sentences using an adjectival verb, the word order is:

noun subject + **hěn** + adjectival verb

The word **hěn** has little meaning, unless it is stressed, when it means 'very'.

sùcài hěn suān	**shū dōu hěn piányi**
soo-tsai hun swahn	shoo doh hun pyen-yee
the vegetable dish is very sour	the books are all cheap

Suàn means 'to be sour' and **piányi** 'to be cheap'.

For greater emphasis, add **tài** to mean 'very', 'really' or 'extremely':

tài hǎole
tai how-lur
that's really great

Comparatives

To form the comparative (more ..., ...-er) in sentences when only one thing is referred to, most often in response to a question, an adjectival verb is used by itself. In the following two examples, the adjectival verbs **hǎokàn** (attractive) and **guì** (expensive) are used:

zhèige hǎokàn
jay-gur how-kahn
this (one) is more attractive

nèige guì
nay-gur gway
that (one) is more expensive

The above phrases can also be translated as 'this one is attractive' and 'that one is expensive', but the exact meaning will be clear from the context. The following are added after the adjective or adjectival verb to indicate the degree of comparison:

... diǎnr	[dyenr]	more ...
... xiē	[hsyeh]	a bit more ...
... yìdiǎnr	[yee-dyenr]	a bit more ...
... de duō	[dur dwor]	much more ...
... duōle	[dwor-lur]	far more ...
... gèng	[gung]	even more ...

zhèige guì (yi)diǎnr/xiē
jay-gur gway (yee-)dyenr/hsyeh
this (one) is (a bit) more expensive

zhèige guì de duō
jay-gur gway dur dwor
this (one) is much more expensive

zhèige guì duōle
jay-gur gway dwor-lur
this (one) is far more expensive

zhèige gèng guì
jay-gur gung gway
this (one) is even more expensive

To compare two nouns, the word order is:

subject + **bǐ** + object of comparison + adjectival verb

Fǎguó bǐ Zhōngguó xiǎo
fah-gwor bee joong-gwor hsyow
France is smaller than China

qùnián bǐ jīnnián rè
chew-nyen bee jin-nyen rur
last year was hotter than this year

zhèige bǐ nèige gèng měilì
jay-gur bee nay-gur gung may-lur
this one is even more beautiful than that one

Superlatives

To form the superlative (most ..., ...-est), place **zuì** before the adjective or adjectival verb:

zuì guì de zìxíngchē
dzway gway dur dzur-hsing-chur
the most expensive bicycle

zhèige fàndiàn zuì dà
jay-gur fahn-dyen dzway dah
this hotel is the largest

Adverbs

Adverbs usually have the same form as adjectives, but are sometimes repeated for emphasis (**mànmàn** below):

tā mànmàn de kànle nǐde xìn
tah mahn-mahn dur kahn-lur nee-dur hsin
he/she read your letter slowly

Adverbs can also be formed by placing **de** after an adjective:

nǐ dàshēng de gēn tā shuō ba
nee dah-shung dur gun tah shwor bah
speak loudly to him/her

When **de** appears after a verb, the subsequent adjective takes on an adverbial function:

tāmen qǐde hén wǎn
tah-mun chee-dur hun wahn
they got up late

tā zúqiu tīde hén hǎo
tah dzoo-chyew tee-dur hun how
he plays football well

Pronouns

Personal Pronouns

wǒ	[wor]	I; me
nǐ	[nee]	you (sing)
nín	[nin]	you (sing, pol)
tā	[tah]	he; him; she; her; it
wǒmen	[wor-mun]	we; us
nǐmen	[nee-mun]	you (pl)
tāmen	[tah-mun]	they; them

There are no different forms for subject and object in Chinese:

wǒ rènshi tā
wor run-shur tah
I know him/her

tā rènshi wǒ
tah runshur wor
he/she knows me

zhèi shì géi nǐ de
jay shur gay nee dur
this is for you

Tà can also mean 'it', though this is not a common usage. Generally, there is no need to refer to 'it' in a sentence as the context usually makes it clear:

shū hěn wúqù – wǒ bù xǐhuan
shoo hun woo-choo – wor boo hshee-hwahn
the book is boring – I don't like it

wó xǐhuan nèiběn shū – hén yǒu yìsi
wor hshee-hwahn nay-bun shoo – hun yoh yee-sur
I like that book – it's very interesting

Like **tà**, **tàmen** referring to inanimate things is rarely used.

Demonstrative Pronouns

zhè [jur] this

zhè búshì tāde
jur boo-shur tah-dur
this is not his

nà [nah] that

nà tèbié hǎo
nah tur-byeh how
that's awfully good

In order to translate 'this one' or 'that one' as the object of a sentence, a measure word (see page 22) must be added:

wǒ xǐhuan zhèige/nèige
wor hshee-hwahn jay-gur/nay-gur
I like this (one)/that (one)

Possessives

In order to form possessive adjectives and pronouns, add the suffix **-de** to the personal pronouns on page 20:

wǒde	[wor-dur]	my; mine
nǐde	[nee-dur]	your; yours (sing)
nínde	[nin-dur]	your; yours (sing, pol)
tāde	[tah-dur]	his; her; hers; its
wǒmende	[wor-mun-dur]	our; ours
nǐmende	[nee-mun-dur]	your; yours (pl)
tāmende	[tah-mun-dur]	their; theirs

wǒde zhuōzi	**tāde péngyou**
wor-dur jwor-dzur	tah-dur pung-yoh
my table	his/her friend
tāmende péngyou	**zhè shì nǐde**
tah-mun-dur pung-yoh	jur shur nee-dur
their friend	this is yours

De equates to 'of' or apostrophe 's' in English. **De** phrases always precede the noun to be described:

Shànghǎi de fēngjǐng	**qiūtian de tiānqi**
shahng-hai dur fung-jing	chyew-tyen dur tyen-chee
the scenery of Shanghai	autumn weather
wǒ qīzi de yīxiāng	
wor chee-dzur dur yee-hsyang	
my wife's suitcase	

If a relationship or possession is obvious from the context, it is common to omit **de**:

wǒ àiren	tā jiā	wǒ péngyou
wor ai-run	tah jyah	wor pung-yoh
my wife	his/her home	my friend

wó mǎile chēpiào le
wor mai-lur chur-pyow lur
I've bought my train ticket

Dependent Clauses and 'de'

Dependent clauses precede the noun to be modified and **de** is inserted between the clause and the noun:

tā jì de xìn	wǒ kàn de shū
tah jee dur hsin	wor kahn dur shoo
the letter which he sent	the book(s) (which/that) I read

zuótian kàn de nèibù diànyǐng
dzwor-tyen kahn dur nay-boo dyen-ying
that film I saw yesterday

Measure Words

Demonstrative Adjectives and Measure Words

Nouns or groups of nouns in Chinese have specific measure words which are used when counting or quantifying the noun or nouns, i.e. which are used in conjunction with demonstratives and numerals. The demonstrative adjective is usually formed with the demonstrative **nèi** (that) or **zhèi** (this) followed by a measure word. Measure words, of which there are around fifty in common usage, are added to the end of the demonstrative (or numeral) and precede the noun. Some measure words can be readily translated into English while others cannot, for example:

gōngjīn   **mǐ**   **píng**
goong-jin   mee   ping
kilogram   metre   bottle

sāngōngjīn lí   **sānmǐ miánbù**
sahng-goong-jin lee   sahn-mee myen-boo
three kilos of pears   three metres of cotton

nèipíng píjiǔ
nay-ping pee-yoh
that bottle of beer

The most common measure words are:

bǎ	[bah]	chairs, knives, teapots, tools or implements with handles, stems, bunches of flowers
bēi	[bay]	cups, glasses
běn	[bun]	books, magazines
fēng	[fun]	letters
ge	[gur]	general measure word
jiàn	[jyen]	things, affairs, shirts etc
kē	[kur]	trees
kuài	[kwai]	lumps, pieces
liàng	[lyang]	vehicles
pán	[pahn]	round objects
suǒ	[swor]	buildings
tiáo	[tyow]	fish and various long narrow things
wèi	[way]	polite measure word used for gentlemen, ladies, guests etc
zhāng	[jahng]	tables, beds, tickets, sheets of paper
zhī	[jur]	hands, birds, suitcases, boats

zhèiběn shū   **nèijiàn lǐwù**
jay-bun shoo   nay-jyen lee-woo
this book   that present

nèikē shù   **zhèiliàng zìxíngchē**
nay-kur shoo   jay-lyang dzur-hsing-chur
that tree   this bicycle

23

nèisuǒ yīyuàn	**sāntiáo chuán**
nay-swor yee-ywahn	sahn-tyow chwahn
that hospital	three boats
nèiwèi láibīn	**sānzhāng piào**
nay-way lai-bin	sahn-jahng pyow
that guest	three tickets

The most common of all measure words is **ge**:

zhèige shāngdiàn	**nèige zhěntou**
ay-gur shang-dyen	nay-gur jun-toh
this shop	that pillow

When the correct measure word is not known, the best solution is to use **ge**.

In a dialogue, when it is clear from the context what is being referred to, then the noun may be omitted and only the demonstrative and measure word are used:

wó xǐhuan nèige	**zhèibēi chá hén hǎohē**
wor hshee-hwahn nay-gur	jay-bay chah hun how-hur
I like that (one)	this is a lovely cup of tea

zhèiwèi shì ...
jay-way shur
this is ... (introducing people)

Numbers and Measure Words

As is the case with demonstrative adjectives, you must use a measure word with numbers when they are linked with nouns:

sìkē shù	**sānshíwúběn shū**	**sìshíge rén**
sur-kur shoo	sahn-shur-woo-bun shoo	sur-shur-gur run
four trees	thirty-five books	forty people

See page 42 for the use of **liǎng** (two) with measure words. Similarly, when ordinal numbers are linked with a noun, it is necessary to include a measure word:

dìsānsuǒ fángzi
dee-sahn-swor fahng-dzur
the third house

dìsìtiáo lù
dee-sur-tyow loo
the fourth road

Demonstratives and Numbers

If a demonstrative and a number are used together in a sentence, the word order is:

demonstrative + number + measure word + noun

nèi sānběn shū
nay sahn-bun shoo
those three books

zhèi bāwèi láibīn
jay bah-way lal-bin
these eight guests

nèi liùge
nay lyoh-gur
those six

Verbs

There is no change in Chinese verbs for first, second or third person subjects, both singular and plural:

wó zǒu
wor dzoh
I walk, I am walking

tā zǒu
tah dzoh
he/she walks, he/she is walking

tāmen zǒu
tah-mun dzoh
they walk, they are walking

Chinese verbs also have no tenses:

wǒ míngtian zǒu
wor ming-tyen dzoh
I will go for a walk tomorrow

wǒ zuótian zǒu de shíhou, tiānqi hén hǎo
wor dzwor-tyen dzoh dur shur-hoh tyen-chee hun how
when I was walking yesterday, the weather was lovely

The future and past are indicated in the above sentences by the time words **míngtian** (tomorrow) and **zuótian** (yesterday), while the form of the verb **zǒu** does not change.

The meaning of verbs is also influenced by a number of suffixes and sentence particles (see pages 28 and 30).

A verb used by itself usually implies either a habitual action:

Zhōngguórén chī mǐfàn
joong-gwor-run chur mee-fahn
Chinese people eat rice

or an imminent action:

nǐ qù nǎr?
nee chew nar
where are you going?

To Be

The verb 'to be', when followed by a noun, is **shì**, which corresponds to all the forms of the verb 'to be' in English ('am', 'are', 'is', 'were' etc):

tā shì wǒde péngyou
tah shur wor-dur pung-yoh
she is my friend

zhè shì shénme?
jur shur shun-mur
what is this?

tāmen shì xuésheng
tah-mun shur hway-shung
they are students

The verb **shì** is not required when adjectival verbs are used (see page 17).

The preposition **zài** (in, at) is used as a verb to convey the meaning of 'to be in or at' a particular place (see page 34).

Negatives

To form a negative sentence, use the word **bù** (not); when **bù** precedes a word with a fourth tone, the tone changes to a second tone (**bú**):

wǒ búyào nèiběn shū
wor boo-yow nay-bun shoo
I do not want that book

tā bú qù
tah boo chew
he's not going

nà wǒ bù zhīdao
nah wor boo jur-dow
I didn't know that

Bù is also the negative used with adjectives/adjectival verbs:

bùmǎn
boo-mahn
dissatisfied, discontented

fángzi bú dà
fahng-dzur boo dah
the building isn't big

With the verb **yǒu** (to have), **méi** is used as a negative rather than **bù**:

tā yǒu kòng
tah yoh koong
he/she has time

wǒ méiyǒu kòng
wor may-yoh koong
I don't have time

Méi can also be used on its own to mean 'have not':

wǒ méishìr
wor may-shur
I have nothing to do

Yǒu also means 'there is/are':

shāngdiànli méiyǒu niúnǎi
shahng-dyen-lee may-yoh nyoh-nai
there's no milk in the shop

méiyǒu bànfǎ
may-yoh bahn-fah
there's nothing to be done,
   there's nothing you can do
   about it

yǒu rén
yoh run
there is someone there; engaged, occupied (on a toilet door)

Verb Suffixes

Suffixes are added to Chinese verbs to modify their meaning.

The addition of the suffix **-le** indicates a changed situation; often this means that the action of the verb has been completed:

wó mǎile sānge píngguǒ
wor mai-lur sahn-gur ping-gwor
I bought three apples

tā yǐjing líkāile
tah yee-jing lee-kai-lur
he/she has left already

wǒ zài nàr zhùle jiǔnián
wor dzai nar joo-lur jyoh-nyen
I lived there for nine years

hēwánle chá wǒ jiù kàn diànshì
hur-wahn-lur chah wor jyoh kahn dyen-shur
when I have finished my tea, I am going to watch television

As the fourth example shows, the completed action need not necessarily be in the past.

In order to express the negative form of a completed action, either **méi** or **méi yǒu** is placed before the verb and **-le** is omitted:

wǒ méi(yǒu) kàn diànshì
wor may(-yoh) kahn dyen-shur
I didn't watch television

tā méi(yǒu) líkāi
tah may(-yoh) lee-kai
he hasn't left

Continuous or prolonged action is expressed by the suffix **-zhe**:

tā chōuzhe yān
tah choh-jur yahn
he/she is smoking a cigarette

tā zài shāfāshang zuòzhe
tah dzai shah-fah-shahng dzwor-jur
he/she is sitting on the sofa

The suffix **-zhe** can also be used to convey the idea of doing more than one thing at the same time:

tā hēzhe chá kàn shū
tah hur-jur chah kahn shoo
he read a book while drinking tea

When the **-zhe** suffix is used, **méi** is placed before the verb to form the negative:

tā méi chuānzhe zhōngshānzhuāng
tah may chwahn-jur joong-shahn-jwahng
he/she isn't wearing a Mao suit

Note that **-zhe** has no connection with tense. Depending on the context, the above sentences could be translated as: 'he/she was smoking a cigarette', 'he/she wasn't wearing a Mao suit'.

Another way of indicating continuous action is to place the word **zài** in front of the verb:

tā zài chōuyān
tah dzai choh-yahn
he is smoking

nǐ zài kàn shénme?
nee dzai kahn shun-mur
what are you reading?

The suffix **-guo** is used to indicate a past experience:

wǒ qùguo Zhōngguó
wor chew-gwor joong-gwor
I have been to China

wǒ kànguo nèibēn shū
wor kahng-gwor nay-bun shoo
I have read that book

When the suffix **-guo** is used, **méi** is placed before the verb to form the negative:

wǒ méi qùguo Shànghǎi
wor may chew-gwor shahng-hai
I have never been to
   Shanghai

tā méi hēguo Yìndù chá
tah may hur-gwor yin-doo chah
he's/she's never drunk
   Indian tea

Sentence Particles

The particle **le** at the end of a sentence either indicates that something happened in the past which is still relevant to the present or implies a change of circumstances in the present or future:

tā mǎi bàozhǐ qù le
tah mai bow-jur chew lur
he/she has gone to buy a paper

wǒ zài Lúndūn zhùle liùnián le
wor dzai lun-dun joo-lur lyoh-nyen lur
I have been living in London for six years

gūafēng le
gwah-fung lur
it's windy (now)

wǒ xiànzai bú è le
wor hsyahn-dzai boo ur lur
I'm not hungry any more

píngguǒ dōu huài le
ping-gwor doh hway lur
the apples have all gone bad

wǒmen zǒu le
wor-mun dzoh lur
we are leaving (now)

The particle **ne** adds emphasis to what is said:

tā hái méi líkāi ne
tah hai may lee-kai nur
he still hasn't gone

zuò chángtú qìchē kě bù fāngbiàn ne
dzwor chahng-too chee-chur kur boo fahng-byen nur
(but) it's so inconvenient to go by bus

nǐ zuò shénme ne?
nee dzwor shun-mur nur
well, what are you going to do?

On its own, often in response to an earlier question, **ne** can be used to express the idea 'and what about ...?':

zhèishuāng xié tài guì – nèishuāng ne?
jay-shwahng hsyeh tai gway – nay-shwahng nur
this pair of shoes is too expensive – what about that pair?

The particle **ba** indicates a suggestion:

zǒu ba!
dzoh bah
let's go!

nǐ kǎolǜ yíxià ba
nee kow-lyew yee-syah bah
think about it, consider it

It can also mean 'I suggest' or 'I suppose':

nǐ shì lǎo Zhāng ba?
nee shur low jahng bah
I suppose you must be old Zhang?

nǐmen dōu hěn lèi ba?
nee-mun doh hun lay bah
you are all very tired, aren't you?

Questions

There are a number of ways of forming questions in Chinese. One way is to add the particle **ma** to the end of a sentence to turn it into a question without changing the word order:

tā shì Rìběrén ma?
tah shur ree-bur-run mah
is he/she Japanese?

nǐ mǎi zhèifèn bàozhǐ ma?
nee mai jay-fun bow-jur mah
are you buying this newspaper?

nǐ è ma?
nee ur mah
are you hungry?

nǐ qùguo Běijīng ma?
nee choo-gwor bay-jing mah
have you ever been to Beijing?

nǐ yǒu háizi ma?
nee yoh hai-dzur mah
do you have any children?

Alternatively, the verb is repeated along with the negative **bù** or **méi**:

tāmen shì búshì Yīngguórén?
tah-mun shur boo-shur ying-gwor-run
are they British?

jīntian rè bú rè?
jin-tyen rur boo rur
is it hot today?

nǐ è bú è?
nee ur boo ur
are you hungry?

tā chīguo Zhōngcān méiyǒu?
tah chur-gwor joong-tsahn may-yoh
has he/she ever eaten
    Chinese food?

ní yǒu méiyou háizi?
nee yoh may-yoh hai-dzur
do you have any children?

Shéi (who?) and **shénme** (what?) are the main interrogative pronouns. Interrogative pronouns are placed in the same position in the sentence as the noun in the answer that is implied:

tā shì shéi?
tah shur shay
who is he?

tā shì wǒ péngyou
tah shur wor pung-yoh
he's my friend

shéi fù qián?
shay foo chyen
who is going to pay?

tā fùqián
tah foo-chyen
he is going to pay

ní mǎi shénme?
nee mai shun-mur
what are you going to buy?

wó mǎi yìjié diànchí
wor mai yee-jyeh dyen-chur
I'm going to buy a battery

The other common interrogatives are:

nǎr/nǎli?	[nar/nah-lee]	where?
duōshǎo?	[dwor-show]	how many?, how much?
nèi?	[nay]	which?
shéide?	[shay-dur]	whose?
zěnme?	[dzun-mur]	how?
wèishénme?	[way-shun-mur]	why?

shāngdiàn zài nǎr?
shahng-dyen dzai nar
where is the shop?

duōshǎo qián?
dwor-show chyen
how much is that?

něige fàndiàn zuì guì?
nay-gur fahn-dyen dzway gway
which hotel is most expensive?

ní xǐhuan něige?
nee hshee-hwahn nay-gur
which one would you like?

zhè shì shéide?
jur shur shay-dur
whose is this?

ní shì zěnme láide?
nee shur dzun-mur lai-dur
how did you get here?

tāmen wèishénme bú shàng huǒchē?
tah-mun way-shun-mur goo shahng hwor chur
why aren't they getting on the train?

Háishi (or) is used in questions posing alternatives:

ní xiáng mǎi zhèige háishi nèlge?
nee hsyahng mai jay-gur hai-shur nay-gur
do you wish to buy this one or that one?

Prepositions

Some common prepositions are:

cóng	[tsoong]	from
dào	[dow]	to
duì	[dway]	towards, with regard to
gěi	[gay]	for
gēn	[gun]	with
lí	[lee]	from/to (in expressions of distance)
wèile	[way-lur]	because of
yòng	[yoong]	with, by means of,
zài	[dzai]	in, at (see page 34)

wǒmen míngtian dào Shànghǎi qù
wor-mun ming-tyen dow shahng-hai chew
we're going to Shanghai tomorrow

cóng sāndiǎnbàn dào sìdiǎn
tsoong sahn-dyen-bahn dow sur-dyen
from three thirty to four o'clock

Yīngguó lí Fǎguó bù yuǎn
ying-gwor lee fah-gwor boo ywahn
Britain is not far from France

wǒmen shì zuò chuán láide
wor-mun shur dzwor chwahn lai-dur
we came by boat

wó géi ní mǎile yìxiē píngguǒ
wor gay nee mai-lur yee-hsyeh ping-gwor
I've bought some apples for you

qǐng gēn wǒ lái
ching gun wor lai
please come with me

tā wèi tā háizi hěn zháojí
tah way tah hai-dzur hun jow-jee
she was very worried about her child

Zài (in, at) is also used as a verb meaning 'to be in/at':

tā zài nǎr?	**tāmen zài Shànghǎi**
tah dzai nar	tah-mun dzai shahng-hai
where is he/she?	they are in Shanghai
zhuōzi zài wàibiānr	**wǒ zài Shànghǎi méiyǒu qīnqī**
jwor-dzur zai wai-byenr	wor dzai shahng-hai may-yoh ching-chee
the table is outside	I don't have any relatives in Shanghai

Place Word Suffixes

Various suffixes are added to nouns to indicate location and are nearly always used in conjunction with the preposition **zài**. The most important are:

lǐ	[lee]	inside, in
shàng	[shahng]	above, on
wài	[wai]	outside
xià	[hsyah]	below
zhōng	[joong]	in the middle, between

nǐde bàozhǐ zài dàizili
nee-dur bow-jur dzai dai-dzur-lee
your newspaper is in your bag

chéngwài yǒu fēijīchǎng
chung-wai yoh fur-jee-chahng
there's an airport outside the town

nǐde zhàoxiàngjī zài chuángshàng
nee-dur jow-hsyahng-jee dzai chwahng-shahng
your camera is on the bed

nǐde yīxiāng zài chuángxià
nee-dur yee-hsyahng dzai chwahng-hsyah
your suitcase is under the bed

zài shānlǐ
dzai shahn-lee
in the mountains

Yes and No

Chinese has no standard words for 'yes' and 'no', but you can often use **shì(de)** (yes, it is the case), **duìle** (yes, that's right) and **bú shì** (no, it is not the case).

The most common way of saying 'yes' is to repeat the verb of the question; to say 'no', repeat the verb of the question together with **bù** or **méi** as required:

ní yǒu kòng ma?		yǒu	méi yǒu
nee yoh koong mah		yoh	may yoh
do you have any free time?		yes	no

tā shì xuésheng ma?		**shì**	**bú shì**
tah shur hsyeh-shung mah		shur	boo shur
is he a student?		yes	no

nǐ qùguo Chángchéng méi yǒu?
nee chew-gwor chahng-chung may yoh
have you been to see the Great Wall?

qùguo	**méi yǒu/méi qùguo**
chew-gwor	may yoh/may chew-gwor
yes	no

Imperatives

To make an imperative in Chinese, pronounce the verb in an emphatic way:

zhànzhù!	**gǔnchūqu!**
jahn-joo	gun-choo-chew
stop!	get out!

Imperatives are rarely used because they sound too abrupt. The verb is more likely to be preceded by **qǐng** (please) or followed by **ba** (see page 31) to make the command sound more polite:

qǐng zuò ba
ching dzwor bah
please sit down

Negative imperatives are formed using either **bié** or **bú yào** (don't):

bié zǒule	**bú yào zài shūo**
byeh dzoh-lur	boo yow dzai shwor
don't go	say no more

Dates

Dates in Chinese are written in the following order:

year + month + number

To write the year, place the relevant numbers in front of **nián** (year); this is followed by the month and then the number of the day plus **hào**:

九月一号
jiǔyuè yīhào
jyoh-yew-eh yee-how
the first of September

十二月二号
shíèryuè èrhào
shur-er-yew-eh er-how
the second of December

五月三十号
wǔyuè sānshíhào
woo-yew-eh sahn-shur-how
the thirtieth of May

一九九七年五月三十一号
yījiǔ jiǔqī nián wǔyuè sānshíyīhào
yee-jyoh jyoh-chee nyen woo-yew-eh
   sahn-shur-yee-how
the thirty-first of May, 1997

一九四二年
yījiǔ sìèr nián
yee-jyoh sur-er nyen
1942

Days

Sunday xīngqītiān 〖hsing-chee-tyen〗 星期天
Monday xīngqīyī 〖hsing-chee-yee〗 星期一
Tuesday xīngqīèr 〖hsing-chee-er〗 星期二
Wednesday xīngqīsān 〖hsing-chee-sahn〗 星期三
Thursday xīngqīsì 〖hsing-chee-sur〗 星期四
Friday xīngqīwǔ 〖hsing-chee-woo〗 星期五
Saturday xīngqīliù 〖hsing-chee-lyoh〗 星期六

Months

January yīyuè [yee-yew-eh] 一月

February èryuè [er-yew-eh] 二月

March sānyuè [sahn-yew-eh] 三月

April sìyuè [sur-yew-eh] 四月

May wǔyuè [woo-yew-eh] 五月

June liùyuè [lyoh-yew-eh] 六月

July qīyuè [chee-yew-eh] 七月

August bāyuè [bah-yew-eh] 八月

September jiǔyuè [jyoh-yew-eh] 九月

October shíyuè [shur-yew-eh] 十月

November shíyīyuè [shur-yee-yew-eh] 十一月

December shíèryuè [shur-er-yew-eh] 十二月

Time

When telling the time, the word **diǎn** is added to the number to indicate the hours. **Zhōng** (clock) is optional and is placed at the end of most time expressions. The word **fēn** (minutes) is added to the number of minutes.

what time is it? jídiǎn le? [jee-dyen lur] 几点了？

o'clock diǎn zhōng [dyen joong] 点钟

one o'clock yīdiǎn (zhōng) [yee-dyen] 一点（钟）

two o'clock liángdiǎn (zhōng) [lyang-dyen] 两点（钟）

at one o'clock yìdiǎn (zhōng) [yee-dyen] 一点（钟）

it's one o'clock yìdiǎn (zhōng) 一点（钟）

it's two o'clock liángdiǎn (zhōng) [lyang-dyen] 两点（钟）

it's ten o'clock shídiǎn (zhōng) [shur-dyen] 十点（钟）

five past one yìdiǎn wǔfēn [yee-dyen woo-fun] 一点五分

ten past two liángdiǎn shifēn [lyang-dyen shur-fun] 两点十分

quarter past one yìdiǎn yíkè [yee-dyen yee-kur] 一点一刻

quarter past two liángdiǎn yíkè [lyang-dyen yee-kur] 两点一刻

half past two liángdiǎn bàn [bahn] 两点半

half past ten shídiǎn bàn [shur-dyen] 十点半

twenty to one yìdiǎn chà èrshí [yee-dyen chah er-shur] 一点差二十

twenty to ten shídiǎn chà èrshí [shur-dyen] 十点差二十

quarter to one yìdiǎn chà yíkè [yee-dyen chah yee-kur] 一点差一刻

quarter to two liǎngdiǎn chà yíkè [lyang-dyen] 两点差一刻

a.m. (early morning up to about 9) zǎoshang [dzow-shahng] 早上

(from about 9 till noon) shàngwǔ 上午

p.m. (afternoon) xiàwǔ [hsyah-woo] 下午

(evening) wǎnshang [wahn-shahng] 晚上

(night) yèlǐ [yur-lee] 夜里

2 a.m. língchén liángdiǎn [ling-chun lyang-dyen] 凌晨两点

2 p.m. (14.00) xiàwǔ liángdiǎn [hsyah-woo] 下午两点

6 a.m. zǎoshang liùdiǎn [dzow-shahng lyoh-dyen] 早上六点

6 p.m. (18.00) wǎnshang liùdiǎn [wahn-shahng] 晚上六点

10 a.m. shàngwǔ shídiǎn [shahng-woo shur-dyen] 上午十点

10 p.m. wǎnshang shídiǎn [wahn-shahng] 晚上十点

noon zhōngwǔ [joong-woo] 中午

midnight bànyè [bahn-yur] 半夜

hour xiǎoshí [hsyow-shur] 小时

minute fēn [fun] 分

two minutes liǎng fēnzhōng [lyang fun-joong] 两分钟

second miǎo [myow] 秒

quarter of an hour yí kèzhōng [kur-joong] 一刻钟

half an hour bàn xiǎoshí [bahn hsyow-shur] 半小时

three quarters of an hour sān kèzhōng [sahn kur-joong] 三刻钟

nearly three o'clock kuài sān diǎn le [kwai sahn dyen lur] 快三点了

Numbers

See **Measure Words** on page 22.

0	líng	零
1	yī [yee]	一
2	èr, liǎng [lyang]	二
3	sān [sahn]	三
4	sì [sur]	四
5	wǔ	五

6	liù [lyoh]	六
7	qī [chee]	七
8	bā [bah]	八
9	jiǔ [jyoh]	九
10	shí [shur]	十
11	shíyī [shur-yee]	十一
12	shíèr [shur-er]	十二
13	shísān [shur-sahn]	十三
14	shísì [shur-sur]	十四
15	shíwǔ [shur-woo]	十五
16	shíliù [shur-lyoh]	十六
17	shíqī [shur-chee]	十七
18	shíbā [shur-bah]	十八
19	shíjiǔ [shur-jyoh]	十九
20	èrshí [er-shur]	二十
21	èrshíyí [er-shur-yee]	二十一
22	èrshíèr [er-shur-er]	二十二
30	sānshí [sahn-shur]	三十
31	sānshíyī [sahn-shur-yee]	三十一
32	sānshíèr [sahn-shur-er]	三十二
40	sìshí [sur-shur]	四十
50	wǔshí [woo-shur]	五十
60	liùshí [lyoh-shur]	六十
70	qīshí [chee-shur]	七十
80	bāshí [bah-shur]	八十
90	jiǔshí [jyoh-shur]	九十
100	yìbǎi	一百
101	yìbǎi líng yī	一百零一
102	yìbǎi líng èr	一百零二
110	yìbǎi yìshí [yee-shur]	一百一十
111	yìbǎi yìshíyī [shur-yee]	一百一十一
200	èrbǎi	二百
201	èrbǎi líng yī	二百零一
202	èrbǎi líng èr	二百零二
210	èrbǎi yīshí [yee-shur]	二百一十

300	sānbǎi [sahn-bai]	三百
1,000	yìqiān [yee-chyen]	一千
2,000	liǎngqiān [lyang-chyen]	两千
3,000	sān qiān [sahn chyen]	三千
4,000	sìqiān [sur-chyen]	四千
5,000	wǔqiān [woo-chyen]	五千
10,000	yíwàn [yee-wahn]	一万
50,000	wǔwàn	五万
100,000	shíwàn [shur-wahn]	十万
1,000,000	bǎiwàn	百万
10,000,000	qiānwàn [chyen-wahn]	千万
100,000,000	yí yì	一亿

When counting 'one, two, three' and so on, **yī** (one) is written and said with the first tone. In other situations, the fourth tone is used:

yī, èr, sān	**yìtiáo yú**	**yìkē shū**
yee er sahn	yee-tyow yoo	yee-kur shoo
one, two, three	a fish	a tree

The exception to the above is if **yì** is followed by a fourth tone, in which case it changes to second tone:

yíjiàn dōngxi
yee-jyen doong-hshee
an object

In number sequences **yāo** is used for 'one' instead of **yī**, as in the two examples below:

sān-èr-wǔ-yāo-bā	**yāoyāojiǔ**
sahn-er-woo-yow-bah	yow-yow-jyoh
32518	number one hundred and nineteen
(phone number)	(room number)

There are two words for two in Chinese: **èr** and **liǎng**. **Èr** is used in counting or for phone, room or bus numbers:

yī, èr, sān ...	èr hào	èr lù chē
yee er sahn	er how	er loo chur
one, two three ...	number two	number two bus
	(room, house etc)	

Èr also occurs in compound numbers:

sānshí'èr [sahn-shur-er] thirty-two

Liǎng is similar to 'a couple' in English and is used with measure words (see page 22):

liǎngwèi péngyou	liǎngsuǒ fángzi
lyang-way pung-yoh	lyang-swor fahng-dzur
two friends	two buildings

The numbers 11-19 are made up of **shí** (ten) followed by the numbers **yī** (one) to **jiǔ** (nine):

shíyī	eleven
shí'èr	twelve
shísān	thirteen

Multiples of ten are formed by adding the numbers two to nine to **shí** (ten):

èrshí	twenty
sānshí	thirty
sìshí	forty

The numbers 21 to 29, 31-39 etc are formed by adding one to nine to the above numbers **èrshí**, **sānshí** and so on:

èrshíyī	twenty-one
sìshíqī	forty-seven
bāshíwǔ	eighty-five

A similar pattern is used with **bǎi** (hundred), **qiān** (thousand) and **wàn** (ten thousand):

sìbǎi	sìbǎi jiǔshí
sur-bai	sur-bai jyoh-shur
four hundred	four hundred and ninety

bābǎi sìshí liù
bah-bai sur-shur lyoh
eight hundred and forty-six

jiǔqiān sìbǎi qīshí
jyoh-chyen sur-bai chee-shur
nine thousand four hundred
and seventy

qīwàn sìqiān bābǎi
chee-wahn sur-chyen bah-bai
seventy-four thousand eight
hundred

For numbers in the thousands and millions, **shí**, **bǎi**, **qiān** and **wàn** are added to **wàn**:

shíwàn
shur-wahn
a hundred thousand

bǎiwàn
bai-wahn
a million

qiānwàn
chyah-wahn
ten million

yí yì
a hundred million

Líng (zero) is used when there are zeros in the middle of a number sequence:

yìbǎi líng sān
yee-bai ling sahn
one hundred and three

yìqiān líng sān
yee-chyen ling sahn
one thousand and three

yìqiān líng bāshí
yee-chyen ling bah-shur
one thousand and eighty

Ordinals

1st	dì yī	第一	6th	dì liù [lyoh]	第六
2nd	dì èr	第二	7th	dì qī [chee]	第七
3rd	dì sān [sahn]	第三	8th	dì bā	第八
4th	dì sì [sur]	第四	9th	dì jiǔ [jyoh]	第九
5th	dì wǔ	第五	10th	dì shí [shur]	第十

Basic Phrases

yes
shìde
shur-dur
是的

no
bù
boo
不

OK
hǎo
how
好

hello
ní hǎo
nee how
你好

good morning
ní zǎo
nee dzow
你早

good evening
ní hǎo
ni how
你好

good night
wǎn'ān
wahn-ahn
晚安

goodbye/see you!
zàijiàn
dzai-jyen
再见

see you later
huítóujiàn
hway-toh-jyen
回头见

please
qǐng
ching
请

yes, please
hǎo, xièxie
how hsyeh-hsyeh
好谢谢

could you please ...?
qǐng nín ..., hǎo ma?
ching nin ... how mah
请您 ..., 好吗？

thank you
xièxie
hsyeh-hsyeh
谢谢

thank you very much
duōxiè
dwor-hsyeh
多谢

no, thank you
xièxie, wǒ bú yào
hsyeh-hsyeh wor boo yow
谢谢我不要

don't mention it
bú kèqi
boo kur-chee
不客气

how do you do?
ní hǎo
ni how
你好？

how are you?
ní hǎo ma?
mah
你好吗？

fine, thanks
hén hǎo, xièxie
hun how hsyeh-hsyeh
很好谢谢

nice to meet you
jiàndào nǐ hěn gāoxìng
jyen-dow nee hun gow-hsing
见到你很高兴

excuse me (to get past)
láojià
low-jyah
劳驾

(to get attention)
láojià, qǐng wèn ...
ching wun
劳驾请问

excuse me/sorry
duìbuqǐ
dway-boo-chee
对不起

sorry?/pardon me?
nǐ shuō shenme?
shwor shun-mur
你说什么？

I see/I understand
wǒ míngbai le
wor ming-bai lur
我明白了

I don't understand
wǒ bù dǒng
wor boo dong
我不懂

do you speak English?
nín huì jiǎng Yīngyǔ ma?
hway jyang ying-yew mah
您会讲英语吗？

I don't speak Chinese
wǒ búhuì jiǎng Hànyǔ
wor boo-hway hahn-yew
我不会讲汉语

could you speak more slowly?
qǐng shuō màn yìdiǎnr
ching shwor mahn yee-dyenr
请说慢一点儿

could you repeat that?
qíng nǐ zài shuō yíbiàn, hǎo ma?
ching nee dzai shwor yee-byen how mah
请你再说一遍好吗？

45

Conversion Tables

1 centimetre = 0.39 inches   1 inch = 2.54 cm

1 metre = 39.37 inches = 1.09 yards   1 foot = 30.48 cm

1 kilometre = 0.62 miles = 5/8 mile   1 yard = 0.91 m

1 mile = 1.61 km

km	1	2	3	4	5	10	20	30	40	50	100
miles	0.6	1.2	1.9	2.5	3.1	6.2	12.4	18.6	24.8	31.0	62.1

miles	1	2	3	4	5	10	20	30	40	50	100
km	1.6	3.2	4.8	6.4	8.0	16.1	32.2	48.3	64.4	80.5	161

1 gram = 0.035 ounces   1 kilo = 1000 g = 2.2 pounds

g	100	250	500
oz	3.5	8.75	17.5

1 oz = 28.35 g
1 lb = 0.45 kg

kg	0.5	1	2	3	4	5	6	7	8	9	10
lb	1.1	2.2	4.4	6.6	8.8	11.0	13.2	15.4	17.6	19.8	22.0

kg	20	30	40	50	60	70	80	90	100
lb	44	66	88	110	132	154	176	198	220

lb	0.5	1	2	3	4	5	6	7	8	9	10	20
kg	0.2	0.5	0.9	1.4	1.8	2.3	2.7	3.2	3.6	4.1	4.5	9.0

1 litre = 1.75 UK pints / 2.13 US pints

1 UK pint = 0.57 l   1 UK gallon = 4.55 l
1 US pint = 0.47 l   1 US gallon = 3.79 l

centigrade / Celsius   °C = (°F − 32) x 5/9

°C	-5	0	5	10	15	18	20	25	30	36.8	38
°F	23	32	41	50	59	64	68	77	86	98.4	100.4

Fahrenheit   °F = (°C x 9/5) + 32

°F	23	32	40	50	60	65	70	80	85	98.4	101
°C	-5	0	4	10	16	18	21	27	29	36.8	38.3

English

→

Chinese

A

a, an*

about: about 20 èr shí zuǒyòu
[dzwor-yoh]
二十左右

it's about 5 o'clock wǔdiǎn
(zhōng) zuǒyòu
五点钟左右

a film about China guānyú
Zhōngguó de diànyǐng
[gwahn-yew – dur dyen-ying]
关于中国的电影

above* (zài) ... shàng [(dzai) ...
shahng]
在 … 上

abroad guówài [gwor-wai]
国外

absorbent cotton yàomián
[yow-myen]
药棉

accept jiēshòu [jyeh-shoh]
接受

accident shìgù [shur-goo]
事故

there's been an accident
chūle ge shìgù
[choo-lur gur]
出了个事故

accommodation
see **room** and **hotel**

accurate zhǔnquè
[jun-chew-eh]
准确

ache téng [tung]
疼

my back aches wǒ hòubèi
téng [wor hoh-bay]
我后背疼

acrobatics zájì [dzah-jee]
杂技

across: across the road zài
mǎlù duìmiànr [dzai mah-loo
dway-myenr]
在马路对面儿

acupuncture zhēnjiǔ [jun-jyoh]
针灸

adapter duōyòng chātóu
[dwor-yoong chah-toh]
多用插头

address dìzhǐ [dee-jur]
地址

what's your address? nín
zhù nǎr? [joo]
您住哪儿？

Addresses are written in
the reverse order to the
way they are written in
the West, beginning with the
country, followed by the province,
town, street number and ending
with the addressee's name. For
example:

People's Republic of China
Shanxi Province
Taiyuan
Donglu (East Road) 15
Wang Shixing

People's Republic of China is sometimes shortened to PRC.

address book tōngxùnlù 〖toong-hsyewn-loo〗
通讯录

admission charge: how much is the admission charge? rùchǎng fèi shì duōshao qián? 〖roo-chahng fay shur dwor-show chyen〗
入场费是多少钱？

 Virtually all tourist sites have some kind of admission charge. This will often come to no more than a few yuan, but discriminatory pricing policies usually mean that foreigners are charged more than locals. In some extreme cases, such as visiting the Forbidden City in Beijing or the Terracotta Warriors in Xi'an, foreigners may find themselves paying many times more than the locals. At the Forbidden City, however, the price for foreigners includes a recorded commentary in English. If you have a student card you can occasionally get in for the Chinese price.

adult dàrén 〖dah-run〗
大人

advance: in advance tíqián 〖tee-chyen〗
提前

aeroplane fēijī 〖fay-jee〗
飞机

after yǐhòu 〖yee-hoh〗
以后

after you nǐ xiān qù ba 〖nee hsyen chew bah〗
你先去吧

after lunch wǔfàn hòu 〖woo-fahn〗
午饭后

afternoon xiàwǔ 〖hsyah-woo〗
下午

in the afternoon xiàwǔ
下午

this afternoon jīntiān xiàwǔ 〖jin-tyen〗
今天下午

aftershave xūhòushuǐ 〖hsyew-hoh-shway〗
须后水

afterwards yǐhòu 〖yee-hoh〗
以后

again zài 〖dzai〗
再

age niánjì 〖nyen-jee〗
年纪

ago: a week ago yíge xīngqī yǐqián 〖yee-gur hsing-chee yee-chyen〗
一个星期以前

an hour ago yíge xiǎoshí yǐqián 〖hsyow-shur〗
一个小时以前

agree: I agree wǒ tóngyì [wor
toong-yee]
我同意

AIDS àizībìng [ai-dzur-bing]
爱滋病

air kōngqì [koong-chee]
空气

by air zuò fēijī [dzwor fay-jee]
坐飞机

air-conditioning kōngtiáo
[koong-tyow]
空调

airmail: by airmail
hángkōng(xìn)
[hahng-koong(-hsin)]
航空信

airmail envelope hángkōng
xìnfēng [hsin-fung]
航空信封

airplane fēijī [fay-jee]
飞机

airport fēijīchǎng [–chahng]
飞机场

to the airport, please qǐng
dài wǒ dào fēijīchǎng [ching
dai wor dow]
请带我到飞机场

airport bus jīchǎng bānchē
[jee-chahng bahn-chur]
机场班车

alarm clock nàozhōng
[now-joong]
闹钟

alcohol (drink) jiǔ [jyoh]
酒

all: all of it quánbù
[chew-ahn-boo]
全部

that's all, thanks gòule,
xièxie [goh-lur hsyeh-hsyeh]
够了谢谢

allergic: I'm allergic to ... wǒ
duì ... guòmǐn [wor dway ...
gwor-min]
我对 ... 过敏

allowed: is it allowed? zhè
yúnxǔ ma? [jur yun-hsyew
mah]
这允许吗？

all right hǎo [how]
好

I'm all right wǒ méi shìr [wor
may shur]
我没事儿

are you all right? nǐ méi shìr
ba? [nee may-shur bah]
你没事儿吧？

(greeting) nǐ hǎo ma? [nee how]
你好吗？

almost chàbuduō
[chah-boo-dwor]
差不多

alone yíge rén [yee-gur run]
一个人

already yǐjing
已经

also yě [yur]
也

although suīrán [sway-rahn]
虽然

altogether yígòng
[yee-goong]
一共

always zǒng [dzoong]
总

am*: I am shì [shur]
是

a.m.: at seven a.m. shàngwǔ
qī diǎn [chee dyen]
上午七点

amazing (surprising) méi
xiǎngdào [may hsyang-dow]
没想到
(very good) liǎobùqǐ
[lyow-boo-chee]
了不起

ambulance jiùhùchē
[jyoh-hoo-chur]
救护车

call an ambulance! (kuài) jiào
jiùhùchē! [(kwai) jyow]
（快）叫救护车

The number for the
ambulance service is
120.

America Měiguó [may-gwor]
美国

American (adj) Měiguó
美国

I'm American wǒ shì
Měiguó rén [wor shur – run]
我是美国人

among zài ... zhī zhōng
[dzai ... jur joong]
在 ... 之中

amp: a 13-amp fuse shísān
ānpéi de bǎoxiǎnsī [shur-sahn
ahn-pay dur bow-hsyen-sur]
十三安培的保险丝

and hé [hur]
和

angry shēngqì [shung-chee]
生气

animal dòngwù [doong-woo]
动物

ankle jiǎobózi [jyow-bor-dzur]
脚脖子

annoying: how annoying! zhēn
tǎoyàn! [jun tow-yahn]
真讨厌

another (different) lìng yíge
[yee-gur]
另一个
(one more) yòu yíge [yoh]
又一个

can we have another room?
wó xiǎng huàn lìngwài yíge
fángjiān [wor hsyang hwahn
ling-wai]
我想换另外一个房间

another beer, please qǐng zài
lái yì bēi píjiǔ [ching dzai lai
yee]
请再来一杯啤酒

antibiotics kàngjūnsù
[kahng-jyewn-soo]
抗菌素

antique: is it a genuine

antique? shì zhēn gǔdǒng ma? [shur jurn goo-doong mah]

是真古董吗？

antique shop wénwù shāngdiàn [wun-woo shahng-dyen]

文物商店

antiseptic fángfǔjì [fahng-foo-jee]

防腐剂

any: do you have any ...? nǐ yǒu ... ma? [nee yoh ... mah]

你有 ... 吗？

sorry, I don't have any duìbuqǐ, wǒ méiyǒu [dway-boo-chur wor may-yoh]

对不起我没有

anybody shéi [shay]

谁

does anybody speak English? shéi huì shuō Yīngyǔ? [hway shwor ying-yoo]

谁会说英语？

there wasn't anybody there zàinàr shénme rén dōu méiyou [zai-nar shun-mur run doh may-yoh]

在那儿什么人都没有

anything shénme [shun-mur]

什么

dialogues

anything else? hái yào shénme? [hai yow]

nothing else, thanks bú yào, xièxie [hsyeh-hsyeh]

would you like anything to drink? nǐ yào hé diǎnr shénme? [hur dyenr]

I don't want anything, thanks wǒ shénme dōu bú yào, xièxie [wor – doh]

apart from chúle ... yǐwài [choo-lur]

除了 ... 以外

apartment dānyuán [dahn-yew-ahn]

单元

aperitif kāiwèijiǔ [kai-way-jyoh]

开胃酒

appendicitis lánwěiyán [lahn-way-yen]

阑尾炎

appetizer lěngpánr [lung-pahnr]

冷盘儿

apple píngguǒ [ping-gwor]

苹果

appointment yuēhuì [yew-eh-hway]

约会

dialogue

good morning, how can I help you? nín zǎo, wǒ néng bāng shénme máng ma? [dzow wor nung bahng

shun-mur mahng mah]
I'd like to make an appointment wó xiăng dìng ge yùehùi [hsyang ding gur]

what time would you like? nín xiăng yuē shénme shíjian[yew-eh]

three o'clock sān diăn (zhōng) [dyen (joong)]

I'm afraid that's not possible, is four o'clock all right? duìbùqǐ sān diăn bù xíng, sì diăn (zhōng) xíng ma? [dway-boo-chee – hsing – mah]

yes, that will be fine xíng, kěyǐ [kur-yee]

the name was? nín guì xìng? [gway]

apricot xìngzi [hsing-dzur]
杏子
April sìyuè [sur-yew-eh]
四月
are*: we are wǒmen shì [wor-mun shur]
我们是
you are (sing) nǐ shì
你是
(pl) nǐmen shì [nee-mun]
你们是
they are tāmen shì [tah-mun]
他们是
area (measurement) miànjì

[myen-jee]
面积
(region) dìqū [dee-chew]
地区
arm gēbo [gur-bor]
胳膊
army jūnduì [chewn-dway]
军队
arrange: will you arrange it for us? nǐ néng tì wǒmen ānpái yí xià ma? [nung tee wor-mun ahn-pai yee hsyah mah]
你能替我们安排一下吗？
arrive dào [dow]
到
when do we arrive? wǒmen shénme shíhou dàodá? [wor-mun shun-mur shur-hoh dow-dah]
我们什么时候到达？
has my fax arrived yet? wó géi nǐ fā de chuánzhēn dàole ma? [wor gay nee fah dur chwahn-jun dow-lur mah]
我给你发的传真到了吗？
we arrived today wǒmen jīntiān gāng dào [jin-tyen gahng]
我们今天刚到
art yìshù [yee-shoo]
艺术
art gallery měishùguǎn [may-shoo-gwahn]
美术馆

as: as big as... gēn ... yíyàng dà [gun ... yee-yang dah]

跟 … 一样大

as soon as possible jǐnkuài [jin-kwai]

尽快

ashtray yānhuī gāng [yahn-hway gahng]

烟灰缸

ask (someone to do something) qǐng [ching]

请

(a question) wèn [wun]

问

could you ask him to ...? nǐ néng bù néng qǐng tā ...? [nung – tah]

你能不能请他 … ?

asleep: she's asleep tā shuìzháole [tah shway-jow-lur]

他睡着了

aspirin āsīpǐlín [ah-sur-pee-lin]

阿斯匹林

asthma qìchuǎn [chee-chwahn]

气喘

at*: at my hotel zài wó zhù de fàndiàn [dzai wor joo dur]

在我住的饭店

at the railway station zài huǒchē zhàn

在火车站

at six o'clock liùdiǎn zhōng [lyoh-dyen joong]

六点钟

at Li Zhen's zài Lǐ Zhēn jiā [jyah]

在李真家

ATM zìdòng qǔkuǎnjī [dzur-doong chew-kwahn-jee]

自动取款机

attendant (on train) chéngwùyuán [chung-woo-yew-ahn]

乘务员

August bāyuè [bah-yew-eh]

八月

aunt (father's sister, unmarried) gūgu

姑姑

(father's sister, married) gūmǔ

姑母

(mother's sister, unmarried) yímǔ

姨母

(mother's sister, married) yímā [yee-mah]

姨妈

Australia Àodàlìyà [or-dah-lee-yah]

澳大利亚

Australian (adj) Àodàlìyà

澳大利亚

I'm Australian wǒ shì Àodàlìyà rén [wor shur – run]

我是澳大利亚人

automatic (adj) zìdòng [dzur-doong]

自动

autumn qiūtiān [chyoh-tyen]

秋天

in the autumn qiūtiān

[hoh-myen]

秋天

在后面

average (ordinary) yíbàn

[yee-bahn]

一般

can I have my money back?
qǐng ba qián huán gěi wǒ ba

[ching bah chyen hwahn gay wor
bah]

on average píngjūn

[ping-jyewn]

平均

请把钱还给我吧

awake: is he awake? tā xǐngle
ma? [tah hsing-lur mah]

他醒了吗 ?

to come back huílai [hway–]

回来

to go back huíqu [–chew]

away: is it far away? yuǎn
ma? [yew-ahn]

远吗 ?

回去

backache bèitòng [bay-toong]

背痛

awful zāogāole [dzow-gow-lur]

糟糕了

bad huài [hwai]

坏

a bad headache tóu téng de
lìhai [toh tung dur lur-hai]

B

头疼得利害

bag dàizi [dai-dzur]

baby yīng'ér [ying-er]

婴儿

袋子

(handbag) shǒutíbāo

[shoh-tee-bow]

baby food yīng'ér shíwù
[shur-woo]

婴儿食物

手提包

(suitcase) shǒutíxiāng

[shoh-tee-hsyang]

baby's bottle nǎipíng

奶瓶

手提箱

baggage xíngli [hsing-lee]

baby-sitter línshí kān xiǎoháir
de [lin-shur kahn hsyow-hair dur]

临时看小孩儿的

行李

baggage check (US) xíngli
jìcúnchù [jee-tsun-choo]

back hòu [hoh]

后

行李寄存处

(of body) hòubèi [bay]

后背

baggage claim xíngli tíqǔchù
[tee-chew-choo]

行李提取处

at the back zài hòumian [dzai

bakery miànbāodiàn

[myen-bow-dyen]

面包店

balcony yángtái

阳台

a room with a balcony dài yángtái de fángjiān [dur fahng-jyen]

带阳台的房间

ball qiú [chyoh]

球

ballet bāléiwǔ [bah-lay-woo]

芭蕾舞

ballpoint pen yuánzhūbǐ [yew-ahn-joo-bee]

圆珠笔

bamboo zhúzi [joo-dzur]

竹子

bamboo shoots zhúsǔn [joo-sun]

竹笋

banana xiāngjiāo [hsyang-jyow]

香蕉

band (musical) yuèduì [yew-eh-dway]

乐队

bandage bēngdài [bung-dai]

绷带

Bandaid® xiàngpí gāo [hsyang-pee gow]

橡皮膏

bank (money) yínháng [yin-hahng]

银行

 Banks in major Chinese cities are sometimes open seven days a week, though foreign exchange is usually only available from Monday to Friday, approximately from 9 a.m. to noon and from 2 to 5 p.m. All banks are closed for the first three days of the Chinese New Year (Spring Festival), with reduced hours for the following eleven days.

bank account zhànghù [jahng-hoo]

帐户

banquet yànhuì [yen-hway]

宴会

bar jiǔbājiān [jyoh-bah-jyen]

酒吧间

a bar of chocolate yí kuàir qiǎokèlì [yee kwair chyow-kur-lee]

一块儿巧克力

 Increasingly, bars are found in China's major cities, both within large hotels and as individual enterprises. There are even a few karaoke bars. Substantial mark-ups are to be expected in such places, especially on foreign spirits.

barber's lǐfàdiàn [lee-fah-dyen]

理发店

bargaining

Bargaining is common practice in markets, but isn't generally pursued with the same enthusiasm as in other Asian countries. Most taxi cars have meters but be prepared to negotiate a price before hiring a motorized or cycle rickshaw or a motorbike taxi.

dialogue

how much is this? zhèi ge duōshao qián? [jay gur dwor-show chyen]

30 yuan sān shí kuài qián [kwai chyen]

that's too expensive, how about 20? tài guì le, èr shí kuài, zénme yàng? [gway lur – dzun-mur]

I'll let you have it for 25 èr shí wŭ kuài ba [bah]

can you reduce it a bit more? zài jiăn yí diănr ba [dzai jyen yee dyenr]

OK, it's a deal hăo ba [how]

basket kuāng [kwahng]
筐

bath xízăo [hshee-dzow]
洗澡

can I have a bath? wŏ néng xĭ ge zăo ma? [wor nung hshee gur dzow mah]
我能洗个澡吗？

bathroom yùshì [yew-shur]
浴室

with a private bathroom dài xízăojiān de fāngjiān [dai hshee-dzow-jyen dur fahng-jyen]
带洗澡间的房间

bath towel yùjīn [yew-jin]
浴巾

bathtub zăopén [dzow-pun]
澡盆

battery diànchí [dyen-chur]
电池

bay hăiwān [hai-wahn]
海湾

be* shì [shur]
是

beach hăitān [hai-tahn]
海滩

on the beach zài hăitānshang [dzai –shahng]
在海滩上

bean curd dòufu [doh-foo]
豆腐

beans dòu [doh]
豆

French beans sìjìdòu [sur-jee-doh]
四季豆

broad beans cándòu [tsahn-doh]
蚕豆

string beans jiāngdòu

[jyang-doh]

豇豆

soya beans huángdòu

[hwahng-doh]

黄豆

bean sprouts dòu yár

豆芽儿

beard húzi [hoo-dzur]

胡子

beautiful (object) měilì

[may-lee]

美丽

(woman) piàoliang [pyow-lyang]

漂亮

(view, city, building) měi

美

(day, weather) hǎo [how]

好

because yīnwéi [yin-way]

因为

because of ... yóuyú ...

[yoh-yew]

由于

bed chuáng [chwahng]

床

I'm going to bed now wǒ

yào shuì le [wor yow shway

lur]

我要睡了

bed and breakfast

see hotel

bedroom wòshì [wor-shur]

卧室

beef niúròu [nyoh-roh]

牛肉

beer píjiǔ [pee-jyoh]

啤酒

two beers, please qǐng lái

liǎng bēi píjiǔ [ching]

请来两杯啤酒

 The popularity of beer in China rivals that of tea, and for men it is the preferred mealtime beverage. (Drinking alcohol in public is considered improper for Chinese women, though not for foreigners.) Chinese beer is produced and drunk throughout the country and closely resembles some European lagers though it is usually served at room temperature. The excellent **Tsingtao** label, established in the eastern city of Qingdao during the time of German jurisdiction, is widely available and just about every province produces at least one brand of 4% pilsner. Sold in litre bottles, it's always drinkable, often pretty good, and is actually cheaper than bottled water. A number of foreign brands, notably San Miguel and Carlsberg, are available in bigger cities.

before: before ... ... yǐqián

[yee-chyen]

... 以前

begin kāishǐ [kai-shur]

开始

when does it begin? shénme shíhou kāishǐ? [shun-mur shur-hoh]

什么时候开始？

beginner chūxuézhě [choo-yew-eh-jur]

初学者

behind zài ... hòumian [dzai ... hoh-myen]

在 ... 后面

behind me zài wǒ hòumian [wor]

在我后面

believe xiāngxìn [hsyang-hsin]

相信

below* zài ... xiàmian [dzai ... hsyah-myen]

在 ... 下面

(less than) zài ... yǐxià [yee-hsyah]

在 ... 以下

belt yāodài [yow-dai]

腰带

bend (in road) lùwánr [loo-wahnr]

路弯儿

berth (on train) wòpù [wor-poo]

卧铺

beside: beside the ... zài ... pángbiān [dzai ... pahng-byen]

在 ... 旁边

best zuìhǎo [dzway-how]

最好

better: even better gèng hǎo [gung how]

更好

a bit better hǎo yì diǎnr [dyenr]

好一点儿

are you feeling better? háo diǎnr le ma? [lur mah]

好点儿了吗？

between zài ... zhī jiān [dzai ... jur-jyen]

在 ... 之间

bicycle zìxíngchē [dzur-hsing-chur]

自行车

China has the highest number of bicycles of any country in the world, with about a quarter of the population owning one. Private car ownership is beyond all but the most affluent. Few cities have any hills, and all have **zūchēbù** (bike rental shops or booths), especially near the train stations, where you can rent a set of wheels for a couple of yuan a day. To do this, you will need to leave a deposit and show some form of ID. You're fully responsible for anything that happens to the bike while it's in your care, so check brakes, tyre pressure and gears before renting. Most rental bikes are very basic old models. Cheap **xiūchēbù** (repair shops) are all over the place should you need a tyre patched or a chain fixed. Note that there is little in the way of private insurance in China, so if the bike sustains any serious damage it's up to the parties involved to sort out responsibility and payment on the spot. To avoid theft always use a bicycle chain or lock – they're available everywhere – and in cities, leave your vehicles in one of the ubiquitous designated parking areas, where it will be guarded by an attendant for a few mao.

An alternative to renting is to buy a bike, a sensible option if you're going to be based anywhere for a while. All department stores stock them and demand is so high that there should be little problem reselling the bike when you leave.

big dà [dah]
大
too big tài dà le [lur]
太大了
it's not big enough búgòu dà [boo-goh]
不够大
bill zhàngdānr [jahng-dahnr]
帐单儿
(US: money) chāopiào [chow-pyow]
钞票
could I have the bill, please?
qǐng bāng wǒ jiézhàng, hǎo ma? [ching bahng wor jyeh-jahng

how mah]
请帮我结帐好吗？

 As in virtually the whole of Asia, restaurant bills are never shared in China and people go to great lengths to claim the honour of paying the whole bill by themselves. Normally that honour falls to the person perceived as the most senior, and if you are a foreigner dining with Chinese you should make some effort to stake your claim, though it is most likely that someone else will grab the bill before you do. Attempting to pay your 'share' of the bill will cause embarrassment.

bin lājī xiāng [lah-jee hsyang]
垃圾箱
bird niǎo [nyow]
鸟
birthday shēngrì [shung-rur]
生日
happy birthday! zhù nǐ shēngrì kuàilè! [joo – kwai-lur]
祝你生日快乐
biscuit bǐnggān [bing-gahn]
饼干
bit: a little bit yìdiǎnr [yee-dyenr]
一点儿
a big bit yídàkuàir [yee-dah-kwair]
一大块儿

a bit expensive yǒu diǎn guì
有点贵

bite (by insect) yǎo [yow]
咬

bitten by a dog ràng gǒu gěi
yǎoshāng le [rahng goh gay
yow-shahng]
让狗给咬伤了

bitter (taste etc) kǔ
苦

black hēi [hay]
黑

blanket tǎnzi [tahn-dzur]
毯子

blind xiā [hsyah]
瞎

blocked dǔzhùle
[doo-joo-lur]
堵住了

blond (adj) jīnhuángsè
[jin-hwahng-sur]
金黄色

blood xiě [hsyeh]
血

high blood pressure gāo
xuèyā [gow hsyew-eh-yah]
高血压

blouse nǚchènshān
[nyew-chun-shahn]
女衬衫

blow-dry: I'd like a cut and
blow-dry wó xiǎng lǐfà hé
chuīfēng [wor hsyang lee-fah hur
chway-fung]
我想理发和吹风

blue lánsè [lahn-sur]
蓝色

blue eyes lán yǎnjing [lahn
yahn-jing]
蓝眼睛

boarding pass dēngjì kǎ
[dung-jee kah]
登记卡

boat chuán [chwahn]
船

(for passengers) kèchuán
[kur-chwahn]
客船

body shēntǐ [shun-tee]
身体

boiled egg zhǔ jīdàn [joo
jee-dahn]
煮鸡蛋

boiled rice mǐfàn [mee-fahn]
米饭

boiled water kāishuǐ
[kai-shway]
开水

bone gǔ [goo]
骨

book (noun) shū
书

(verb) dìng
订

can I book a seat? wǒ néng
dìng ge zuòwei ma? [wor
nung – gur dzwor-way mah]
我能订个座位吗？

dialogue

I'd like to book a table for two/three wǒ xiǎng dìng liǎng/sān ge rén yì zhuō de wèizi [wor hsyang – gur run yee jwor dur way-dszur]
what time would you like it booked for? nǐn yào jǐdiǎn zhōng? [yow jee-dyen joong]
half past seven qī diǎn bàn
that's fine xíng [hsing]
and your name? nín guì xìng? [gway]

bookshop, bookstore shūdiàn [shoo-dyen]
书店
boot (footwear) xuēzi [hsyew-eh-dzur]
靴子
(of car) xínglixiāng [hsing-lee-hsyang]
行李箱
border (of country) biānjiè [byen-jyeh]
边界
border region biānjìng
边境
bored: I'm bored fán sǐ le [fahn sur-lur]
烦死了
boring méi jìnr [may]
没劲儿

born: I was born in Manchester wǒ shì zài Mànchéng shēng de [wor shur dzai – shung dur]
我是在曼城生的
I was born in 1960 wǒ shì yí jiǔ liù líng nián shēng de
我是一九六零年生的
borrow jiè [jyeh]
借
may I borrow ...? wǒ kéyi jiè yíxia ... ma? [wor kur-yee jyeh yee-hsyah ... mah]
我可以借一下 ... 吗？
both liǎngge dōu [lyang-gur doh]
两个都
bother: sorry to bother you duìbuqǐ dájiǎo nín le [dway-boo-chee dah-jyow nin lur]
对不起打搅您了
bottle píngzi [ping-dzur]
瓶子
a bottle of beer yì píng píjiǔ [ping-dzur]
一瓶啤酒
bottle-opener kāi píng qì [chee]
开瓶器
bottom dǐr [deer]
底儿
(of person) pìgu
屁股
at the bottom of the road lù de jìntóu [loo dur jin-toh]
路的尽头

box hézi [hur-dzur]

盒子

a box of chocolates yí hé qiǎokèlì [hur chyow-kur-lee]

一盒巧克力

box office shòupiào chù [shoh-pyow]

售票处

boy nánhái [nahn-hai]

男孩

boyfriend nán péngyou [nahn pung-yoh]

男朋友

bra xiōngzhào [hsyoong-jow]

胸罩

bracelet shǒuzhuó [shoh-jwor]

手镯

brandy báilándì [bai-lahn-dee]

白兰地

bread (baked) miànbāo [myen-bow]

面包

(steamed) mántou [mahn-toh]

馒头

white bread bái miànbāo

白面包

brown bread hēi miànbāo [hay]

黑面包

wholemeal bread quánmài miànbāo [chew-ahn-mai]

全麦面包

 Western-style bread is available in bigger cities but it is usually very light and lacking in flavour. Chinese eat **mántou**, a heavy steamed bread, with their meals. In Xinjiang, wonderful unleavened bread can be found in street markets.

break (verb) dǎpò [dah-por]

打破

I've broken the ... wǒ dǎpòle ... [wor dah-por-lur]

我打破了 ...

I think I've broken my ... wǒde ... kěnéng huàile [wor-dur ... kur-nung hwai-lur]

我的 ... 可能坏了

breakdown gùzhàng [goo-jahng]

故障

breakfast zǎofàn [dzow-fahn]

早饭

break-in: I've had a break-in (in room) wǒde fángjiān ràng rén gěi qiàole mén le [wor-dur fahng-jyen rahng run gay chyow-lur mun lur]

我的房间让人给撬了门了

breast xiōng [hsyoong]

胸

breeze wēifēng [way-fung]

微风

bridge (over river) qiáo [chyow]

桥

brief duǎn [dwahn]
短

briefcase gōngwénbāo
[goong-wun-bow]
公文包

bright (light etc) míngliàng
[ming-lyang]
明亮

brilliant (idea, person) gāomíng
[gow-ming]
高明

bring dàilái
带来

I'll bring it back later wǒ guò
xiē shíhou dàihuílái [wor gwor
hsyeh shur-hoh dai-hway-lai]
我过些时候带回来

Britain Yīngguó [ying-gwor]
英国

British (adj) Yīngguó
英国

I'm British wǒ shì Yīngguó
rén [wor shur – run]
我是英国人

brochure shuōmíng shū
[shwor-ming]
说明书

broken (object) pòle [por-lur]
破了
(leg etc) duànle [dwahn-lur]
断了
(not working) huàile [hwai-lur]
坏了

brooch xiōngzhēn [hsyoong-jun]
胸针

brother xiōngdì
[hsyoong-dee]
兄弟
(older) gēge [gur-gur]
哥哥
(younger) dìdi
弟弟

brother-in-law (elder sister's
husband) jiěfū [jyeh-foo]
姐夫
(younger sister's husband) mèifu
[may-foo]
妹夫
(wife's elder brother) nèixiōng
[nay-hsyoong]
内兄
(wife's younger brother) nèidì
[nay-dee]
内弟
(husband's elder brother) dàbó
[dah bor]
大伯
(husband's younger brother)
xiǎoshū [hsyow-shoo]
小叔

brown zōngsè [dzoong-sur]
棕色

brush shuāzi [shwah-dzur]
刷

bucket tǒng [toong]
桶

Buddha Fó [for]
佛

Buddhism Fójiào [for-jyow]
佛教

Buddhist (adj) Fójiàotú
佛教徒

buffet car cānchē
[tsahn-chur]
餐车

building fángzi [fahng-dzur]
房子
(multi-storey) dàlóu [dah-loh]
大楼

bunk: bottom bunk xià pù
[hsyah]
下铺

middle bunk zhōng pù [joong]
中铺

top bunk shàng pù [shahng]
上铺

bureau de change wài huì
duìhuàn bù [hway dway-hwahn]
外汇兑换部
see **bank**

burglary dàoqiè [dow-chyeh]
盗窃

Burma Miǎndiàn [myen-dyen]
缅甸

burn (noun) shāoshāng
[show-shahng]
烧伤
(verb) ránshāo [rahn-show]
燃烧

burnt: this is burnt (food)
shāojiāole [show-jyow-lur]
烧焦了

bus (public transport) gōnggòng
qìchē [goong-goong chee-chur]
公共汽车

(limited stop) shìqūchē
[shur-chew-chur]
市区车
(in suburbs) jiāoqūchē
[jyow-chew-chur]
郊区车
(long-distance) chángtú qìchē
[chahng-too chee-chur]
长途汽车

what number bus is it to ...?
dào ... qù zuò jǐ lù chē? [dow
... chew dzwor jee lu chur]
到 ... 去坐几路车？

when is the next bus to ...?
dào ... qù de xià (yì) bān chē
shì jídiǎn? [dow ... chew dur
hsyah (yee) bahn chur shur jee-dyen]
到 ... 去的下一班车是几
点？

what time is the last bus?
mòbānchē shì jǐ diǎn?
[mor-bahn-chur shur jee dyen]
末班车是几点？

 All Chinese cities have a
very extensive public
transport system. Beijing
and Shanghai have efficient
underground railways, with
Guangzhou's still being constructed.
Elsewhere in cities, buses are the
main form of transport. These are
cheap and run from around 6 a.m. to 9
p.m. or later, but are usually slow and
crowded. Pricier private minibuses

often run the same routes in similar comfort and at greater speed.

The bus is the cheapest (and often only) way of getting from town to town. However, bus travel is very slow: there are breakdowns from time to time and stops every few minutes to pick up or set down passengers. There are a few new expressways, but poor surfaces and maintenance mean that country roads can be downright dangerous, as is the habit of saving fuel by coasting down hills or mountainsides with the engine off. Take some food along because though buses usually pull up at inexpensive roadhouses at mealtimes, they have been known to take two drivers and plough on for 24 hours without stopping.

The standard Chinese long-distance bus is fairly ramshackle, with wooden or lightly padded seats, and is neither heated nor air-conditioned. Luggage racks are tiny, and you'll have to put anything bulkier than a satchel on the roof, on your lap, or beside the driver. On popular routes you'll also find more comfortable options, although these are more expensive than an ordinary bus. Luxury buses have larger and better padded seats which often recline; sometimes there's even air-conditioning and a video.

Sleeper buses have basic bunks instead of seats, and can be comfortable if a little cramped; they tend to be harder to book, however, and road travel at night is always more dangerous.

Minibuses are common on routes of less than 100km or so, and can be immensely useful. If you've missed the only bus to where you're going, you can usually hop there in stages by minibus. All are privately run and prices vary around the country, but they typically cost a little more than the same journey by public bus. Tickets are sold at the point of departure, whether this is a proper bus station or just a kerb stop – in which case you'll pay on board; you'll do this too if you hail a bus in passing. Destinations are always displayed (in Chinese characters) on the front of the vehicle. It's best to buy your ticket a day or two in advance if possible.

dialogue

does this bus go to ...?
zhèi liàng chē qù ... ma?
[jay lyang chur chew ... mah]
no, you need a number ...
bú qù, nǐ yào zùo ... hào
chē [chew nee yow zwor ... how chur]

business shēngyì [shung-yee]
生意
(firm, company) gōngsī
[goong-sur]
公司
bus station gōnggòng qìchē
zǒngzhàn [goong-goong
chee-chur dzoong-jahn]
公共汽车总站
bus stop gōnggòng qìchē
zhàn [jahn]
公共汽车站
busy (road etc) rènào [rur-now]
热闹
(person) hěn máng [hun mahng]
很忙
I'm busy tomorrow wǒ
míngtiān hěn máng [wor
ming-tyen hun mahng]
我明天很忙
but kěshì [kur-shur]
可是
butcher's ròu diàn [roh dyen]
肉店
butter huángyóu [hwahng-yoh]
黄油
button niǔkòu [nyoh-koh]
纽扣
buy mǎi
买
where can I buy ...? zài nǎr
néng mǎidào ...? [dzai nar nung
mai-dow]
在哪儿能买到 ... ？
by: by bus zuò gònggōng

qìchē [dzwor]
坐公共汽车
written by ... shì ... xiě de
[shur ... sheh dur]
是 ... 写的
by the window zài chuānghu
pángbiān [dzai]
在窗户旁边
by the sea zài hǎibiān
在海边
by Thursday xīngqī sì zhī
qián [jur chyen]
星期四之前
bye zàijiàn [dzai-jyen]
再见

C

cabbage báicài [bai-tsai]
白菜
cabin (on ship) chuáncāng
[chwahn-tsahng]
船舱
cake dàngāo [dahn-gow]
蛋糕
cake shop gāodiǎndiàn
[gow-dyen-dyen]
糕点店
call (verb: to phone) dǎ diànhuà
[dah dyen-hwah]
打电话
what's it called? zhège jiào
shénme? [jay-gur jyow shun-mur]
这个叫什么？

he/she is called ... (given name)
tā jiào ... [tah jyow]

他叫 ...

(surname) tā xìng ... [hsing]

他姓 ...

please call the doctor qǐng
bǎ yīshēng jiào lái [chǐng bah
yee-shung jyow]

请把医生叫来

**please give me a call at 7.30
a.m. tomorrow** qǐng
míngtiān zǎoshàng qī diǎn
bàn gěi wó dǎ diànhuà
[ching ming-tyen dzow-shahng
chee dyen bahn gay wor dah
dyen-hwah]

请明天早上七点半给
我打电话

please ask him to call me
qǐng tā dǎ diànhuà géi wǒ
[tah dah – gay]

请他打电话给我

call back: I'll call back later
(phone back) wǒ guò yì huìr
zài dǎ lái [gwor yee hwayr dzai
dah]

我过一回儿再打来

**call round: I'll call round
tomorrow** wǒ míngtiān lái
zhǎo nǐ [jow]

我明天来找你

camcorder shèxiàngjī
[shur-hsyang-jee]

摄相机

camera zhàoxiàngjī
[jow-hsyang-jee]

照相机

camping
Camping rough for
foreigners is officially not
allowed. Camping is only really
feasible in the wildernesses of
western China, where you are not
going to wake up under the prying
eyes of local villagers. In parts of
Tibet, Qinghai, Xinjiang, Gansu and
Inner Mongolia there are places
within reach for hikers or cyclists
where camping is possible. All
equipment would have to be brought
in from outside the country. There
are no official campsites.

can (noun) guàntou [gwahn-toh]

罐头

a can of beer yí guànr píjiǔ

一罐儿啤酒

can: can you ...? nǐ néng ...
ma? [nung ... mah]

你能 ... 吗？

can I have ...? qǐng géi wǒ
...? [ching gay wor]

请给我 ... ？

I can't ... wǒ bù néng ...

我不能 ...

Canada Jiānádà [jyah-nah-dah]

加拿大

Canadian (adj) Jiānádà

加拿大

I'm Canadian wǒ shì Jiānádàrén [wor shur –run]

我是加拿大人

canal yùnhé [yewn-hur]

运河

cancel (reservation etc) tuì [tway]

退

candies tángguǒ [tahng-gwor]

糖果

candle làzhú [lah-joo]

蜡烛

can-opener kāiguàn dāojù [kai-gwahn dow-joo)

开罐刀具

Cantonese (adj) Guǎngdōng [gwahng-doong]

广东

(language) Guǎngdōnghuà [–hwah]

广东话

(person) Guǎngdōng rén [run]

广东人

cap (hat) màozi [mow-dzur]

帽子

(of bottle) pínggài [ping-gai]

瓶盖

car xiǎo qìchē [hsyow chee-chur]

小汽车

by car zuò xiǎo qìchē [dzwor]

坐小汽车

card kǎpiàn [kah-pyen]

卡片

here's my (business) card zhèi shì wǒde míngpiàn [jay shur wor-dur ming-pyen]

这是我的名片

Christmas card shèngdàn kǎ [shung-dahn kah]

圣诞卡

birthday card shēngrì kǎ [shung-rur kah]

生日卡

cardphone cíkǎ diànhuà [tsur-kah dyen-hwah]

磁卡电话

careful: be careful! xiǎoxīn! [hsyow-hsin]

小心

car ferry lúndù [lun-doo]

轮渡

car park tíngchēchǎng [ting-chur-chahng]

停车场

carpet dìtǎn [dee-tahn]

地毯

car rental qìchē chūzū [chee-chur choo-dzoo]

汽车出租

carriage (of train) chēxiāng [chur-hsyang]

车厢

carrot húluóbo [hoo-lwor-bor]

胡萝卜

carry ná [nah]

拿

cash (noun) xiànqián [hsyen-chyen]

现钱

will you cash this for me? nǐ

néng tì wǒ huàn chéng xiàn qián ma? [nung tee wor hwahn chung – mah]

你能替我换成现钱吗？

cash desk jiāokuǎnchù [jyow-kwahn-choo]

交款处

cash dispenser zìdòng qúkuǎnjī [dzur-doong chew-kwahn-jee]

自动取款机

cassette cídài [tsur-dai]

磁带

cassette recorder lùyīnjī [loo-yin-jee]

录音机

castle chéngbǎo [chung-bow]

城堡

casualty department jíjiùshì [jee-jyoh-shur]

急救室

cat māo [mow]

猫

catch (verb) zhuā [jwah]

抓

where do we catch the bus to ...? qù ... zài nǎr shàng chē? [chew ... dzai – chur]

去 ... 在哪儿上车？

cathedral dà jiàotáng [dah jyow-tahng]

大教堂

Catholic (adj) tiānzhǔjiào [tyen-joo-jyow]

天主教

cauliflower càihuā [tsai-hwah]

菜花

cave shāndòng [shahn-doong]

山洞

(dwelling) yáodòng [yow-doong]

窑洞

cemetery mùdì

墓地

centigrade shèshì [shur-shur]

摄氏

centimetre límǐ [lee-mee]

厘米

central zhōngyāng [joong-yang]

中央

central heating nuǎnqì [nwahn-chee]

暖气

centre zhōngxīn [joong-hsin]

中心

how do we get to the city centre? qù shì zhōngxīn zénme zǒu? [chew shur joong-hsin dzun-mur dzoh]

去市中心怎么走？

certainly dāngrán [dahn-grahn]

当然

certainly not dāngrán bù

当然不

chair yǐzi [yee-dzur]

椅子

Chairman Mao Máo zhǔxí [mow jyew-hshee]

毛主席

change (noun: money) língqián

[ling-chyen]

零钱

(verb: money) duìhuàn

[dway-hwahn]

兑换

can I change this for ...? nín néng bāng wǒ duìhuàn chéng ... ma? [nung bahng wor dway-hwahn chung ... mah]

您能帮我兑换成 ... 吗？

I don't have any change wǒ yìdiǎnr língqián yě méi yǒu [wor yee-dyenr ling-chyen yur may yoh]

我一点儿零钱也没有

can you give me change for a hundred-yuan note? yí bǎi kuài nín zhǎodekāi ma? [kwai nin jow-dur-kai mah]

一百块您找得开吗？

dialogue

do we have to change (trains)? zhōngtú yào huàn chē ma? [joong-too yow hwahn chur mah]

yes, change at Hangzhou yào zài Hángzhōu huàn chē [yow dzai]

no, it's a direct train bú yòng huàn chē, zhè shì zhídáchē [yoong – jur shur jur-dah-chur]

changed: to get changed huàn yīfu [hwahn yee-foo]

换衣服

character (in Chinese writing) zì [dzur]

字

charge (noun) shōufèi [shoh-fay]

收费

charge card see **credit card**

cheap piányi [pyen-yee]

便宜

do you have anything cheaper? yǒu piányi diǎnr de ma? [yoh pyen-yee dyenr dur mah]

有便宜点儿的吗？

check: could you check the bill, please? qǐng bǎ zhàngdān jiǎnchá yíxià, hǎo ma? [ching bah jahng-dahn jyen-chah yee-syah how mah]

请把帐单检查一下好吗？

check (US: bill) zhàngdānr [jahng-dahnr]

帐单儿

check in dēngjì [dung-jee]

登记

where do we have to check in? wǒmen yào zài nǎr dēngjì? [wor-men yow dzai nar]

我们要在哪儿登记？

cheerio! zàijiàn! [dzai-jyen]

再见

cheers! (toast) gānbēi!
[gahn-bay]
干杯

cheese nǎilào [nai-low]
奶酪

chemist's yàofáng [yow-fahng]
药房

cherry yīngtao [ying-tow]
樱桃

chess guójì xiàngqí [gwor-jee
hsyang-chee]
国际象棋

  to play chess xià qí [hsyah
  chee]
  下棋

  Chinese chess xiàngqí
  [hsyang-chee]
  象棋

chest (body) xiōng [hsyoong]
胸

chicken (meat) jīròu [jee-roh]
鸡肉

child háizi [hai-dzur]
孩子

 Anyone taking children
into China should be
aware that they will
attract a great deal of friendly
interest. Care should be taken with
hygiene, food etc.
see **health**

child minder báomǔ [bow-moo]
保姆

chin xiàba [hsyah-bah]
下巴

china cíqì [tsur-chee]
瓷器

China Zhōngguó [joong-gwor]
中国

China tea Zhōngguo chá
[chah]
中国茶

Chinese (adj) Zhōngguó
[joong-gwor]
中国

  (person) Zhōngguó rén [run]
  中国人

  (spoken language) Hànyǔ
  [hahn-yew]
  汉语

  (written language) Zhōngwén
  [joong-wun]
  中文

  the Chinese Zhōngguó
  rénmín [run-min]
  中国人民

Chinese leaf báicài [bai-tsai]
白菜

Chinese-style Zhōngshì
[joong-shur]
中式

chips zhá tǔdòu tiáo [jah
too-doh tyow]
炸土豆条

  (US) (zhá) tǔdòupiànr [too-
  doh-pyenr]
  （炸）土豆片儿

chocolate qiǎokèlì

【chyow-kur-lee】
巧克力
milk chocolate nǎiyóu
qiǎokèlì 【nai-yoh】
奶油巧克力
plain chocolate chún
qiǎokèlì
纯巧克力
a hot chocolate yì bēi rè
qiǎokèlì (yǐnliào) 【bay rur –
(yin-lyow)】
一杯热巧克力（饮料）
choose xuǎn 【hsyew-ahn】
选
chopsticks kuàizi 【kwai-dzur】
筷子
Christmas Shèngdàn jié
【shung-dahn jyeh】
圣诞节
Christmas Eve
Shèngdànqiányè 【–chyen-yur】
圣诞前夜
Merry Christmas! Shèngdàn
kuàilè! 【kwai-lur】
圣诞快乐
church jiàotáng 【jyow-tahng】
教堂
cigar xuějiā 【hsyew-eh-jyah】
雪茄
cigarette xiāngyān 【hsyang-yen】
香烟

Smoking is an almost
universal habit among
Chinese men. In the few

places where non-smoking stickers
have been posted (soft-seat train
compartments for example), the
signs are rarely observed. Handing
out cigarettes is one of the most
basic ways to establish trust and
non-smokers should be apologetic
about turning down cigarettes. Many
foreign brands are on sale, with
Marlboro being by some way the
most popular.

cinema diànyǐng yuàn
【dyen-ying yew-ahn】
电影院
circle yuánquān 【ywahn-kwahn】
圆圈
(in theatre) lóutīng 【loh-ting】
楼厅
city chéngshì 【chung-shur】
城市
city centre shì zhōngxīn 【shur
joong-hsin】
市中心
clean (adj) gānjìng 【gahn-jing】
干净
can you clean these for me?
nǐ néng tì wǒ xǐyìxǐ, ma?
【nung tee wor hshee-yee-hshee
mah】
你能替我洗一洗吗？
clear (water) qīngchè
【ching-chur】
清澈
(speech, writing) qīngxī

[ching-hshee]

清晰

(obvious) míngxiǎn [–hsyen]

明显

clever cōngming [tsoong-ming]

聪明

cliff xuányá [hsyew-ahn-yah]

悬崖

climbing páshān [pah-shahn]

爬山

clinic zhénsuǒ [jun-swor]

诊所

cloakroom yīmàojiān
[yee-mow-jyen]

衣帽间

clock zhōng [joong]

钟

close (verb) guān [gwahn]

关

dialogue

what time do you close?
nǐmen shénme shíhou
guān mén? [nee-mun
shun-mur shur-hoh – mun]
we close at 8 p.m. on
weekdays and 6 p.m. on
Saturdays zhōurì xiàwǔ
bā diǎn, xīngqī liù xiàwǔ
liù diǎn [joh-rur]
do you close for lunch?
chī wǔfàn de shíhou guān
mén ma? [chur woo-fahn dur
shur-hoh – mah]

yes, between 1 and
3.30 p.m. shì de, cóng yī
diǎn dào sān diǎn bàn yě
guān mén [shur dur tsoong –
dow – yur]

closed guānménle
[gwahn-mun-lur]

关门了

cloth (fabric) bùliào
[bool-yow]

布料

(for cleaning etc) mābù
[mah-boo]

抹布

clothes yīfu [yee-too]

衣服

clothes line shàiyīshéng
[shai-yee-shung]

晒衣绳

clothes peg yīfu jiāzi [yee-foo
jyah-dzur]

衣服夹子

cloudy duōyún [dwor-yewn]

多云

coach (bus) chángtú qìchē
[chahng-too chee-chur]

长途汽车

(tourist bus) lǚyóu chē
[lyew-yoh chur]

旅游车

(on train) kèchē [kur-chur]

客车

coach station chángtú
qìchēzhàn [chang-too

chee-chur-jahn]
长途汽车站

coach trip zuò chángtú qìchē
lǚxíng [dzwor chahng-too
chee-chur lyew-hsing]
坐长途汽车旅行

coast hǎibīn
海滨

coat (long coat) dàyī [dah-yee]
大衣

coathanger yījià [yee-jyah]
衣架

cockroach zhāngláng
[jahng-lahng]
蟑螂

code (for phoning) diànhuà
qūhào [dyen-hwah chew-how]
电话区号

**what's the (dialling) code for
Beijing?** Běijīng de diànhuà
qūhào shì duōshao? [dur –
shur dwor-show]
北京的电话区号是多
少？

coffee kāfēi [kah-fay]
咖啡

two coffees, please qǐng lái
liǎng bēi kāfēi [ching]
请来两杯咖啡

Coffee is grown and drunk
in Yunnan and Hainan, and
available as instant powder
elsewhere; Hainan produces a nice
instant variety with coconut essence.

Jars of Nescafé are on sale
throughout the country. Milk is
generally sold in powder form as baby
food, though you sometimes find
cartons of UHT in supermarket fridges.

coin yìngbì [ying-bee]
硬币

Coke® Kěkǒukělè
[kur-koh-kur-lur]
可口可乐

cold lěng [lung]
冷

I'm cold wó juéde hén
lěng [wor jyew-eh-dur hun lung]
我觉得很冷

I have a cold wǒ gǎnmào le
[gahn-mow lur]
我感冒了

collapse: he's collapsed tā
kuǎle [tah kwah-lur]
他垮了

collar yǐlǐng
衣领

collect qǔ ... [chew]
取

I've come to collect ... wǒ lái
qǔ ... [wor]
我来取

collect call duìfāng fùkuǎn
[dway-fahng foo-kwahn]
对方付款

college xuéyuàn
[hsyew-eh-yew-ahn]
学院

colour yánsè [yahn-sur]
颜色
do you have this in other colours? yǒu biéde yánsè de ma? [yoh byeh-dur – dur mah]
有别的颜色吗？
colour film cǎisè jiāojuǎnr [tsai-sur jyow-jyew-ahnr]
彩色胶卷儿
comb shūzi [shoo-dzur]
梳子
come lái
来

dialogue

where do you come from? nǐ shì cóng nǎr láide? [shur tsoong nar lai-dur]
I come from Edinburgh wǒ shì cóng Àidīngbǎo lái de [wor]

come back huílai [hway-lai]
回来
I'll come back tomorrow wǒ míngtiān huílai [ming-tyen]
我明天回来
come in qǐng jìn [ching jin]
请进
comfortable shūfu [shoo-foo]
舒服
communism gòngchánzhǔyì [goong-chahn-joo-yee]
共产主义

Communist Party Gòngchándǎng [–dahng]
共产党
Communist Party member gòngchándǎngyuán [–dahng-yew-ahn]
共产党员
compact disc jīguāng chàngpiàn [jee-gwahng chahng-pyen]
激光唱片
company (business) gōngsī [goong-sur]
公司
compass zhǐnánzhēn [jur-nahn-jun]
指南针
complain mányuàn [mahn-yew-ahn]
埋怨
complaint bàoyuàn [bow-yew-ahn]
抱怨
I have a complaint to make wó xiǎng tí yí ge yìjiàn [wor hsyang tee yee gur yee-jyen]
我想提一个意见
completely wánwánquánquán [wahn-wahn-chahn-chahn]
完完全全
computer diànnǎo [dyen-now]
电脑
concert yīnyuèhuì [yin-yew-eh-hway]
音乐会

concussion nǎozhèndàng
[now-jun-dahng]
脑震荡

conditioner (for hair) hùfàsù
[hoo-fah-soo]
护发素

condom bìyùntào
[bee-yewn-tow]
避孕套

conference huìyì [hway-yee]
会议

congratulations! gōngxǐ!
gōngxǐ! [goong-hsee]
恭喜恭喜

connecting flight xiánjiē de
bānjī [hsyen-jyeh dur bahn-jee]
衔接的班机

connection (in travelling)
liányùn [lyen-yewn]
联运

(rail) zhōngzhuǎn
[joong-jwahn]
中转

constipation biànbì [byen-bee]
便秘

consulate lǐngshìguǎn
[ling-shur-gwahn]
领事馆

contact (verb) liánxi
[lyen-hshee]
联系

contact lenses yǐnxíng
yǎnjìng [yin-hsing yahn-jing]
隐型眼镜

contraceptive bìyùn yòngpǐn

[bee-yewn yoong-pin]
避孕用品

convenient fāngbiàn
[fahng-byen]
方便

that's not convenient bù
fāngbiàn
不方便

cooker lúzào [loo-dzow]
炉灶

cookie xiǎo bǐnggān [hsyow
bing-gahn]
小饼干

cool liángkuai [lyang-kwai]
凉快

corner: on the corner jiējiǎor
[jyeh-jyowr]
街角儿

in the corner qiángjiǎor
[chyang-jyowr]
墙角儿

correct (right) duì [dway]
对

corridor zǒuláng [dzoh-lahng]
走廊

cosmetics huàzhuāngpǐn
[hwah-jwahng-pin]
化妆品

cost (noun) jiàqián
[jyah-chyen]
价钱

how much does it cost?
duōshao qián? [dwor-show
chyen]
多少钱？

cotton miánhuā [myen-hwah]
棉花

cotton wool yàomián
[yow-myen]
药棉

couchette wòpù [wor-poo]
卧铺

cough késou [kur-soh]
咳嗽

cough medicine zhǐké yào
[jur-kur yow]
止咳药

could: could you ...? nín
kěyi ... ma? [kur-yee ... mah]
您可以 ... 吗？

I couldn't ... wǒ bù néng ...
[wor boo nung]
我不能

country (nation) guójiā
[gwor-jyah]
国家

(countryside) xiāngcūn
[hsyang-tsun]
乡村

couple (two people) fūfù
[foo-foo]
夫妇

a couple of ... liǎngge ...
[lyang-gur]
两个 ...

courier xìnshǐ [hsin-shur]
信使

course: of course dāngrán
[dahn-grahn]
当然

of course not dāngrán bù
当然不

cousin (son of mother's brother:
older than speaker) biǎogē
[byow-gur]
表哥

(younger than speaker) biǎodì
表弟

(son of father's brother: older than
speaker) tángxiōng
[tahng-hsyoong]
堂兄

(younger than speaker) tángdì
堂弟

(daughter of mother's brother: older
than speaker) biáojiě [byow-jyeh]
表姐

(younger than speaker) biǎomèi
[byow-may]
表妹

(daughter of father's brother: older
than speaker) tángjiě
[tahng-jyeh]
堂姐

(younger than speaker) tángmèi
[tahng-may]
堂妹

cow nǎiniú [nain-yoh]
奶牛

crab pángxiè [pahng-hsyeh]
螃蟹

craft shop gōngyìpǐn
shāngdiàn [goong-yee-pin
shahng-dyen]
工艺品商店

crash (noun: vehicle) zhuàng
chē [jwahng chur]
撞车
crazy fēng [fung]
疯
credit card xìnyòng kǎ
[hsin-yoong kah]
信用卡
do you take credit cards?
shōu xìnyòng kǎ ma?
[show – mah]
收信用卡吗？

 Visa, American Express
and Mastercard are
accepted at big tourist
hotels, and you can obtain a cash
advance with a Visa card within an
hour at many Chinese banks. Wiring
money through the Bank of China
will take weeks even in Beijing,
Shanghai, or Guangzhou, and rates
charged at both ends make it a poor
option except as a last resort. In
cases of dire emergency, you will
either have to rely on the good will
of fellow travellers or get in touch
with your embassy.

dialogue

can I pay by credit card?
wǒ kéyǐ yòng xìnyòng kǎ
jiāo kuǎn ma? [wor kur-yee
yoong hsin-yoong kah jyow

kwahn mah]
**which card do you want to
use?** nín yóng de shì
shénme kǎ? [dur shur
shun-mur kah]
Mastercard/Visa
yes, sir kéyǐ [kur-yee]
what's the number?
duōshao hàomǎ?
[dwor-show how-mah]
and the expiry date? jǐ shí
guòqī? [jee shur gwor-chee]

crisps (zhá) tǔdòupiànr [(jah)
too-doh-pyenr]
（炸）土豆片儿
crockery cānjù [tsahn-jew]
餐具
crossing (by sea) guòdù
[gwor-doo]
过渡
crossroads shízì lùkǒu
[shur-dzur loo-koh]
十字路口
crowd rénqún [run-chewn]
人群
crowded yōngjǐ [yoong-jee]
拥挤
crown (on tooth) yáguàn
[yah-gwahn]
牙冠
cruise zuò chuán lǚxíng
[dzwor chwahn lyew-sing]
坐船旅行
crutches guǎizhàng

[gwai-jahng]

拐杖

cry (verb) kū

哭

Cultural Revolution wénhuà dà gémìng [wun-hwah dah gur-ming]

文化大革命

cup bēizi [bay-dzur]

杯子

a cup of tea/coffee, please yì bēi chá/kāfēi [bay]

一杯茶／咖啡

cupboard guìzi [gway-dzur]

柜子

cure (verb) zhìyù [jur-yew]

治愈

curly juǎnqūde [jwahn-chew-dur]

卷曲的

currency

Chinese currency is formally called **yuán**, more colloquially known as **kuài**, and breaks down into units of ten **máo** or **jiǎo**, and one hundred **fēn**. The last are effectively worthless and you'll only ever be given them in official currency transactions, or see the tiny yellow or green notes folded up into little twists and used to build model dragons or boats. Paper money was invented in China and is still the main form of exchange, available in 100, 50, 20, 10, 5, and 1 yuan notes, with a similar selection of mao; you occasionally come across tiny mao or fen coins, and rare brass 1 yuan pieces. Tourist hotels in Beijing, Shanghai and Guangzhou also sometimes accept, or even insist on, payment in Hong Kong or US dollars. Yuan are not available overseas, though they can be obtained in Hong Kong.

current (electric) diànliú [dyen-lyoh]

电流

(in water) shuǐliú [shway-lyoh]

水流

curry gālì [gah-lee]

咖喱

curtains chuānglián [chwahng-lyen]

窗帘

cushion diànzi [dyen-dzur]

垫子

custom fēngsú [fung-soo]

风俗

Customs hǎiguān [hai-gwahn]

海关

You are allowed to import up to six hundred cigarettes, two litres of alcohol and twenty fluid ounces of perfume. It's illegal to import printed matter, tapes or videos of a politically sensitive nature. There is

CU

no restriction on the amount of
foreign currency you are allowed to
bring into China.

Export restrictions apply to items
more than a hundred years old, for
which you require an export form
available from a friendship store in
Beijing or another major city. You
could be asked to show receipts for
any cultural relics you have.

cut (noun) dāoshāng
〖dow-shahng〗
刀伤
I've cut myself wó bǎ zìjǐ
gēshāng le 〖wor bah dzur-jee gur-
shahng lur〗
我把自己割伤了
cutlery dāochā cānjù
〖dow-chah tsahn-jyew〗
刀叉餐具
cycling qí zìxíngchē 〖chee
dzur-hsing-chur〗
骑自行车
cyclist qí zìxíngchē de rén
〖dur run〗
骑自行车的人

D

dad bàba 〖bah-bah〗
爸爸
daily měi tiān 〖may tyen〗
每天

damage (verb) sǔnhuài
〖syewn-hwai〗
损坏
damaged sǔnhuài le
损坏了
I'm sorry, I've damaged this
duìbùqǐ, wó bǎ zhèi ge
nòng huài le 〖dway-boo-chee
wor bah jay gur noong hwai lur〗
对不起我把这个弄坏了
damn! zāole! 〖dzow-lur〗
糟了
damp (adj) cháoshī 〖chow-shur〗
潮湿
dance (noun) wúdǎo 〖woo-dow〗
舞蹈
(verb) tiàowǔ 〖tyow-woo〗
跳舞
would you like to dance? ní
xiǎng tiàowǔ ma? 〖hsyang –
mah〗
你想跳舞吗？
dangerous wēixiǎn
〖way-hsyen〗
危险
Danish (adj) Dānmài
〖dahn-mai〗
丹麦
dark (adj) àn 〖ahn〗
暗
(colour) shēnsè 〖shunsur〗
深色
it's getting dark tiān hēile
〖tyen hay-lur〗
天黑了

date*: what's the date today?
jīntiān jǐ hào? [jin-tyen jee how]
今天几号？

let's make a date for next Monday zánmen xiàge xīngqīyī jiànmiàn [zahn-mun hsyah-gur – jyen-myen]
咱们下个星期一见面

daughter nǚ'ér [nyew-er]
女儿

daughter-in-law érxífur
[er-hshee-foor]
儿媳妇儿

dawn límíng
黎明

at dawn tiān gāng liàng [tyen gahng lyang]
天刚亮

day tiān [tyen]
天

the day after dìèr tiān
第二天

the day after tomorrow hòutiān [hoh-tyen]
后天

the day before qián yì tiān [chyen]
前一天

the day before yesterday qiántiān [chyen-tyen]
前天

every day měitiān [may-tyen]
每天

all day zhěngtiān [jung-tyen]
整天

in two days' time liǎng tiān nèi [nay]
两天内

have a nice day zhù nǐ wánr de gāoxìng [joo nee wahnr dur gow-hsing]
祝你玩儿得高兴

day trip yírìyóu [yee-rur-yoh]
一日游

dead sǐle [sur-lur]
死了

deaf ěr lóng [loong]
耳聋

deal (business) mǎimài
买卖

it's a deal! yì yán wéi dìng! [yee yahn way]
一言为定

death sǐwáng [sur-wahng]
死亡

December shí'èr yuè [shur-er yew-eh]
十二月

decide juédìng [jyew-eh-ding]
决定

we haven't decided yet wǒmen hái méi juédìng [wor-mun hai may]
我门还没决定

decision juédìng
决定

deck (on ship) jiábǎn [jyah-bahn]
甲板

deep shēn [shun]
深

definitely yídìng
一定
definitely not yídìng bù
一定不
degree (qualification) xuéwèi
[hsyew-eh-way]
学位
delay (noun) wándiǎn
[wahn-dyen]
晚点
deliberately gùyì [goo-yee]
故意
delicious hǎochī [how-chur]
好吃
deliver sòng [soong]
送
delivery (of mail) sòngxìn
[soong-hsin]
送信
Denmark Dānmài [dahn-mai]
丹麦
dentist yáyī [yah-yee]
牙医

Avoid going to the dentist in China. In many places dentists can be seen operating on street corners without the benefit of anaesthetic. If at all possible, wait until you get home, or at least to Beijing or Hong Kong, where any treatment will be extremely expensive, though it should be covered by insurance.

dialogue

it's this one here zhèr zhèi
kē [jer jay kur]
这儿这棵
this one? zhèi kē ma?
[mah]
这棵吗？
no, that one bù, shì nèi kē
[shur nay]
不，是那棵
here? zhèr?
这儿？
yes duì [dway]
对

dentures jiǎyá [jee-ah-yah]
假牙
deodorant chúchòujì
[choo-choh-jee]
除臭剂
department (administrative) bù
部
(academic) xì [hshee]
系
department store bǎihuò
dàlóu [bai-hwor dah-loh]
百货大楼
departure lounge hòujīshì
[hoh-jee-shur]
侯机室
depend: it depends on ... nà
yào kàn ... [nah yow kahn]
那要看 ...
deposit yājīn [yah-jin]
押金
dessert tiánpǐn [tyen-pin]
甜品
destination mùdìdì
目的地

develop (film) chōngxǐ
[choong-hshee]
冲洗

dialogue

> **could you develop these
> films?** qǐng nín bāng wǒ
> chōngxǐ yíxià zhèi xiē
> jiāojuǎnr, hǎo ma? [ching
> nin bahng wor choong-hshee
> yee-hsyah jay hsyeh
> jyow-jyew-ahnr how mah]
> **yes, certainly** kěyǐ [kur-yee]
> **when will they be ready?**
> shénme shíhou néng
> chōng hǎo? [shun-mur
> shur-hoh nung choong how]
> **tomorrow afternoon**
> míngtiān xiàwǔ [ming-tyen
> hsyah-woo]
> **how much is the four-hour
> service?** sì xiǎoshí fúwù
> duōshao qián? [sur
> hsyow-shur foo-woo dwor-show]

diabetic (noun) tángniàobìng
rén [tahng-nyow-bing run]
糖尿病人
dial (verb) bōhào [bor-how]
拨号
dialling code diànhuà qūhào
[dyen-hwah chew-how]
电话区号

To call abroad from
mainland China dial 00 +
country code (see below)
+ area code minus initial zero +
number:

UK 44	US 1
Canada 1	Australia 61
New Zealand 64	Ireland 353

diamond zuànshí [dzwahn-shur]
钻石
diaper niàobù [nyow-boo]
尿布
diarrhoea lā dùzi [lah doo-dzur]
拉肚子
**do you have something for
diarrhoea?** ní yǒu zhì lā dùzi
de yào ma? [nee yoh jur lah
doo-dzur dur yow mah]
你有治拉肚子的药吗？
diary rìjì [rur-jee]
日记
dictionary cídiǎn [tsur-dyen]
词典
didn't* see not
die sǐ [sur]
死
diet jìkǒu [jee-koh]
忌口
I'm on a diet wǒ zài jìkǒu
[wor dzai]
我在忌口
I have to follow a special diet
wó děi chī guīdìng de
yǐnshí [day chur gway-ding dur

yin-shur]

我得吃规定的饮食

difference bùtóng [boo-toong]

不同

 what's the difference? yǒu
 shénme bùtóng? [yoh
 shun-mur]

有什么不同？

different bùtóng

不同

difficult kùnnan [kun-nahn]

困难

difficulty kùnnan

困难

dining room cāntīng [tsahn-ting]

餐厅

dinner (evening meal) wǎnfàn
 [wahn-fahn]

晚饭

 to have dinner chī wǎnfàn

吃晚饭

direct (adj) zhíjiē [jur-jyeh]

直接

 (flight) zhífēi [jur-fay]

直飞

 is there a direct train? yǒu
 zhídá huǒchē ma? [yoh jur-dah
 hwor-chur mah]

有直达火车吗？

direction fāngxiàng
 [fahng-hsyang]

方向

 which direction is it? zài
 nǎige fāngxiàng? [dzai nay-gur]

在哪个方向？

is it in this direction? shì
 zhèige fāngxiàng ma? [shur
 jay-gur – mah]

是这个方向吗？

director zhǔrén [joo-run]

主任

dirt wūgòu [woo-goh]

污垢

dirty zāng [dzahng]

脏

disabled cánfèi [tsahn-fay]

残废

 **is there access for the
 disabled?** yǒu cánjírén de
 tōngdào ma? [you tsahn-jee-run
 dur toong-dow mah]

有残疾人的通道吗？

disaster zāinàn [dzai-nahn]

灾难

disco dísīkē [dee-sur-kur]

迪斯科

discount jiǎnjià [jyen-jyah]

减价

 is there a discount? néng
 jiǎnjià ma? [nung – mah]

能减价吗？

disease jíbìng

疾病

disgusting ěxīn [ur-hsin]

恶心

dish (meal) cài [tsai]

菜

 (bowl) diézi [dyeh-dzur]

碟子

disk (for computer) ruǎnpán

[rwahn-pahn]

软盘

disposable nappies/diapers
(yícìxìng) niàobù
[(yee-tsur-hsing) nyow-boo]

（一次性）尿布

distance jùlí

距离

in the distance zài yuǎnchù
[dzai yew-ahn-choo]

在远处

district dìqū [dee-chew]

地区

disturb dárǎo [dah-row]

打扰

divorced líhūn [lee-hun]

离婚

dizzy: I feel dizzy wǒ tóuyūn
[wor toh-yewn]

我头晕

do (verb) zuò [dzwor]

作

what shall we do? ní xiǎng
zuò shénme? [hsyang –
shun-mur]

你想作什么？

how do you do it? gāi zěnme
zuò? [dzun-mur]

该怎么做？

will you do it for me? máfan
nǐ bāng wǒ zuò yíxià, hǎo
ma? [mah-fahn nee bahng wor
dzwor yee-hsyah how mah]

麻烦你帮我做一下好
吗？

dialogues

how do you do? nín hǎo?
[how]

nice to meet you jiàn dào
nín zhēn gāoxìng [jyen dow
nin jun gow hsing]

what do you do? (work) nǐ
shì zuò shénme gōngzuò
de? [shur – goong-dzwor dur]

I'm a teacher, and you?
wǒ shì jiàoshī, nǐ ne? [wor
– nur]

I'm a student wǒ shì
xuésheng

**what are you doing this
evening?** nǐ jīnwǎn zuò
shénme? [jin-wahn]

**we're going out for a drink,
do you want to join us?**
wǒmen chū qù hē jiǔ, nǐ
xiǎng gēn wǒmen yí
kuàir qù ma? [wor-mun choo
chew hur jyoh nee hsyang gun –
kwair chew mah]

do you want more rice? nǐ
hái yào fàn, ma? [yow fahn]

I do, but she doesn't wǒ
yào, tā bú yào [wor yow tah]

doctor yīshēng [yee-shung]

医生

please call a doctor qǐng nǐ
jiào ge yīshēng [ching nee jyow

gur]
请你叫个医生

Medical facilities are good, at least in the big cities. Low standards of public hygiene and overcrowded conditions are to blame for most of the problems that beset visitors. If you do get ill, international clinics in Beijing, Shanghai and Guangzhou can provide diagnosis and treatment for minor complaints; also, every town has a pharmacy which can suggest remedies and doctors who can treat you with traditional Chinese or Western techniques. You can't expect to find English-speaking medical or pharmacy staff. Large hotels usually have a clinic offering diagnosis, advice and prescriptions and there'll be someone who speaks English. If you are seriously ill, it's best to head straight to a hospital (don't get the police involved as they are rarely helpful) – though you could try giving CITS (the state tour operator) a ring for advice on where to go. You will be expected to pay for your treatment on the spot, so keep the receipt and you can claim the money back from your insurance policy when you get home.
see **health**

dialogue

where does it hurt? nár téng? [tung]
right here jiù zài zhèr [jyoh dzai jer]
does that hurt now? xiànzài hái téng ma? [hsyahn-dzai – mah]
yes hái téng
take this prescription to the chemist ná zhèi gè yàofāng dào yàodiàn qù pèi yào [nah jay gur yow-fahng dow yow-dyen chew pay yow]

document wénjiàn [wun-jyen]
文件
dog gǒu [goh]
狗
domestic flight guónèi hángbān [gwor-nay hahng-bahn]
国内行班
don't!* búyào! [boo-yow]
不要
don't do that! bié zhème zuò [byeh jur-mur zwor]
别这么做
see **not**
door mén [mun]
门
doorman bǎménrde [bah-munr-dur]
把门儿的

Do

double shuāng [shwahng]

双

double bed shuāngrén

chuáng [–run chwahng]

双人床

double room shuāngrén

fáng(jiān) [fahng(jyen)]

双人房（间）

down xià [hsyah]

下

  down here jiù zài zhèr [jyoh

dzai jer]

就在这儿

  put it down over there gē zài

nàr

搁在那儿

  it's down there on the right

jiù zài yòubian [yoh-byen]

就在右边

  it's further down the road zài

wǎng qián [wahng chyen]

再往前

downstairs lóuxià [loh-hsyah]

楼下

dozen yì dá [dah]

一打

  half a dozen bàn dá [bahn]

半打

dragon lóng [loong]

龙

draught beer shēng píjiǔ

[shung pee-jyoh]

生啤酒

draughty: it's draughty

zhèr tōngfēng [jer

toong-fung]

这儿通风

drawer chōuti [choh-tee]

抽屉

drawing huìhuà [hway-hwah]

绘画

dreadful zāotòule [dzow-toh-lur]

糟透了

dress (noun) liányīqún

[lyen-yee-chewn]

连衣裙

 Judging what clothing is
appropriate is generally a
matter of common sense.
Shorts are OK for temples, but
women should not wear anything
too revealing.

dressed: to get dressed

chuān yīfu [chwahn]

穿衣服

dressing gown chényī

[chun-yee]

晨衣

drink (noun: alcoholic) jiǔ [jyoh]

酒

(non-alcoholic) yǐnliào [yin-lyow]

饮料

(verb) hē [hur]

喝

  a cold drink yì bēi léngyǐn

[yee bay lung-yin]

一杯冷饮

  can I get you a drink?

hēdiǎnr shénme ma? [dyenr
shun-mur mah]

喝点儿什么吗？

**what would you like (to
drink)?** ní xiǎng hē diǎnr
shénme? [hsyang]

你想喝点儿什么？

no thanks, I don't drink
xièxie, wǒ bú huì hē jiǔ
[hsyeh-hsyeh wor boo hway hur jyoh]

谢谢我不会喝酒

I'll just have a drink of water
wǒ hē diǎnr shuǐ ba [shway
bah]

我喝点儿水吧

see **bar**

drinking water yǐnyòngshuǐ
[yin-yoong-shway]

饮用水

is this drinking water? zhè
shuǐ kěyǐ hē ma? [jur shway
kur-yee hur ma]

这水可以喝吗？

drive (verb) kāichē [kai-chur]

开车

we drove here wǒmen
kāichē lái de [wor-mun kai-chur
lai dur]

我们开车来的

I'll drive you home wǒ kāichē
sòng nǐ huíjiā [wor kai-chur
soong nee hway-jyah]

我开车送你回家

driver sījī [sur-jee]

司机

driving

Renting a car to drive
yourself is impossible for
a tourist, but it is possible to rent
vehicles with a driver for local use in
Beijing, Shanghai and Sanya, on
Hainan Island.

Prices are set by negotiating and
you'll be expected to provide lunch
for the driver. It's easiest to arrange
this type of rental through a hotel,
though some tour operators rent out
vehicles too – which might be more
useful as they often include the
services of an interpreter. In Tibet,
hiring a jeep with driver is pretty
much the only way to get to many
destinations.

driving licence jiàshǐ zhízhào
[jyah-shur jur-jow]

驾驶执照

drop: just a drop, please (of
drink) zhēn de yì diǎnr,
xièxie [jun dur yee dyen
hsyeh-hsyeh]

真的一点儿谢谢

drugs (narcotics) dúpǐn [doo-pin]

毒品

drunk (adj) hēzuìle
[hur-dzway-lur]

喝醉了

dry (adj) gān [gahn]

干

dry-cleaner gānxǐdiàn

[gahn-hshee-dyen]
干洗店

duck (meat) yā [yah]
鸭

due: he was due to arrive
yesterday tā yīnggāi shì
zuótiān dào [tah ying-gai
dzwor-tyen dow]
他应该昨天到

when is the train due?
huŏchē jĭ diăn dào?
[hwor-chur jee shur]
火车几点到？

dull (pain) yínyĭn zuòtòng
[dzwor-toong]
隐隐作痛

(weather) yīntiān [yin-tyen]
阴天

during zài ... de shíhou [dzai ...
dur shur-hoh]
在 ... 的时候

dust huīchén [hway-chun]
灰尘

dustbin lājīxiāng [lah-jee-hsyang]
垃圾箱

Dutch (adj) Hélán [hur-lahn]
荷兰

duty-free (goods) miănshuì
[myen-shway]
免税

duty-free shop miănshuì
shāngdiàn [shahng-dyen]
免税商店

dynasty cháodài [chow-dai]
朝代

E

each (every) měi [may]
每

how much are they each? yí
ge yào duōshao qián? [yee gur
yow dwor-show chyen]
一个要多少钱？

ear ěrduo [er-dwor]
耳朵

earache: I have earache wó
ěrduo téng [wor – tung]
我耳朵疼

early zăo [dzow]
早

early in the morning yì zăo
一早

I called by earlier wó zăo xiē
shíhou láiguo [wor – hsyeh
shur-hoh lai-gwor]
我早些时候来过

earrings ěrhuán [er-hwahn]
耳环

east dōng [doong]
东

in the east dōngbiān
[doong-byen]
东边

East China Sea Dōng Hăi
东海

easy róngyì [roong-yee]
容易

eat chī [chur]
吃

we've already eaten, thanks
xièxie, wǒmen yǐjing chīle
[hsyeh-hsyeh wor-mun –chur-lur]
谢谢我们已经吃了

economy class jīngjìcāng
[–tsahng]
经济舱

egg jīdàn [jee-dahn]
鸡蛋

either: either ... or ...
huòzhe ... huòzhe ...
[hwor-jur]
或者 ... 或者 ...

either of them něi liǎngge
dōu kéyǐ [nay lyang-gur doh
kur-yee]
那两个都可以

elastic band xiàngpíjīnr
[hsyahng–]
橡皮筋儿

elbow gēbozhǒur [gur-bor-johr]
胳膊肘儿

electric diàn [dyen]
电

electric fire diàn lúzi [loo-dzur]
电炉子

electrician diàngōng
[dyen-goong]
电工

electricity diàn [dyen]
电
see **voltage**

elevator diàntī [dyen-tee]
电梯

else: something else biéde

dōngxi [byeh-dur doong-hshee]
别的东西

somewhere else biéde dìfāng
[dee-fahng]
别的地方

dialogue

> would you like anything
> else? hái yào biéde ma?
> [yow – mah]
> no, nothing else, thanks
> bú yào le, xièxie [lur
> hsyeh-hsyeh]

email diànzi yóujiàn [dyen-dzur
yoh-jyen]
电子邮件

embassy dàshǐguǎn
[dah-shur-gwahn]
大使馆

embroidery cìxiù [tsur-hsyoh]
刺绣

emergency jǐnjí qíngkuàng
[ching-kwahng]
紧急情况

this is an emergency!
jiùmìng! [jyoh-ming]
救命

emergency exit ānquánmén
[ahn-choo-en-mun]
安全门

emperor huángdì
[hwahng-dee]
皇帝

empress huánghòu
皇后

empty kōng [koong]
空

end (noun) mòduān
[mor-dwahn]
末端

at the end of the street zhèi
tiáo jiē de jìntóu [jay tyow jyeh
dur jin-toh]
这条街的尽头

when does it end? shénme
shíhou jiéshù? [shun-mur
shur-hoh jyeh-shoo]
什么时候结束？

engaged (toilet) yǒurén
[yoh-run]
有人

(phone) zhànxiàn [jahn-hsyen]
占线

(to be married) dìnghūnle
[ding-hun-lur]
定婚了

England Yīngguó [ying-gwor]
英国

English (adj) Yīngguó
[ying-gwor]
英国

(language) Yīngyǔ [ying-yew]
英语

I'm English wǒ shì Yīngguó
rén [wor shur – run]
我是英国人

do you speak English? ni
huìbuhuì shuō Yīngyǔ?
[hway-boo-hway shwor]
你会不会说英语？

enjoy: to enjoy oneself wánr
de hěn kāixīn [wahnr dur hun
kai-hsin]
玩儿得很开心

dialogue

how did you like the film?
nǐ juéde diànyǐng zěnme
yàng? [jyew-ch dur dyen-ying
dzun-mur yang]
I enjoyed it very much, did
you enjoy it? wǒ juéde
hén hǎo, nǐ ne? [wor – hun
how nee nur]

enjoyable lìng rén yúkuàide
[run yew-kwai-dur]
令人愉快的

enormous dàjíle [dah-jee-lur]
大极了

enough: that's enough gòule
[goh-lur]
够了

there's not enough bú gòu
不够

it's not big enough bú gòu dà
不够大

entrance (noun) rùkǒuchù
[roo-koh-choo]
入口处

envelope xìnfēng [hsin-fung]
信封

equipment shèbèi [shur-bay]
设备
(for climbing, sport etc) qìxiè
[chee-hsyeh]
器械
especially tèbié [tur-byeh]
特别
essential zhòngyào [joong-yow]
重要
it is essential that ... ... shì
juéduì bìyào de [shur
jyew-eh-dway bee-yow dur]
... 是决对必要的
Europe Ōuzhōu [oh-joh]
欧洲
European (adj) Ōuzhōu
欧洲
even shènzhi [shun-jur]
甚至
even if ... jìshǐ ... yě [jee-shur ...
yur]
即使 ... 也
evening wǎnshang
[wahn-shahng]
晚上
this evening jīntiān
wǎnshang [jin-tyen]
今天晚上
in the evening wǎnshang
晚上
evening meal wǎnfàn
[wahn-fahn]
晚饭
eventually zuìhòu [dzway-hoh]
最后

ever céngjīng [tsung-jing]
曾经

dialogue

have you ever been to the
Great Wall? nǐ qùguo
Chángchéng ma?
[chew-gwor – mah]
**yes, I was there two years
ago** qùguo, liǎng nián
qián qùguo [chew-gwor
lyang nyen chyen chew-gwor]

every měige [may-gur]
每个
every day měitiān [may-tyen]
每天
everyone měige rén [may-gur
run]
每个人
everything měijiàn shìr
[may-jyen shur]
每件事儿
(objects) suóyǒu de dōngxi
[swor-yoh dur doong-hshee]
所有的东西
everywhere měige dìfāng
[may-gur dee-fahng]
每个地方
exactly! duìjíle!
[dway-jee-lur]
对极了
exam kǎoshì [kow-shur]
考试

example lìzi [lee-dzur]

例子

for example lìrú

例如

excellent hǎojíle [how-jee-lur]

好极了

except chúle ... yǐwài
[choo-lur]

除了 ... 以外

excess baggage chāozhòng
xíngli [chow-joong hsing-lee]

超重行李

exchange rate duìhuàn lǜ
[dway-hwahn lyew]

兑换率

exciting (day) cìji [tsur-jee]

刺激

excuse me (to get past) láojià
[low-jyah]

劳驾

(to get attention) láojià, qǐng
wèn ... [ching wun]

劳驾请问

(to say sorry) duìbuqǐ
[dway-boo-chee]

对不起

exhausted (tired) lèisǐle
[lay-sur-lur]

累死了

exhibition (of paintings etc)
zhánlǎn [jan-lan]

展览

(trade fair etc) jiāoyì huì
[jyow-yee hway]

交易会

exit chūkǒu [choo-koh]

出口

where's the nearest exit? zuì
jìn de chūkǒu zài nǎr? [dzway
jin dur choo-koh dzai]

最近的出口在哪儿？

expensive guì [gway]

贵

experienced yǒu jīngyàn [yoh
jing-yen]

有经验

explain jiěshì [jyeh shur]

解释

can you explain that? nǐ
néng jiěshì yíxià ma? [nung –
yee-syah mah]

你能解释一下吗？

express (mail) kuàidì
[kwai-dee]

快递

(train) kuàichē [kwai-chur]

快车

extension (telephone) fēnjī
[fun-jee]

分机

extension 221, please qǐng
guà èr èr yāo [ching gwah er er
yow]

请挂二二一

extra: can we have an extra
one? qǐng zài lái yíge? [dzai
lai yee-gur]

请再来一个？

do you charge extra for that?
hái yào qián ma? [hai yow

chyen mah]

还要钱吗？

extremely fēicháng [fay-chahng]

非常

eye yǎnjing [yahn-jing]

眼睛

will you keep an eye on my suitcase for me? máfan nín bāng wǒ kān yíxià tíbāo, hǎo ma? [mah-fahn nin bahng wor kahn yee-hsyah tee-bow how mah]

麻烦您帮我看一下提包好吗？

eyeglasses yǎnjìng [yahn-jing]

眼镜

F

face liǎn [lyen]

脸

factory gōngchǎng [goong-chahng]

工厂

Fahrenheit huáshì [hwah-shur]

华氏

faint (verb) yūn [yewn]

晕

she's fainted tā yūndàole [tah yewn-dow-lur]

她晕倒了

I feel faint wǒ juéde yóu diǎn (tóu) yūn [wor jyew-eh-dur yoh dyen (toh)]

我觉得有点（头）晕

fair (adj) gōngpíng [goong-ping]

公平

fake màopái [mow-pai]

冒牌

fall (verb: person) shuāidǎo [shwai-dow]

摔倒

she's had a fall tā shuāile yì jiāo [tah shwai-lur yee jyow]

她摔了一交

fall (US) qiūtiān [chyoh-tyen]

秋天

in the fall qiūtiān

秋天

false jiǎ [jyah]

假

family jiātíng [jyah-ting]

家庭

famous yǒumíng [yoh-ming]

有名

fan (electrical) fēngshàn [fung-shahn]

风扇

(hand-held) shànzi [shahn-dzur]

扇子

(sports) qiúmí [chyoh-mee]

球迷

fantastic (wonderful) tàihǎole [tai-how-lur]

太好了

far yuǎn [yew-ahn]

远

dialogue

is it far from here? lí zhèr yuǎn ma? [jer – mah]

no, not very far bú tài yuǎn

well, how far? duō yuǎn ne? [dwor – nur]

it's about 20 kilometres èr shí gōnglǐ zuǒyòu [goong-lee dzwor-yoh]

fare chēfèi [chur-fay]
车费

Far East Yuǎndōng [yew-ahn-doong]
远东

farm nóngchǎng [noong-chahng]
农场

fashionable shímáo [shur-mow]
时髦

fast kuài [kwai]
快

fat (person) pàng [pahng]
胖
(on meat) féiròu [fay-roh]
肥肉

father fùqīn [foo-chin]
父亲

father-in-law yuèfù [yew-eh-foo]
岳父

faucet shuǐlóngtóu [shway-loong-toh]
水龙头

fault cuò [tswor]
错

sorry, it was my fault duìbuqǐ shì wǒde cuò [dway-boo-chee shur wor-dur tswor]
对不起是我的错

it's not my fault bú shì wǒde cuò
不是我的错

faulty yǒu máobìng [yoh mow-bing]
有毛病

favourite zuì xǐhuan de [dzway hshee-hwahn dur]
最喜欢的

fax (noun) chuánzhēn [chwahn-jun]
传真

to send a fax fā chuánzhēn [fah]
发传真

February èryuè [er-yew-eh]
二月

feel gǎnjué [gahn-jyew-eh]
感觉

I feel hot wǒ juéde hěn rè [wor jyew-eh-dur hun rur]
我觉得很热

I feel unwell wǒ juéde bú tài shūfu [–dur – shoo-foo]
我觉得不太舒服

I feel like going for a walk wó xiǎng qù zóuzǒu [hsyahng chew dzoh-dzoh]
我想去走走

how are you feeling? nǐ juéde zěnme yàng le? [nee jyew-eh-dur dzun-mur – lur]
你觉得怎么样了？

I'm feeling better wǒ hǎo diǎnr le [how dyenr]
我好点儿了

fence zhàlan [jah-lahn]
栅栏

ferry bǎidù
摆渡

There are any number of river and sea journeys to make while in China, though passenger ferries are generally on the decline as new roads are built with buses providing a faster service. It might not always be the quickest or cheapest form of transport, but a boat ride can be a refreshing change from the tribulations of train or bus travel, and it's always affordable. Conditions on board are greatly variable, but on overnight trips there's always a choice of classes – sometimes as many as six – which can range from a bamboo mat on the floor, right through to the luxury of private cabins. Toilets and food can be basic, though, so plan things as best you can.

festival jiérì [jyeh-ree]
节日

Traditionally, there were a large number of festivals in China, many of which marked different stages of the agricultural year. In recent years, some have been revived.

Moon Festival celebrations are held to mark the middle of autumn on the fifteenth day of the eighth lunar month; they always feature fireworks and lanterns, large mooncakes (with images of three-legged toads and rabbits and symbols of the moon carved on the top) and Maotai (a clear spirit distilled from rice or millet). Poems are composed and recited in honour of the full moon.

The birthday of Confucius on 28 September is marked by celebrations at all Confucian temples. It is a good time to visit his birthplace, Qufu, which is located in Shandong Province, elaborate ceremonies being held in the temple there.

On **Dēngjié** (Lantern Festival), which takes place on the fifteenth day of the New Year, all shops and houses display lanterns in recognition of the coming of greater light and warmth.

The **Qīngmíng** (Pure Brightness) festival, held on 5 April, is the day for honouring ancestors. Graves are swept and various paper objects, such as money and sacrificial utensils, are displayed before being burnt.

On the fifth day of the fifth month, the **Dragon-Boat Festival** is held in honour of the great poet Qu Yuan who drowned in a river on this day. In many towns of southern China, races are held between long dragon boats. **Zhōng Yuán**, which takes place on the fifteenth day of the seventh month, is another festival in honour of ancestors. Traditionally on this day, lanterns are lit and sutras recited in Buddhist temples in order to lead the souls of the departed through the sea of suffering.

On **Chóng Yáng** (Double Yang), held on the ninth day of the ninth month, people climb hills to recite poems, drink wine and enjoy nature.

fetch qǔ [chew]
取
I'll fetch him wǒ qù jiào tā lái [wor – jyow tah]
我去叫他来
will you come and fetch me later? děng huìr nǐ lái jiē wǒ, hǎo ma? [dung hwayr – jyeh]
等会儿你来接我好吗？
feverish fāshāo [fah-show]
发烧
few: a few yì xiē [yee-hsyeh]
一些

a few days jǐ tiān [tyen]
几天
fiancé wèihūnfū [way-hun-foo]
未婚夫
fiancée wèihūnqī [way-hun-chee]
未婚妻
field tiándì [tyen-dee]
田地
(paddy) dàotián [dow-tyen]
稻田
fill in tián [tyen]
填
do I have to fill this in? wǒ yào tián zhèi zhāng biǎo ma? [wor yow tyen jay jahng byow mah]
我要填这张表吗？
filling (in cake, sandwich) xiànr [hsyenr]
馅儿
(in tooth) bǔ yá [byew yah]
补牙
film (movie) diànyǐng [dyen-ying]
电影
(for camera) jiāojuǎnr [jyow-jew-ahnr]
胶卷儿

dialogue

do you have this kind of film? nǐ yǒu zhèi zhǒng jiāojuǎnr ma? [yoh jay-joong

jyow-jyew-ahnr mah]
yes, how many exposures?
yǒu, nǐ yào duōshao
zhāng de? [yow dwor-show
jahng dur]
36 sān shí liù zhāng (de)

filthy zāng [dzahng]
脏
find (verb) zhǎodào [jow-dow]
找到
I can't find it wó zhǎobúdào
[wor jow-boo-dow]
我找不到
I've found it zhǎodàole [jow-
dow-lur]
找到了
find out zhǎochū [jow-choo]
找出
could you find out for me? nǐ
néng tì wǒ diàochá yíxià
ma? [nung tee wor dyow-chah
yee-hsyah mah]
你能替我调查一下吗？
fine (weather) qínglǎng
[ching-lang]
晴朗
(punishment) fákuán [fah-kwahn]
罚款

dialogues

how are you? nǐ hǎo ma?
[how mah]
I'm fine, thanks hén hǎo,

xièxie [hun how hsyeh-hsyeh]

is that OK? zhèyàng xíng
ma? [jur-yang hsing mah]
that's fine, thanks xíng,
xièxie

finger shóuzhǐ [shoh-jur]
手指
finish (verb) zuò wán [dzwor
wahn]
作完
I haven't finished yet wǒ hái
méi nòng wán [wor hai may
noong wahn]
我还没弄完
when does it finish? shénme
shíhou néng wán? [shun-mur
shur-hoh nung]
什么时候能完？
fire huǒ [hwor]
火
(blaze) huǒzāi [hwor-dzai]
火灾
fire! zháohuǒle! [jow-hwor-lur]
着火了
can we light a fire here? zhèr
néng dián huǒ ma? [jer nung
dyen hwor mah]
这儿能点火吗？
fire alarm huójǐng [hwor-jing]
火警
fire brigade xiāofǎngduì
[hsyow-fahng-dway]
消防队

The phone number for the fire brigade is 119.

fire escape tàipíngtī
太平梯

fire extinguisher mièhuǒqì
[myeh-hwor-chee]
灭火器

first dìyī
第一

I was first wǒ dìyī [wor]
我第一

first of all shǒuxiān
[shoh-hsyen]
首先

at first qǐchū [chee-choo]
起初

the first time dīyí cì [tsur]
第一次

first on the left zuǒbian dì
yīge [zwor-byen – gur]
左边第一个

first aid jíjiù [jee-jyoh]
急救

first-aid kit jíjiùxiāng
[–hsyahng]
急救箱

first class (travel etc) yīděng
[yee-dung]
一等

first floor èr lóu [er loh]
二楼

(US) yī lóu
一楼

first name míngzi [ming-dzur]
名子

fish (noun) yú [yew]
鱼

fit: it doesn't fit me zhè duì
wǒ bù héshì [jur dway wor boo
hur-shur]
这对我不合适

fitting room shì yī shì [shur yee
shur]
试衣室

fix: can you fix this? (repair) nǐ
néng bǎ zhèige xiū hǎo ma?
[nung bah jay-gur hsyoh how mah]
你能把这个修好吗？

fizzy yǒuqìde [yoh-chee-dur]
有气的

flag qí [chee]
旗

flannel (xǐliǎn) máojīn
[(hshee-lyen) mow-jin]
洗脸毛巾

flash (for camera)
shǎnguāngdēng
[shahn-gwahng-dung]
闪光灯

flat (noun: apartment) dānyuán
[dahn-yew-ahn]
单元

(adj) píngtǎn [ping-tahn]
平坦

I've got a flat tyre wǒde
chētāi biěle [wor-dur chur-tai
byeh-lur]
我的车胎瘪了

FI

flavour wèidao [way-dow]
味道

flea tiàozǎo [tyow-dzow]
跳蚤

flight hángbān [hahng-bahn]
航班

flight number hángbān hào
[how]
航班号

flood hóngshuǐ [hoong-shway]
洪水

floor (of room: wooden) dìbǎn
地板
(storey) lóu [loh]
楼
(in hotel etc) céng [tsung]
层
on the floor zài dìshang [dzai
dee-shahng]
在地上

florist huādiàn [hwah-dyen]
花店

flower huā [hwah]
花

flu liúgǎn [lyoh-gahn]
流感

**fluent: he speaks fluent
Chinese** tā Hànyǔ jiǎngde
hěn liúlì [tah hahn-yew jyang-dur
hun lyoh-lee]
他汉语讲得很流利

fly (noun) cāngying [tsahng-ying]
苍蝇
(verb) fēi [fay]
飞

can we fly there? dào nàr
yǒu fēijī ma? [dow nar yoh
fay-jee mah]
到那儿有飞机吗？

fog wù
雾

foggy: it's foggy yǒu wù [yoh
有雾

folk dancing mínjiān wúdǎo
[min-jyen woo-dow]
民间舞蹈

folk music mínjiān yīnyuè
[yin-yew-eh]
民间音乐

food shíwù [shur-woo]
食物
(in shops) shípǐn [shur-pin]
食品

food poisoning shíwù
zhòngdú [joong-doo]
食物中毒

food shop, food store shípǐn
diàn [shur-pin dyen]
食品店

foot (measurement) yīngchǐ
[ying-chur]
英尺
(of person) jiǎo [jyow]
脚
to go on foot bùxíng
[boo-hsing]
步行

football (game) zúqiúsài
[dzoo-chyoh-sai]
足球赛

(ball) zúqiú [dzoo-chyoh]
足球

for*: do you have something for ...? (illness) nǐ yǒu zhì... de yào ma? [yoh –jur yow mah]
你有治 ... 的药吗？

dialogues

who are the dumplings for? zhèi xiē jiǎozi shì shéi (jiào) de? [jay hsyeh jyow-dzur shur shay (jyow) dur]
that's for me shì wǒ de [shur wor]
and this one? zhèi gè ne? [jay gur ne]
that's for her shì tā de [shur tah]

where do I get the bus for Beijing? qù Běijīng zài nár zuò chē? [chew – dzai nar dzwor chur]
the bus for Beijing leaves from Donglu Street qù Běijīng de chē zài Dōnglù kāi [chew – dur chur dzai]

how long have you been here? nǐ lái zhèr duō cháng shíjiān le? [jer dwor chahng shur-jyen lur]
I've been here for two days,

how about you? wǒ láile liǎng tiān le, nǐ ne? [wor lai-lur lyang tyen lur nee nur]
I've been here for a week wǒ láile yíge xīngqī le [yee-gur hsing-chee lur]

Forbidden City Gùgōng [goo-goong]
故宫
foreign wàiguó [wai-gwor]
外国
foreigner wàiguó rén [run]
外国人

 Foreigners are highly conspicuous in China and local people are profoundly curious to see them, particularly in remote rural areas. When they appear, people run up and shout **Lǎo Wài!** ('old outside person'), and although this is not intended to be rude or insulting, it can give foreigners the uncomfortable feeling of being like an animal in a zoo. The best way to diffuse this sensation is to address the onlookers in Chinese, if you can. Visitors who speak Chinese will encounter an endless series of delighted and amazed people who will invariably ask about their age and marital status before anything else. Even if you don't speak

Chinese, you will run into enough locals eager to practise their English. Surprisingly, the main gripe of foreign travellers concerns the widespread Chinese attitude that foreigners should pay double. This attitude is so deeply rooted in the Chinese sense of justice that you would do well to indulge it. The average rickshaw driver would consider it a humiliating defeat to carry a foreigner for the same price as a local.

Foreign teachers or students may find themselves expelled from the country for talking about politics or religion. The Chinese they talk to will be treated less leniently.

forest sēnlín [sun-lin]
森林

forget wàng [wahng]
忘

I forget, I've forgotten wǒ wàngle [wor –lur]
我忘了

fork (for eating) chā [chah]
叉

(in road) chàlù [chah-loo]
岔路

form (document) biǎo [byow]
表

formal (dress) zhèngshì [jung-shur]
正式

fortnight liǎngge xīngqī [lyang-gur hsing-chee]
两个星期

fortunately xìngkuī [hsing-kway]
幸亏

forward: could you forward my mail? nín néng bāng wǒ zhuǎn yíxià xìn ma? [nung bahng wor jwahn yee-hsyah hsin mah]
您能帮我转一下信吗？

forwarding address zhuǎnxìn dìzhǐ [jwahn-hsin dee-jur]
转信地址

fountain pēnquán [pun-chew-ahn]
喷泉

foyer xiūxītīng [hsyoh-see-ting]
休息厅

fracture (noun) gǔzhé [gyew-jur]
骨折

France Fǎguó [fah-gwor]
法国

free zìyóu [dzur-yoh]
自由

(no charge) miǎn fèi [myen fay]
免费

is it free (of charge)? miǎn fèi de ma? [dur mah]
免费的吗？

French (adj) Fǎguó [fah-gwor]
法国

(language) Fǎyǔ [fah-yew]
法语

French fries zhá tǔdòu tiáo
[jah too-doh tyow]
炸土豆条

frequent jīngcháng
[jing-chahng]
经常

**how frequent is the bus to
the Forbidden City?** dào
Gùgōng qù de gōnggòng
qìchē duōcháng shíjian kāi
yì bān? [dow goo-goong chew dur
goong-goong chee-chur
dwor-chahng shur-jyen kai yee bahn]
到故宫去的公共汽车
多长时间开一班？

fresh (weather, breeze) qīngxīn
[ching-hsin]
清新

(fruit etc) xiān [hsyen]
鲜

fresh orange juice xiān júzhī
[jyew-jur]
鲜桔汁

Friday xīngqī wǔ
[hsing-chee-woo]
星期五

fridge bīngxiāng [–hsyahng]
冰箱

fried (shallow-fried) jiānde
[jyen-dur]
煎的

(deep-fried) zháde [jah-dur]
炸

(stir-fried) chǎode [chow-dur]
炒

fried egg jiān jīdàn [jyen
jee-dahn]
煎鸡蛋

fried noodles chǎomiàn
[chow-myen]
炒面

fried rice chǎofàn [chow-fahn]
炒饭

friend péngyou [pung-yoh]
朋友

friendly yóuhǎo [yoh-how]
友好

friendship yǒuyì [yoh-yee]
友谊

friendship store yǒuyì
shangdiàn [yoh-yee
shahng-dyen]
友谊商店

 Friendship stores are
state-run shops where
you can buy genuine
antiques and paintings, good silks
and souvenirs. Prices are high, but
you may get the occasional bargain.
The larger stores have a reasonable
selection of Western foodstuffs.

from* cóng [tsoong]
从

how far is it from here? lí
zhèr duō yuǎn? [jer dwor
ywahn]
离这儿多远？

when does the next train

from Suzhou arrive? cóng Sūzhōu lái de xià yì bān huǒchē jídiǎn dàodá? [tsoong soo-joh lai dur hsyah yee bahn hwor-chur jee-dyen dow-dah]

从苏州来的下一班火车几点到达？

from Monday to Friday cóng xīngqī yī dào xīngqī wǔ [tsoong hsing-chee-yee dow hsing-chee]

从星期一到星期五

from next Thursday cóng xià xīngqī sì qǐ [hsyah – sur chee]

从下星期四起

dialogue

where are you from? nǐ shì nǎr de rén? [shur nar-duh run]

I'm from Slough wǒ shì Slough láide rén [wor shur – lai-dur]

front qiánmian [chyen-myen]

前面

in front, at the front zài qiánbianr [dzai chyen-byenr]

在前边儿

in front of the hotel zài fàndiàn qiánmian [dzai fahn-dyen chyen-myen]

在饭店前面

frozen bīngdòngde [bing-doong-dur]

冰冻的

fruit shuíguǒ [shway-gwor]

水果

fruit juice guǒzhī [gwor-jur]

果汁

full mǎn [mahn]

满

it's full of ... lǐmian dōu shì ... [lee-myen doh shur]

里面都是 ...

I'm full wó bǎole [wor bow-lur]

我饱了

full board shí zhù quán bāo [shur joo choo-en bow]

食住全包

fun: it was fun hén hǎo wánr [hun how wahnr]

很好玩儿

funeral zànglǐ [dzahng-lee]

葬礼

funny (strange) qíguài [chee-gwai]

奇怪

(amusing) yǒu yìsi [yoh yee-sur]

有意思

(comical) huájī [hwah-jee]

滑稽

furniture jiājù [jyah-jyew]

家具

further: it's further down the road zài wǎng qián zǒu [dzai wahng chyen soh]

再往前走

dialogue

how much further is it to the Forbidden City? dào Gùgōng hái yǒu duōshao lù? [dow – yoh dwor-show] about 5 kilometres dàyuē wǔ gōnglǐ (lù) [dah-yew-eh woo goong-lee]

future jiānglái [jyang-lai]
将来
in future jiānglái
将来

G

game (cards etc) yóuxì
[yoh-hshee]
游戏
(match) bǐsài
比赛
(meat) yěwèi [yur-way]
野味
garage (for fuel) jiāyóu zhàn
[jyah-yoh jahn]
加油站
(for repairs) qìchē xiūlíchǎng
[chee-chur hsyoh-lee-chahng]
汽车修理厂
(for parking) chēkù [chur-koo]
车库
garden huāyuán [hwah-yew-ahn]
花园

garlic dàsuàn [dah-swahn]
大蒜
gas méiqì [may-chee]
煤气
gasoline qìyóu [chee-yoh]
气油
gas station jiāyóu zhàn
[jyah-yoh jahn]
加油站
gate dàmén [dah-mun]
大门
(at airport) dēngjīkǒu
[dung-jee-koh]
登机口
gay tóngxìngliàn
[toong-hsing-lyen]
同性恋
general (adj) yì bān [yee bahn]
一般
gents' toilet nán cèsuǒ [nahn tsur-swor]
男厕所
genuine (antique etc)
zhēnzhèng [jun-jung]
真正
German (adj) Déguó [dur-gwor]
德国
(language) Déyǔ [dur-yew]
德语
Germany Déguó
德国
get (fetch) qǔ [chew]
取
could you get me another one, please? qǐng nǐ zài géi

wǒ yí ge hǎo ma? [ching nee dzai gay wor yee gur how mah]

请你再给我一个好吗 ？

how do I get to ...? qù ... zěnme zǒu? [chew ... dzun-mur dzoh]

去 ... 怎么走 ？

do you know where I can get them? nǐ zhīdao wǒ zài nǎr néng mǎi dào ma? [jee-dow wor dzai nar nung mai dow mah]

你知道我在哪儿能买到吗 ？

dialogue

can I get you a drink? hē diǎnr shénme ma? [hur dyenr shun-mur mah]

no, I'll get this one, what would you like? zhèi huí wǒ lái mǎi, nǐ xiǎng hē shénme? [jay hway wor – hsyahng hur]

a glass of Maotai (lái) yì bēi Máotáijiǔ [bay]

get back huílai [hway-lai]
回来

get in (arrive) dàodá [dow-dah]
到达

get off: where do I get off? wǒ zài nǎr xià chē? [wor dzai nar hsyah chur]

我在哪儿下车 ？

get on (to train etc) shàng chē [shahng chur]
上车

get out (of car etc) xià chē [hsyah-chur]
下车

get up (in the morning) qǐchuáng [chee-chwahng]
起床

gift lǐwù [lee-woo]
礼物

 If you are invited to someone's home a gift might well be expected, though people will not open it in front of you, nor will they express profuse gratitude for it. The Chinese way is to express gratitude through reciprocal actions rather than words, and elaborate protestations of thanks can be interpreted as an attempt to avoid obligation.

gift shop lǐwù shāngdiàn [shahng-dyen]
礼物商店

ginger shēngjiāng [shung-jyang]
生姜

girl nǚ hái'r [nyew]
女孩儿

girlfriend nǚ péngyou [pung-yoh]
女朋友

give gěi [gay]

给

can you give me some change? qǐng gěi wǒ líng qián, hǎo ma? [ching gay wor ling chyen how mah]

请给我零钱好吗？

I gave ... to him wǒ bǎ ... sòng gěi tā [wor bah ... soong gay tah]

我把 ... 送给他

will you give this to ...? qǐng bǎ zhèige sònggěi ...? [ching bah jay-gur soong-gay]

请把这个送给 ... ？

give back huán [hwahn]

还

glad gāoxìng [gow-sing]

高兴

glass (material) bōli [bor-lee]

玻璃

(for drinking) bōli bēi [bay]

玻璃杯

a glass of wine yì bēi jiǔ

一杯酒

glasses yǎnjìng [yahn-jing]

眼镜

gloves shǒutào [shoh-tow]

手套

glue jiāoshuǐr [jyow-shwayr]

胶水儿

go qù [chew]

去

we'd like to go to the Summer Palace wǒmen

xiǎng qù Yíhéyuán [wor-mun hsyahng]

我们想去颐和园

where are you going? nǐ qù nǎr?

你去哪儿？

where does this bus go? zhèi liàng chē qù nár? [jay lyang chur]

这辆车去哪儿？

let's go! wǒmen zǒu ba! [wor-mun dzoh bah]

我们走吧

she's gone tā yǐjing zǒule [tah yee-ying zoh-lur]

她已经走了

where has he gone? tā dào nǎr qù le? [dow]

他到哪儿去了？

I went there last week wǒ shì shàng xīngqī qù nàr de [wor shur shahng hsing-chee]

我是上星期去那儿的

go away líkāi

离开

go away! zǒu kāi! [dzoh]

走开

go back (return) huí [hway]

回

go down (the stairs etc) xià [hsyah]

下

go in jìn

进

go out (in the evening) chūqu

[choo-chew]

出去

do you want to go out tonight? nǐ jīntiān wǎnshang xiǎng chūqù ma? [jin-tyen wahn-shahng hsyahng – mah]

你今天晚上想出去吗？

go through chuān [chwahn]

穿

go up (the stairs etc) shàng [shahng]

上

God shàngdì

上帝

gold (metal) huángjīn [hwahng-jin]

黄金

(colour) jīnsè [jin-sur]

金色

good hǎo [how]

好

good! hǎo!

好

it's no good bù hǎo

不好

goodbye zàijiàn [dzai-jyen]

再见

good evening ní hǎo [how]

你好

good morning ní zǎo [zow]

你早

good night wǎn'ān [wahn-ahn]

晚安

goose é [ur]

鹅

gorge xiá [hsyah]

峡

got: we've got to leave wǒmen déi zǒu le [wor-mun day zoh lur]

我们得走了

have you got any ...? ní yǒu ... ma? [yoh ... mah]

你有 ... 吗？

government zhèngfǔ [jung-foo]

政府

gradually jiànjiàn de [jyen-jyen dur]

渐渐地

grammar yúfǎ [yew-fah]

语法

gram(me) kè [kur]

克

granddaughter (daughter's daughter) wàisūnnǚr [wai-sun-nyewr]

外孙女儿

(son's daughter) sūnnǚr

孙女儿

grandfather (maternal) wàigōng [wai-goong]

外公

(paternal) yéye [yur-yur]

爷爷

grandmother (maternal) wàipó [wai-por]

外婆

(paternal) nǎinai

奶奶

grandson (daughter's son) wài

sūnzi [sun-dzur]

外孙子

(son's son) sūnzi

孙子

grapefruit pútáoyòu

[poo-tow-yoh]

葡萄柚

grapes pútáo [poo-tow]

葡萄

grass cǎo [tsow]

草

grateful gǎnjī [gahn-jee]

感激

great (excellent) hǎojíle

[how-jee-lur]

好极了

a great success jùdà

chéngjiù [joo-dah chung-jyoh]

巨大成就

greedy (for money etc) tānxīn

[tahn-hsin]

贪心

(for food) chán [chahn]

馋

green lǜsè(de) [lyew-sur(-dur)]

绿色的

greengrocer's càidiàn [tsai-dyen]

菜店

greetings

The Chinese do not have elaborate methods of greeting, although the shaking of hands is quite normal among men. It is very common to see young men and women displaying affection for a friend of the same sex. This can involve holding hands or even stroking legs. Generally the Chinese are less physical in their affections between the sexes than Westerners and are embarrassed by over-enthusiastic displays of affection by Western couples.

grey huīsè(de) [hway-sur(-dur)]

灰色的

grilled kǎo [kow]

烤

grocer's záhuòdiàn

[dzah-hwor-dyen]

杂货店

ground: on the ground zài dì

shàng [dzai dee shahng]

在地上

ground floor yī lóu [loh]

一楼

group (tourist etc) cānguāntuán

[tsahn-gwahn-twahn]

参观团

(study, work etc) xiáozǔ

[hsyow-dzyew]

小组

guarantee (noun) bǎozhèng

[bow-jung]

保证

is it guaranteed? bǎo bù

bǎoxiū? [bow – hsyoh]

保不保修？

guest kèrén [kur-run]

客人

guesthouse bīnguǎn
[bing-wahn]
宾馆
see hotel

guide (tour guide) dǎoyóu
[dow-yoh]
导游

guidebook dǎoyóu shǒucè
[shoh-tsur]
导游手册

guided tour yóu dǎoyóu de
yóulǎn [yoh – dur yoh-lahn]
有导游的游览

guitar jítā [jee-tah]
吉他

gum (in mouth) chǐyín [chur-yin]
齿龈

gym tǐyùguǎn [tee-yoo-gwahn]
体育馆

H

hair tóufa [toh-fah]
头发

haircut lǐfà [lee-fah]
理发

hairdresser's lǐfàdiàn [dyen]
理发店

hairdryer diànchuīfēng
[dyen-chway-fung]
电吹风

hair spray pēnfàjì
[pun-fah-jee]
喷发剂

half* (adj) bàn [bahn]
半
(noun) yí bàn
一半

half an hour bàn xiǎoshí
[hsyow-shur]
半小时

half a litre bàn shēng [shung]
半升

about half that nàme duō yí
bàn [nah-mur dwor]
那么多一半

half board bàn shísù
[shur-soo]
半食宿

half-bottle bàn píng
半瓶

half fare bànfèi [bahn-fay]
半费

half price bànjià [bahn-jyah]
半价

ham huótuǐ [hwor-tway]
火腿

hamburger hànbǎobāo
[hahn-bow-bow]
汉堡包

hand shǒu [shoh]
手

handbag shǒutíbāo
[shoh-tee-bow]
手提包

handkerchief shǒujuànr
[shoh-jwahnr]
手绢儿

hand luggage shǒutí xíngli

[shoh-tee hsing-lee]

手提行李

happen fāshēng [fah-shung]

发生

what's happening? zěnme huí shìr? [dzun-mur hway shur]

怎么回事儿？

what has happened? fāshēng le shénme shìr la? [fah-shung lur shun-mur lah]

发生了什么事儿啦？

happy kuàilè [kwai-lur]

快乐

I'm not happy about this wǒ duì zhèige bù mǎnyì [wor dway jay-gur boo mahn-yee]

我对这个不满意

harbour gǎngkǒu [gahng-koh]

港口

hard yìng

硬

(difficult) nán [nahn]

难

hardly: hardly ever hén shǎo [hun show]

很少

hard seat yìngxí [ying-hshee]

硬席

see **train**

hardware shop wǔjīn (shāng) diàn [woo-jin (shahng) dyen]

五金（商）店

hat màozi [mow-dzur]

帽子

hate (verb) hèn [hun]

恨

have* yǒu [yoh]

有

can I have a ...? (asking for something) qǐng géi wǒ ... hǎo ma? [ching gay wor ... how]

请给我 ... 好吗？

(ordering food) qǐng lái ..., hǎo ma? [ching]

请来 ... 好吗？

(in shop) wó xiáng mǎi ... [wor hsyahng]

我想买 ...

do you have ...? nímen yǒu ... ma? [nee-mun yoh ... mah]

你们有 ... 吗？

what'll you have? ní xiǎng hē shénme? [hsyahng hur shun-mur]

你想喝什么？

I have to leave now wó déi zǒu le [wor day dzoh lur]

我得走了

do I have to ...? wó děi ... ma?

我得 ... 吗？

hayfever huāfěnrè [hwah-fun-rur]

花粉热

he* tā [tah]

他

head tóu [toh]

头

113

headache tóuténg [toh-tung]
头疼

health

There is no point in getting paranoid about your health while travelling in China but it's worth being aware of the dangers and taking sensible precautions. It's advisable not to walk around in bare feet and to wear flip-flops in the shower. As for food, the two most important considerations are to eat at places which look busy and clean, and to stick to fresh, thoroughly cooked food. Seafood is risky as the water pollution levels in China are high. Fresh fruit you've peeled yourself is safe; other uncooked foods are risky. The other thing to watch out for is dirty chopsticks; the disposable chopsticks provided in most restaurants are fine, but if you want to be really sure, bring your own pair.

Probably the biggest hazard to your health in China is the host of flu infections that strike down a large proportion of the population, mostly in the winter months. The problem is compounded by the overcrowded conditions, chain smoking, pollution and the widespread habit of spitting. Parts of China are tropical and here

it can require a couple of weeks to acclimatize to the temperature and humidity. High humidity causes heat rashes, prickly heat and fungal infections. Prevention and cure are the same: wear loose clothes made of natural fibres, wash frequently and dry off thoroughly afterwards. Talcum powder and the use of mild antiseptic soap helps too. And don't underestimate the strength of the sun in tropical areas such as Hainan Island, in desert regions such as Xinjiang or very high up, for example on the Tibetan plateau.

At the other extreme, there are plenty of parts of China that get very cold indeed. If you're trekking in Tibet or visiting northern China during the winter, it is essential to be prepared. Hypothermia is sometimes fatal. To prevent the condition, wear lots of layers and a hat, and try to stay dry and out of the wind.

see **water** and **mosquito**

hear tīngjian [ting-jyen]
听见

dialogue

can you hear me? nǐ néng tīngjiàn ma? [nung ting-jyen mah]

I can't hear you, could you repeat that? duìbuqǐ, tīngbujiàn, nǐ néng zài shuō yí biàn ma? [dway-boo-chee ting-boo-jyen – dzai shwor yee byen]

hearing aid zhùtīngqì [joo-ting-chee]
助听器

heart xīnzàng [hsin-dzahng]
心脏

heart attack xīnzàngbìng [–bing]
心脏病

heat rè [rur]
热

heater sànrèqì [sahn-rur-chee]
散热器

heating nuǎnqì [nwahn-chee]
暖器

heavy zhòng [joong]
重

heel (of foot) jiǎogēn [jyow-gun]
脚跟
(of shoe) xié hòugēn [hsyeh]
鞋后跟

could you heel these? qíng géi wǒ dǎ hòugēn, hǎo ma? [ching gay wor dah – how mah]
请给我打后跟好吗？

heelbar xiūxiépù [hsyoh-hsyeh-poo]
修鞋铺

helicopter zhíshēng fēijī

[jur-shung fay-jee]
直升飞机

hello nǐ hǎo [nee how]
你好
(answer on phone) wéi [way]
喂

help bāngzhù [bahng-joo]
帮助

help! jiùmìng! [jyoh-ming]
救命

can you help me? nǐ néng bù néng bāngbāng wǒ? [nung bahng-bahng wor]
你能不能帮帮我？

thank you very much for your help xièxie nǐde bāngmáng [hsyeh-hsyeh nee-dur]
谢谢你的帮忙

helpful bāngle bú shǎo máng [bahng-lur boo show mahng]
帮了不少忙

hepatitis gānyán [gah-nyen]
肝炎

her* tā [tah]
她

that's her towel nà shì tāde máojīn [nah shur tah-dur mow-jin]
那是她的毛巾

herbs (for cooking) zuóliào [dzwor-lyow]
作料
(medicinal) cǎoyào [tsow-yow]
草药

here zhèr [jer]
这儿

here is/are ... zhèr shì ... [shur]
这儿是 ...

here you are géi nǐ [gay]
给你

hers* tāde [tah-dur]
她的

that's hers zhè shì tāde [jur shur]
这是她的

hey! hēi! [hay]
嘿

hi! (hello) nǐ hǎo! [how]
你好

high gāo [gow]
高

hill shān [shahn]
山

him* tā [tah]
他

hip túnbù [tun-boo]
臀部

hire (bike, car) zū [dzoo]
租

(guide, interpreter) gù
顾

for hire chūzū [choo-dzoo]
出租

where can I hire a bike? zài nǎr néng zū dào zìxíngchē? [dzai nar nung zoo dow dzi-hsing-chur]
在哪儿能租到自行车？

his* tāde [tah-dur]
他的

hit (verb) dǎ [dah]
打

hitch-hike dā biànchē [byen-chur]
搭便车

hobby shìhào [shur-how]
嗜好

hole dòng [doong]
洞

holiday (public) jiàqī [jyah-chee]
假期

(festival) jiérì [jyeh-ree]
节日

on holiday dùjià [doo-jyah]
度假

home jiā
家

at home (in my house etc) zài jiā [dzai]
在家

we go home tomorrow (to country) wǒmen míngtiān huí guó [wor-mun ming-tyen hway gwor]
我们明天回国

honest chéngshí [chung-shur]
诚实

honey fēngmì [fung-mee]
蜂蜜

honeymoon mìyuè [mee-yew-eh]
蜜月

Hong Kong Xiānggǎng [hsyahng-gahng]
香港

hope xīwàng [hshee-wahng]

希望

I hope so wǒ xīwàng shì
zhèi yàng [wor – shur jay yang]

我希望是这样

I hope not wǒ xīwàng bú shì
zhèi yàng

我希望不是这样

hopefully xīwàng rúcǐ

[hshee-wahng roo-tsur]

希望如此

horrible kěpà [kur-pah]

可怕

horse mǎ [mah]

马

horse riding qí mǎ [chee]

骑马

hospital yīyuàn [yee-yew-ahn]

医院

hospitality hàokè [how-kur]

好客

**thank you for your
hospitality** xièxie nínde
shèngqíng kuǎndài

[hsyeh-hsyeh nin-dur shung-ching
kwahn-dai]

谢谢您的盛情款待

hot rè [rur]

热

(spicy) là [lah]

辣

I'm hot wǒ juéde hěn rè [wor
jyew-eh-dur hun rur]

我觉得很热

it's hot today jīntiān hěn rè

[jin-tyen]

今天很热

hotel (small) lǚguǎn

[lyew-gwahn]

旅馆

(luxury) fàndiàn [fahn-dyen]

饭店

 In Chinese there are
several different words for
hotel, which give a vague
indication of the status of the place.
A more upmarket hotel might be
called **dà jiǔlóu** or **dà jiǔdiàn**,
which translates as something like
'big wine bar'. The far more
common term **bīnguǎn** is similarly
used for smart new establishments.
Fàndiàn (literally: restaurant) is the
least reliable term as it is used fairly
indiscriminately for top-class hotels,
as well as humble and obscure
ones.
Reliably downmarket – and rarely
accepting foreigners – is
zhāodàisuǒ, while the humblest of
all is **lǚguǎn** (sometimes translated
as 'inn'), where you might
occasionally get to stay in some
rural areas.
In the larger cities – including
virtually all provincial capitals –
you'll find upmarket four- or
five-star hotels, often managed by
foreigners and offering all the usual

international facilities.

Mid-range hotels will generally have clean, spacious, standard double rooms with attached bathroom, 24-hour hot water, TV and air-conditioning, but often have dodgy plumbing, poor temperature control and insufficient lift capacity. Single rooms are rarely available.

In budget hotels, you'll notice that the local Chinese routinely rent beds rather than rooms – doubling up with one or more strangers – as a means of saving money. Foreigners are only very occasionally allowed to share rooms with Chinese people, but tourist centres tend to have one or two budget hotels with special foreigners' dormitory accommodation. Cheap hotels are often perfectly comfortable, but hot water is usually available for only limited hours in the evening, and you would be advised not to leave valuables in the rooms.

Guests are not normally entrusted with keys; instead reception gives you a ticket which you hand to the floor attendant, who opens the door for you. It is normal to pay in full for the room when you check in; a refundable deposit against theft or damage is nearly always required at the same time.

Some hotels have arbitrary rules stipulating that foreigners pay as much as a hundred per cent extra. With polite, friendly bargaining, it is possible to reduce or eliminate such surcharges.

Whatever type of hotel you are staying in, there are two things you can rely on. One is a pair of plastic slippers under the bed that you use for walking to the bathroom, and the other is a Thermos of drinkable water that can be refilled any time by the floor attendant.

Checking into a hotel involves filling in a detailed form. Upmarket hotels have English versions of these forms, but hotels unaccustomed to foreigners usually have them in Chinese only. Filling in forms correctly is a serious business in bureaucratic China and if potential guests are unable to carry out this duty, they may not be allowed to stay.

hour xiǎoshí 〖hsyow-shur〗
小时
house fángzi 〖fahng-dzur〗
房子
how zěnme 〖dzun-mur〗
怎么 ?
how many? (if answer is likely to be more than ten) duōshao?
〖dwor-show〗
多少 ?

(if answer is likely to be ten or less)
jǐge? [jee-gur]
几个？
how do you do? ní hǎo
[how]
你好？

dialogues

how are you? ní hǎo ma?
[mah]
fine, thanks, and you?
hén hǎo, nǐ ne? [hun –
nur]

how much is it? duōshao
qián? [chyen]
17 yuan shí qī kuài [shur
chee kwai]
I'll take it wǒ mǎi [wor]

humid cháoshī [chow-shur]
潮湿
hungry è [ur]
饿
are you hungry? nǐ èle ma?
[ur-lur mah]
你饿了吗？
hurry: I'm in a hurry wó hěn jí
de [wor hun jee dur]
我很急的
there's no hurry mànmàn lái
[mahn-mahn]
慢慢来
hurry up! kuài diǎnr! [kwai

dyenr]
快点儿
hurt (verb) téng [tung]
疼
it really hurts zhēn téng [jun
tung]
真疼
husband zhàngfu [jahng-foo]
丈夫

I

I wǒ [wor]
我
ice bīng
冰
with ice jiā bīngkuàir [jyah
bing-kwair]
加冰块儿
no ice, thanks bù jiā
bīngkuàir, xièxie [boo jyah
bing-kwair hsyeh-hsyeh]
不加冰块儿谢谢
ice cream bīngqílín
[bing-chee-lin]
冰淇淋
ice-cream cone dànjuǎnr
bīngqílín [dahn-jyew-ahnr]
蛋卷儿冰淇淋
ice lolly bīnggùnr
[bing-gunr]
冰棍儿
idea zhǔyi [joo-yee]
主意

119

idiot shǎguā [shah-gwah]
傻瓜

if rúguǒ [roo-gwor]
如果

ill bìngle [bing-lur]
病了

I feel ill wǒ juéde bù shūfu
[wor jyew-eh-dur]
我觉得不舒服

illness jíbìng
疾病

imitation (leather etc) fǎng
[fahng]
仿

immediately mǎshàng
[mah-shahng]
马上

important zhòngyào
[joong-yow]
重要

it's very important hěn
zhòngyào [hun joong-yow]
很重要

it's not important bú
zhòngyào
不重要

impossible bù kěnéng
[kur-nung]
不可能

impressive (building, view)
xióngwěi [hsyoong-way]
雄伟

improve tígāo [tee-gow]
提高

I want to improve my Chinese

wó xiǎng tígāo wǒde Hàyǔ
shuǐpíng [wor hsyahng – wor-dur
hah-yew shway-ping]
我想提高我的汉语水平

in*: it's in the centre zài
zhōngjiān [dzai joong-jyen]
在中间

in my car zài wǒde chē lǐ
[wor-dur chur lee]
在我的车里

in London zài Lúndūn
在伦敦

in two days from now liǎng
tiān zhī hòu [tyen jur hoh]
两天之后

in five minutes wǔ fēn zhōng
(zhī) nèi [fun joong (jur) nay]
五分钟（之）内

in May zài wǔyuè
在五月

in English yòng Yīngyǔ
用英语

in Chinese yòng Hànyǔ
用汉语

is Mr Li in? Lǐ xiānsheng zài
ma? [hsyahng-shung dzai mah]
李先生在吗？

inch yīngcùn [ying-tsun]
英寸

include bāokuò [bow-kwor]
包括

does that include meals? zhè
bāokuò fàn qián ma? [jur –
fahn chyen mah]
这包括饭钱吗？

is that included? nèige yě
bāokuò zài nèi ma? [nay-gur
yur]

那个也包括在内吗？

inconvenient bù fāngbiàn
[fahng-byen]

不方便

India Yìndù [yin-doo]

印度

Indian (adj) Yìndù

印度

indigestion xiāohuà bù liáng
[hsyow-hwah boo lyang]

消化不良

Indonesia Yìndùníxīyà
[yin-doo-nee-hshee-yah]

印度尼西亚

indoor pool shìnèi
yóuyǒngchí [shur-nay
yoh-yoong-chur]

室内游泳池

indoors shìnèi [shur-nay]

室内

inexpensive piányi [pyen-yee]

便宜

infection gǎnrǎn [gahn-rahn]

感染

infectious chuánrǎn
[chwahn-rahn]

传染

inflammation fāyán [fah-yen]

发炎

informal (clothes) suíbiàn
[sway-byen]

随便

(occasion) fēi zhèngshì [fay
jung-shur]

非正式

information xiāoxi
[hsyow-hshee]

消息

**do you have any information
about ...?** ní yǒu guānyú ...
de xiāoxi ma? [nee yoh
gwahn-yew dur – mah]

你有关于 ... 的消息吗？

information desk wènxùnchù
[wun-hsyewn-choo]

问讯处

injection dǎzhēn [dah-jun]

打针

injured shòushāng
[shoh-shahng]

受伤

she's been injured tā
shòushāng le [tah – lur]

她受伤了

inner tube (for tyre) nèitāi
[nay–]

内胎

innocent wúgū

无辜

insect kūnchóng [kun-choong]

昆虫

insect bite chóngzi yǎo de
[choong-dzur yow dur]

虫子咬的

**do you have anything for
insect bites?** yǒu zhì chóng
yǎo de yào ma? [yoh jur choong

121

yow dur yow mah]

有治虫咬的药吗？

insect repellent qūchóngjì
[chew-choong-jee]

驱虫剂

inside* zài ... lǐ [dzai ... lee]

在 ... 里

inside the hotel zài lǚguǎn
lǐmiàn

在旅馆里面

let's sit inside wǒmen jìnqù
zuò ba [wor-mun jin-chew dzwor
bah]

我们进去坐吧

insist: I insist wǒ jiānchí [wor
jyen-chur]

我坚持

instant coffee sùróng kāfēi
[soo-roong kah-fay]

速溶咖啡

insulin yídǎosù [yee-dow-soo]

胰岛素

insurance bǎoxiǎn [bow-hsyen]

保险

intelligent cōngming
[tsoong-ming]

聪明

interested: I'm interested in ...
wǒ duì ... hén gǎn xìngqù
[wor dway ... hun gahn
hsing-chew]

我对 ... 很感兴趣

interesting yǒu yìsi [yoh
yee-sur]

有意思

that's very interesting hén
yǒu yìsi [hun]

很有意思

international guójì
[gwor-jee]

国际

Internet guójì wǎngluò
[gwor-jee wahng-luo]

国际网罗

interpreter fānyì [fahn-yee]

翻译

intersection (US) shízì lùkǒu
[shur-dzur loo-koh]

十字路口

interval (at theatre) mùjiān
xiūxi [moo-jyen hsyoh-hshee]

幕间休息

into: I'm not into ... wǒ duì ...
bù gǎn xìngqù [wor dway ...
boo gahn hsing-chew]

我对 ... 不感兴趣

introduce jièshào [jyeh-show]

介绍

may I introduce ...? wǒ lái
jièshào yíxià, zhèi wèi
shì ... [wor – yee-hsyah jay-way
shur]

我来介绍一下这位是 ...

invitation yāoqǐng
[yow-ching]

邀请

invite yāoqǐng
[yow-ching]

邀请

Ireland Ài'ěrlán [ai-er-lahn]

爱尔兰

Irish Ài'ěrlán [ai-er-lahn]

爱尔兰

I'm Irish wǒ shì Ài'ěrlán rén

[wor shur ai-er-lahn run]

我是爱尔兰人

iron (for ironing) yùndǒu

[yewn-doh]

熨斗

can you iron these for me?

qǐng nǐ bāng wǒ yùnyùn

zhè xié yīfu, hǎo ma? [ching

nee bahng wor yun-yun jur hsyeh

yee-foo how mah]

请你帮我熨熨这些衣

服好吗？

is* shì [shur]

是

island dǎo [dow]

岛

it tā [tah]

它

it is ..., it was ... shì ... [shur]

是 …

is it ...? shì ... ma? [mah]

是 …吗？

where is it? zài nǎr? [dzai]

在哪儿？

Italian (adj) Yìdàlì

[yee-dah-lee]

意大利

Italy Yìdàlì

意大利

itch: it itches yǎng

痒

J

jacket jiākè [jyah-kur]

茄克

jade yù [yew]

玉

jam guǒjiàng [gwor-jyang]

果酱

January yīyuè [yee-yew-eh]

一月

Japan Rìběn [ree-hun]

日本

jar guànzi [gwahn-dzur]

罐子

jasmine tea mòlìhua chá

[mor-lee hwah chah]

茉莉花茶

jaw xiàba [hsyah-bah]

下巴

jazz juéshì yuè [jyeweh-shur

yeweh]

爵士乐

jealous jìdù

忌妒

jeans niúzǎikù [nyoh-dzai-koo]

牛仔裤

jetty mǎtóu [mah-toh]

码头

jeweller's zhūbǎo (shāng)diàn

[joo-bow (shahng-)dyen]

珠宝（商）店

jewellery zhūbǎo

珠宝

Jewish Yóutàirén de

[yoh-tai-run dur]

犹太人的

job gōngzuò [goong-dzwor]

工作

jogging pǎobù [pow-boo]

跑步

to go jogging qù pǎobù

[chew]

去跑步

joke wánxiào [wahn-hsyow]

玩笑

journey lǚxíng [lyew-sing]

旅行

have a good journey! yílù

shùnfēng! [shun-fung]

一路顺风

jug guàn [gwahn]

罐

a jug of water yí guànr shuǐ

一罐儿水

July qīyuè [chee-yew-eh]

七月

jumper tàoshān [tow-shahn]

套衫

junction (road) jiāochākǒu

[jyow-chah-koh]

交叉口

June liùyuè [lyoh-yew-eh]

六月

just (only just) jínjǐn

仅仅

(with numbers) zhǐ [jur]

只

just two zhǐ yào liǎngge [yow]

只要两个

just for me jiù wǒ yào [jyoh

wor]

就我要

just here jiù zài zhèr [dzai jer]

就在这儿

not just now xiànzài bùxíng

[hsyen-dzai boo-hsing]

现在不行

we've just arrived wǒmen

gāng dào [wor-mun gahng dow]

我们刚到

K

keep liú [lyoh]

留

keep the change búyòng

zhǎo le [boo-yoong jow lur]

不用找了

can I keep it? wó kéyǐ liúzhe

ma? [wor kur-yee lyoh-jur mah]

我可以留着吗？

please keep it qǐng liúzhe ba

[ching – bah]

请留着吧

kettle shuǐhú [shway-hoo]

水壶

key yàoshi [yow-shur]

钥匙

the key for room 201, please

qǐng géi wǒ èr líng yāo fǎng

de yàoshi [ching gay wor er ling

yow fahng dur yow-shur]

请给我二零一房的钥匙

see **hotel**

keyring yàoshi quān [yow-shur choo-en]
钥匙环

kidneys (in body) shènzàng [shun-dzahng]
肾脏

(food) yāozi [yow-dzur]
腰子

kill shā [shah]
杀

kilo gōngjīn [goong-jin]
公斤

kilometre gōnglǐ [goong-lee]
公里

how many kilometres is it to ...? qù ... yǒu duōshao gōnglǐ? [chew ... yoh dow-show]
去 ... 有多少公里？

kind (type) zhǒng [joong]
种

that's very kind nǐ zhēn hǎo [nee jun how]
你真好

dialogue

which kind do you want? nǐ yào nǎ yí zhǒng? [yow nah]
I want this/that kind wǒ yào zhèi/nèi yì zhǒng [wor yow jay/nay]

king guówáng [gwor-wahng]
国王

kiosk shòuhuòtíng [shoh-hwor-ting]
售货亭

kiss wěn [wun]
吻

kitchen chúfáng [choo-fahng]
厨房

Kleenex® zhǐjīn [jur-jin]
纸巾

knee xīgài [hshee-gai]
膝盖

knickers sānjiǎokù [sahn-jyow-koo]
三角裤

knife dāozi [dow-dzur]
刀子

knock (verb) qiāo [chyow]
敲

knock over (object) dǎ fān [dah fahn]
打翻

(pedestrian) zhuàng dǎo [jwahng dow]
撞倒

know (somebody) rènshi [run-shur]
认识

(something, a place) zhīdao [jur-dow]
知道

I don't know wǒ bù zhīdao
我不知道

I didn't know that nà wǒ bù zhīdao [nah]
那我不知道

do you know where I can
buy ...? nǐ zhīdao wǒ zài nǎr
néng mǎi dào ...? [wor dzai nar
nung mai dow]

你知道我在哪儿能买
到 ... ?

Korean (adj) Cháoxiān
[chow-hsyen]

朝鲜

L

lacquerware qīqì [chee-chee]

漆器

ladies' room, ladies' toilets nǚ
cèsuǒ [nyew tsur-swor]

女厕所

ladies' wear nǚzhuāng
[nyew-jwahng]

女装

lady nǚshì [nyew-shur]

女士

lager píjiǔ [pee-jyoh]

啤酒

see **beer**

lake hú [hoo]

湖

lamb (meat) yángròu [yang-roh]

羊肉

lamp dēng [dung]

灯

lane (motorway) chēdào
[chur-dow]

车道

(small road) hútòng [hoo-toong]

胡同

language yǔyán [yew-yen]

语言

language course yǔyán kè
[kur]

语言课

Laos Lǎowō [low-wor]

老挝

large dà [dah]

大

last (final) zuìhòu [dzway-hoh]

最后

last week shàng xīngqī
[shahng hsing-chee]

上星期

last Friday shàng xīngqī wǔ

上星期五

last night zuótiān wǎnshang
[dzwor-tyen wahn-shahng]

昨天晚上

what time is the last train to
Beijing? qù Běijīng de
zuìhòu yì bān huǒchē jí
diǎn kāi? [chew – dur
dzway-hoh yur bahn hwor-chur jee
dyen]

去北京的最后一班火
车几点开 ?

late (at night) wǎn [wahn]

晚

(delayed) chí [chur]

迟

sorry I'm late duìbuqǐ, wǒ lái
wǎnle [dway-boo-chee wor lai

对不起我来晚了
the train was late huǒchē lái wǎnle [hwor-chur]
火车来晚了
we must go – we'll be late wǒmen děi zǒulc láibujíle [wor-mun day dzoh-lur lai-boo-jee-lur]
我们得走了来不及了
it's getting late bù zǎole [dzow-lur]
不早了
later hòulái [hoh-lai]
后来
I'll come back later wǒ guò yihuǐr zài lái [wor gwor yee-hwayr dzai]
我过一会儿再来
see you later huítóujiàn [hway-toh-jyen]
回头见
later on hòulái
后来
latest zuìhòu [dzway-hoh]
最后
(most recent) zuìjìn [dzway-jin]
最近
by Wednesday at the latest zuìwǎn xīngqīsān
最晚星期三
laugh (verb) xiào [hsyow]
笑
laundry (clothes) xǐyī

[hshee-yee]
洗衣
(place) xǐyīdiàn [–dyen]
洗衣店
lavatory cèsuǒ [tsur-swor]
厕所
law fǎlǜ [fah-lyew]
法律
lawyer lǜshī [lyew-shur]
律师
laxative xièyào [hsyeh-hyow]
泄药
lazy lǎn [lahn]
懒
lead: where does this road lead to? zhè tiáo lù tōng nǎr qù? [jur tyow loo toong nar chew]
这条路通哪儿去？
leak: the roof leaks wūdǐng lòule [woo-ding loh-lur]
屋顶漏了
learn xuéxí [hsyew-eh-hshee]
学习
least: not in the least yìdiǎnr dōu bù [yee-dyenr doh bu]
一点儿都不
at least zhìshǎo [jee-show]
至少
leather pígé [pee-gur]
皮革
leave (depart) zǒu [dzoh]
走
I am leaving tomorrow wǒ míngtiān zǒu [wor ming-tyen]
我明天走

 English → Chinese

Le

127

when does the bus for Beijing leave? qù Běijīng de qìchē jǐ diǎn kāi? [chew – dur chee-chur jee dyen]

去北京的汽车几点开？

may I leave this here? wǒ néng bǎ zhèige liú zài zhèr ma? [wor nung bah jay-gur lyoh dzai jer mah]

我能把这个留在这儿吗？

he left yesterday tā shì zuótiān líkāi de [tah shur dzwor-tyen lee-kai dur]

他是昨天离开的

I left my coat in the bar wǒ bǎ wǒde dàyī liú zài jiǔbājiān [bah wor-dur dah-yee lyoh dzai jyoh-bah-jyen]

我把我的大衣留在酒吧间

there's none left shénme dōu búshèng [shun-mur doh boo-shung]

什么都不剩

left zuǒ [dzwor]

左

on the left zài zuǒbiānr [dzai dzwor-byenr]

在左边儿

to the left wáng zuǒ [wahng]

往左

turn left wáng zuǒ guǎi [gwai]

往左拐

left-handed zuópiězi [dzwor-pyeh-dzur]

左撇子

left luggage (office) xíngli jìcúnchù [hsing-lee jee-tsun-choo]

行李寄存处

 Most big hotels have reliable left luggage offices for those who have checked out and are awaiting an evening departure.

leg tuǐ [tway]

腿

lemon níngméng [ning-mung]

柠檬

lemonade níngméng qìshuǐr [chee-shwayr]

柠檬汽水儿

lemon tea níngméngchá [–chah]

柠檬茶

lend jiè [jyeh]

借

will you lend me your ...? qǐng bǎ nǐde ... jiè géi wǒ [ching bah nee-dur ... jyeh gay wor]

请把你的 ... 借给我？

lens (of camera) jìngtóu [jing-toh]

镜头

less shǎo [show]

少

less than ... bǐ ... shǎo
比 ...少

less expensive than ... bǐ ... piányi [pyen-yee]
比 ...便宜

lesson kè [kur]
课

let: will you let me know? nǐ dào shíhou gàosu wǒ, hǎo ma? [dow shur-hoh gow-soo wor how mah]
你到时候告诉我好吗？

I'll let you know wǒ dào shíhou gàosu nǐ
我到时候告诉你

let's go for something to eat chīfàn, ba [chur-fahn bah]
吃饭吧

let off: will you let me off at ...? wǒ zài ... xià, xíng ma? [dzai ... hsyah hsing]
我在 ...下行吗？

letter xìn [hsin]
信

do you have any letters for me? yǒu xìn, ma? [yoh hsin mah]
有信吗？

letterbox xìnxiāng [hsin-hsyahng]
信箱

see postal service

library túshūguǎn [too-shoo-gwahn]
图书馆

lid gàir [gair]
盖儿

lie (tell untruth) shuōhuǎng [shwor-hwahng]
说谎

lie down tǎng [tahng]
躺

life shēnghuó [shung-hwor]
生活

lifebelt jiùshēngquān [jyoh-shung-choo-en]
救生圈

lifeguard jiùshēngyuán [jyoh-shung-yew-ahn]
救生员

life jacket jiùshēngyī [jyoh-shung-yee]
救生衣

lift (in building) diàntī [dyen-tee]
电梯

could you give me a lift? nǐ néng bù néng ràng wǒ dāge chē? [nung – rahng wor dah-gur chur]
你能不能让我搭个车？

light (noun) dēng [dung]
灯

(not heavy) qīng [ching]
轻

do you have a light? (for cigarette) ní yóu huǒ ma? [nur yoh hwor mah]
你有火吗？

light bulb dēngpào [dung-pow]
灯泡

I need a new light bulb wǒ xūyào yígè xīn dēngpào [wor hsyoo-yow yee-gur hsin]

我需要一个新灯泡

lighter (cigarette) dáhuǒjī [dah-hwor-jee]

打火机

lightning shǎndiàn [shahn-dyen]

闪电

like xǐhuan [hshee-hwahn]

喜欢

I like it wó xǐhuan [wor]

我喜欢

I don't like it wǒ bù xǐhuan

我不喜欢

I like you wó xǐhuan nǐ

我喜欢你

do you like ...? ní xǐhuan ... ma? [mah]

你喜欢 ... 吗？

I'd like a beer wó xiǎng hē yìpíng píjiǔ [hsyahng hur yee-ping]

我想喝一瓶啤酒

I'd like to go swimming wó xiǎng qù yóuyǒng

我想去游泳

would you like a drink? ní xiǎng hē diǎnr shénme ma? [hur dyenr shun-mur]

你想喝点儿什么吗？

would you like to go for a walk? ní xiǎng bu xiǎng qù zǒuyizǒu? [chew dzoh-yee-dzoh]

你想不想去走一走？

what's it like? tā xiàng shénme? [tah]

它象什么？

I want one like this wǒ yào tónglèide [yow toong-lay-dur]

我要同类的

line xiàn [hsyen]

线

could you give me an outside line? qíng gěi wǒ wàixiàn, hǎo ma? [ching gay wor wai-hsyen how dzwaymah]

请给我外线好吗？

lips zuǐchún [dzway]

嘴唇

lip salve chúngāo [chun-gow]

唇膏

lipstick kǒuhóng [koh-hoong]

口红

listen tīng

听

litre shēng [shung]

升

little xiǎo [hsyow]

小

just a little, thanks jiù yìdiǎnr, xièxie [jyoh yee-dyenr hsyeh-hsyeh]

就一点儿谢谢

a little milk yìdiǎnr niúnǎi [nyoh-nai]

一点儿牛奶

a little bit more duō yìdiǎnr [dwor yee-dyenr]

多一点儿

live (verb) zhù 〖joo〗

住

we live together wǒmen zhù
zài yìqǐ 〖wor-mun joo dzai
yee-chee〗

我们住在一起

dialogue

where do you live? nǐ zhù
zài nǎr? 〖joo dzai〗
I live in London wǒ zhù
zài Lúndūn 〖wor〗

lively (person) huópo
〖hwor-por〗

活泼

(town) rènao 〖rur-now〗

热闹

liver (in body, food) gān 〖gahn〗

肝

lobby (in hotel) qiántīng
〖chyen-ting〗

前厅

lobster lóngxiā 〖loong-hsyah〗

龙虾

local dìfāngde 〖dee-fahng-dur〗

地方的

lock suǒ 〖swor〗

锁

it's locked suǒshang le 〖swor
shahng lur〗

锁上了

lock out: I've locked myself
out wó bǎ zìjǐ suǒ zài

ménwài le 〖wor bah dzur-jee
swor dzai mun-wai lur〗

我把自己锁在门外了

locker (for luggage etc)
xiǎochúguì 〖hsyow-choo-gway〗

小橱柜

London Lúndūn

伦敦

long cháng 〖chahng〗

长

how long does it take? yào
duōcháng shíjiān? 〖yow
dwor-chahng shur-jyen〗

要多长时间？

how long will it take to fix it?
bǎ zhèige dōngxi xiūlǐ hǎo
yào duōcháng shíjian? 〖bah
jay-gur doong-hshee hsyoo-lee hao〗

把这个东西修理好要
多长时间？

a long time hěn cháng
shíjian 〖hun〗

很长时间

one day/two days longer
yí/liǎng tiān duō 〖tyen dwor〗

一／两天多

long-distance call chángtú
diànhuà 〖chahng-too dyen-hwah〗

长途电话

look: I'm just looking, thanks
wó zhǐshi kànyikàn, xièxie
〖wor jur-shur kahn-yee-kahn
hsyeh-hsyeh〗

我只是看一看谢谢

you don't look well kànqǐlái,

131

nǐ shēntǐ bù shūfu
[kahn-chee-lai nee shun-tee boo shoo-foo]

看起来你身体不舒服

look out! xiǎoxīn! [hsyow-hsin]

小心

can I have a look? kéyi kànkan ma? [kur-yee kahn-kahn mah]

可以看看吗？

look after zhàokàn [jow-kahn]

照看

look at kàn [kahn]

看

look for zhǎo [jow]

找

I'm looking for ... wó zhǎo ... [wor jow]

我找 ...

look forward to pànwàng [pahn-wahng]

盼望

I'm looking forward to it wǒ pànwàng [wor]

我盼望

loose (handle etc) sōng [soong]

松

lorry kǎchē [kah-chur]

卡车

lose diū [dyoh]

丢

I'm lost wǒ mílùle [wor mee-loo-lur]

我迷路了

I've lost my bag wǒ bǎ

dàizi diūle [bah dai-dzur dyoh-lur]

我把带子丢了

lost property (office) shīwù zhāolǐng chù [shur-woo jow-ling choo]

失物招领处

lot: a lot, lots hěnduō [hun-dwor]

很多

not a lot bù duō [boo dwor]

不多

a lot of people hěnduō rén [run]

很多人

a lot bigger dà de duō [dah dur]

大得多

I like it a lot wǒ hén xǐhuan [wor hun hshee-hwahn]

我很喜欢

loud dàshēng de [dah-shung dur]

大声的

lounge (in house) kètīng [kur-ting]

客厅

(in hotel) xiūxishì [hsyoh-hshee-shur]

休息室

love (noun) liàn'ài [lyen-ai]

恋爱

(verb) ài

爱

I love China wǒ ài Zhōngguó [wor ai joong-gwor]

我爱中国

lovely (person) kě'ài [kur-ai]
可爱
(thing) hén hǎo [hun how]
很好
low (bridge) dī
低
(prices) piányide [pyen-yee-dur]
便宜的
luck yùnqi [yewn-chee]
运气
good luck! zhù nǐ shùnlì! [joo nee shun-lee]
祝你顺利
luggage xíngli [hsing-lee]
行李
luggage trolley xínglichē [–chur]
行李车
lunch wǔfàn [woo-fahn]
午饭
luxurious háohuá [how-hwah]
豪华
luxury (comfort etc) gāojí [gow-jee]
高级
(extravagance) shēchǐ [shur-chee]
奢侈
lychee lìzhī [lee-jur]
荔枝

M

machine jīqì [jee-chee]
机器

magazine zázhì [dzah-jur]
杂志
maid (in hotel) nǚ fúwùyuán [nyew foo-woo-yew-ahn]
女服务员
mail (noun) yóujiàn [yoh-jyen]
邮件
(verb) jì
寄
is there any mail for me? yóu wǒde xìn ma? [yoh wor-dur hsin mah]
有我的信吗？
see **postal service**
mailbox xìnxiāng [hsin-hsyahng]
信箱
main zhǔyào de [joo-yow dur]
主要的
main course zhǔcài [joo-tsai]
主菜
main post office dà yóujú [dah yoh-joo]
大邮局
main road dàlù [dah-loo]
大路
make (brand name) pái
牌
(verb) zhìzào [jur-dzow]
制造
I make it 10 yuan, OK? wǒ suàn shí kuài qián, hǎo ma? [wor swahn shur kwai chyen how mah]
我算十块钱好吗？

what is it made of? zhè shì yòng shénme zào de? [jur shur yoong shun-mur dzow dur]

这是用什么造的？

make-up huàzhuāngpǐn [hwah-jwahng-pin]

化妆品

Malaysia Mǎláixīyà [mah-lai-hshee-yah]

马来西亚

man nánrén [nahn-run]

男人

manager jīnglǐ

经理

can I see the manager? kéyi jiànjian jīnglǐ ma? [kur-yee jyen-jyen – mah]

可以见见经理吗？

Mandarin Pǔtōnghuà [poo-toong-hwah]

普通话

mandarin orange gānzi [gahn-dzur]

柑子

many hěn duō [hun dwor]

很多

not many bù duō

不多

map dìtú

地图

 Cheap city maps are widely obtainable from hotel shops or street kiosks, though nearly always in Chinese only. Some of the more visited cities do, however, sell different versions of maps, including English-language ones, marking local sights, hotels and restaurants and also giving local train, bus and flight timetables. For Tibet, it is better and cheaper to bring maps with you from outside.

March sānyuè [sahn-yew-eh]

三月

margarine rénzào húangyóu [run-zow hwahng-yoh]

人造黄油

market shìchǎng [shur-chahng]

市场

married: I'm married wǒ jiéhūnle [wor jyeh-hun-lur]

我结婚了

are you married? nǐ jiéhūnle ma? [nee jyeh-hun-lur mah]

你结婚了吗？

martial arts wǔshù

武术

mascara jiémáogāo [jyeh-mow-gow]

睫毛膏

match (sport) bǐsài

比赛

football match zúqiú sài [dzoo-chyoh]

足球赛

matches huǒchái [hwor-]

火柴

material (fabric) bù

布

matter: it doesn't matter méi guānxi [may gwahn-hshee]

没关系

what's the matter? zěnmele? [dzun-mur-lur]

怎么了？

mattress chuángdiàn [chwahng-dyen]

床垫

May wǔyuè [woo-yew-eh]

五月

may: may I have another one? qǐng zài lái yīge [ching dzai lai yee-gur]

请再来一个

may I come in? wǒ néng jìnlái ma? [wor nung jin-lai mah]

我能进来吗？

may I see it? wǒ néng kàn ma? [kahn]

我能看吗？

may I sit here? wǒ néng zuò zhèr ma? [zwor jer]

我能坐这儿吗？

maybe kěnéng [kur-nung]

可能

me* wǒ [wor]

我

that's for me zhè shì wǒde [jer shur wor-dur]

这是我的

send it to me qǐng sòng géi wǒ [ching soong gay]

请送给我

me too wó yě [yur]

我也

meal fàn [fahn]

饭

dialogue

did you enjoy your meal? chīde hái hǎo ma? [chur-dur hai how mah]

it was excellent, thank you hén hǎo, xièxie [hun how hsyeh-hsyeh]

mean: what do you mean? nǐ zhǐde shì shénme? [nee jur-dur shur shun-mur]

你指的是什么？

dialogue

what does this word mean? zhèige cír shì shénme yìsi? [jay-gur tsur – yee-sur]

it means ... in English yòng yīngwen shì ... de yìsi [yoong ying-wun – dur]

meat ròu [roh]

肉

medicine (Western) xīyào [hshee-yow]

西药

(Chinese) zhōngyào [joong-yow]

中药

medium (adj: size) zhōngděng [joong-dung]

中等

medium-rare (steak) bànshēng de [bahn-shung dur]

半生的

medium-sized zhōnghào [joong-how]

中号

meet pèngjiàn [pung-jyen]

碰见

nice to meet you jiàndào nǐ hěn gāoxìng [jyen-dow nee hun gow-hsing]

见到你很高兴

where shall I meet you? wǒ zài nǎr jiàn nǐ? [wor dzai-nar jyen]

我在哪儿见你？

meeting huì(yì) (hway-yee)

会（议）

melon guā [gwah]

瓜

men nánde [nahn-dur]

男的

mend (machine, bicycle) xiūlǐ [hsyoh-lee]

修理

(clothes) féngbǔ [fung-boo]

缝补

could you mend this for me? qíng géi wǒ xiūlǐ yíxià hǎo ma? [ching gay wor – yee-hsyah how mah]

请给我修理一下好吗？

men's room nán cèsuǒ [nahn tsur-swor]

男厕所

menswear nánzhuāng [nahn-jwahng]

男装

mention shuōdào [shwor-dow]

说到

don't mention it búyòng kèqi [boo-yoong kur-chee]

不用客气

menu càidānr [tsai-dahnr]

菜单儿

may I see the menu, please? qǐng lái càidānr, hǎo ma? [ching lai tsai-dahnr – how mah]

请来菜单儿好吗？

see **menu reader** page 269

message xìnr [hsinr]

信儿

are there any messages for me? yóu wǒde xìn shénme ma? [yoh wor-dur hsin shun-mur-dur mah]

有我的信什么的吗？

I want to leave a message for ... wó xiǎng gěi ... liúge xìnr [hsyahng gay ... lyoh-gur]

我想给 ... 留个信儿

metal jīnshǔ [jin-shoo]

金属

metre mǐ

米

midday zhōngwǔ [joong-woo]

中午

at midday zhōngwǔ

中午

middle*: in the middle zài zhōngjiān [dzai joong-jyen]

在中间

in the middle of the night yèli [yur-lee]

夜里

the middle one zhōngjiānde [joong-jyen-dur]

中间的

midnight bànyè [bahn-yur]

半夜

at midnight bànyè [bahn-yur]

半夜

might: I might ... yéxǔ ... [yur-hsoo]

也许

I might not ... yéxǔ bù ...

也许不 ...

mild (taste) wèidàn [wei-dahn]

味淡

(weather) nuǎnhuo [nwahn-hwor]

暖和

mile yīnglǐ

英里

milk niúnǎi [nyoh-nai]

牛奶

millimetre háomǐ [how-mee]

毫米

mind: never mind méi guānxi

[may gwahn-hshee]

没关系

I've changed my mind wó gǎibiàn zhǔyì le [wor gai-byen joo-yee lur]

我改变主意了

dialogue

> **do you mind if I open the window?** wǒ kāi chuāng, xíngbùxíng? [chwahng hsing-boo-hsing]
> **no, I don't mind** xíng [hsing]

mine*: it's mine shì wǒde [shur wor-dur]

是我的

mineral water kuàngquánshuǐr [kwahng-choo-en-shwayr]

矿泉水儿

Ming Tombs shísānlíng [shur-sahn-ling]

十三陵

minute fēn(zhōng) [fun(-joong)]

分（钟）

in a minute yìhuǐr [yee-hwayr]

一会儿

just a minute děng yìhuǐr [dung]

等一会儿

mirror jìngzi [jing-dzur]

镜子

Miss xiáojiě 〖hsyow-jyeh〗
小姐

miss: I missed the bus wǒ
méi gǎnshàng chē 〖wor may
gahn-shahng chur〗
我没赶上车

missing: my ... is missing
wǒde ... diūle 〖wor-dur ...
dyoh-lur〗
我的 ... 丢了

there's a suitcase missing
yíge yīxiāng diūle 〖yee-gur
yee-hsyahng dyoh-lur〗
一个衣箱丢了

mist wù
雾

mistake cuò(wù) 〖tswor–〗
错（误）

I think there's a mistake zhèr
yǒuge cuòr 〖jer yoh-gur〗
这儿有个错儿

sorry, I've made a mistake
dùibùqǐ, wǒ nòngcùole
〖dway-boo-chee wor
noong-tswor-lur〗
对不起我弄错了

misunderstanding wùhuì
〖woo-hway〗
误会

mobile phone shǒutí diànhuà
〖shoh-tee dyen-hwah〗
手提电话

modern xiàndài 〖hsyen-dai〗
现代

moisturizer cāliǎnyóu
〖tsah-lyen-yoh〗
擦脸油

moment: I won't be a moment
jiù yìfēn zhōng 〖jyoh yee-fun
joong〗
就一分钟

monastery (Buddhist) sìyuàn
〖sur-yew-ahn〗
寺院

Monday xīngqīyī
〖hsing-chee-yee〗
星期一

money qián 〖chyen〗
钱

Mongolia Ménggǔ 〖mung-goo〗
蒙古

Mongolian (adj) Ménggǔ
蒙古

monk sēng 〖sung〗
僧

month yuè 〖yew-eh〗
月

monument jìniànbēi
〖jin-yen-bay〗
纪念碑

moon yuèliang 〖yew-eh-lyang〗
月亮

more* gèng duō 〖gung
dwor〗
更多

can I have some more water,
please? qǐng zài lái diǎnr
shuǐ? 〖ching dzai lai shway 〗
请再来点儿水？

more expensive gèng guì

138

[gung gway]

更贵

more interesting than ... bǐ ... gèng yǒu xìngqù [yoh hsing-chew]

比 ... 更有兴趣

more than 50/100 wǔshí/yìbǎi duō

五十／一百多

more than that one bǐ nèige duō [nay-gur]

比那个多

a lot more duōde duō [dwor-dur]

多得多

dialogue

would you like some more? nǐ hái yào diǎnr shénme ma? [yow dyenr shun-mur mah]

no, no more for me, thanks búyào, xièxie [boo-yow hsyeh-hsyeh]

how about you? nǐ ne? [nee-nur]

I don't want any more, thanks wǒ bú zàiyàole, xièxie [wor boo dzai-yow-lur]

morning zǎoshang [dzow-shahng]

早上

this morning jīntiān zǎoshang

[jin-tyen dzow-shahng]

今天早上

in the morning zǎoshang [dzow-shahng]

早上

mosquito wénzi [wun-dzur]

蚊子

 Malaria and dengue fever are not widespread in China: they are only a problem in the south of China in summer and all year round in tropical areas such as Hainan Island. Mosquitoes are most active at dawn and dusk. At these times wear long sleeves and trousers, avoid dark colours and use repellent on exposed skin. Mosquito repellent is usually available in the shops in areas where it is needed.

Most hotels and guesthouses in affected areas provide mosquito nets, but you may want to bring your own if you intend going to any rural areas. Air-conditioning and fans help keep mosquitoes at bay, as do mosquito coils and insecticide sprays, both available in China.

If you're travelling in high-risk areas, it's advisable to take malaria tablets, which you need to start taking a week before exposure, and then continue with them for four weeks after leaving a malarial region.

Mo

mosquito net wénzhàng [wun-jahng]
蚊帐

mosquito repellent qūwénjì [chew-wun-jee]
驱蚊剂

most*: I like this one most of all wǒ zuì xǐhuān zhèige [wor dzway hshee-hwahn jay-gur]
我最喜欢这个

most of the time dàbùfen shíjiān [dah-boo-fun shur-jyen]
大部分时间

most tourists dà duōshù lǚyóuzhe [dah dwor-shoo]
大多数旅游者

mostly dàduō [dah-dwor]
大多

mother mǔqīn [moo-chin]
母亲

mother-in-law pópo [por-por]
婆婆

motorbike mótuōchē [mor-twor-chur]
摩托车

motorboat qìtǐng [chee-ting]
汽艇

mountain shān [shahn]
山

in the mountains zài shānlǐ [dzai shahn-lee]
在山里

mountaineering dēngshān [dung-shahn]
登山

mouse láoshǔ [low-shoo]
老鼠

moustache xiǎo húzi [hsyow hoo-dzur]
小胡子

mouth zuǐ [dzway]
嘴

move: he's moved to another room tā bāndào lìngwài yí jiān qùle [tah bahn-dow ling-wai yee jyen choo-lur]
他搬到另外一间去了

could you move it? qǐng nín nuó yíxià, hǎo ma? [ching nin nwor yee-hsyah how mah]
请您挪一下好吗？

could you move up a little? qíng wǎng qián núo yíxià, hǎo ma? [wahng chyen nwor yee-hsyah]
请往前挪一下好吗？

movie diànyǐng [dyen-ying]
电影

movie theater diànyǐng yuàn [dyen-ying yew-ahn]
电影院

Mr xiānsheng [hsyen-shung]
先生

Mrs fūren [foo-run]
夫人

Ms nǚshì [nyew-shur]
女士

much duō [dwor]
多

much better/worse hǎo/huài

de duō [dur]

好／坏得多

not (very) much bù hěn duō

不很多

I don't want very much wǒ búyào tài dūo [wor boo-yow]

我不要太多

mug (for drinking) bēi [bay]

杯

I've been mugged wó gěi rén qiǎngle [gay run chyang-lur]

我给人抢了

mum māma [mah-mah]

妈妈

museum bówùguǎn [bor-woo-gwahn]

博物馆

see **opening times**

mushrooms mógu [mor-goo]

蘑菇

music yīnyuè [yin-yew-eh]

音乐

Muslim (adj) mùsīlín [moo-sur-lin]

穆斯林

must*: I must wǒ bìxū [wor bee-hsyew]

我必须

I mustn't drink alcohol wǒ búhuì hē jiù [wor-boo-hway hur jyoh]

我不会喝酒

my* wǒde [wor-dur]

我的

myself: I'll do it myself wǒ zìjǐ

lái [wor dzur-jee]

我自己来

by myself wǒ yíge rén [yee-gur run]

我一个人

N

nail (finger) zhǐjiā [jur-jyah]

指甲

(metal) dīngzi [ding-dzur]

钉子

nail varnish zhǐjiā yóu [jur-jyah yoh]

指甲油

name míngzi [ming-dzur]

名子

my name's John wǒde míngzi jiào John [wor-dur – jyow]

我的名子叫 John

what's your name? nǐ jiào shénme? [nee – shun-mur]

你叫什么？

what is the name of this street? zhèi tiào lù jiào shénme? [jay tyow]

这条路叫什么？

 A Chinese name usually comprises three characters. The first character is the family name, inherited from the father. The second two characters are the first name, though strangers find it embarrassing to address each other by their first names – instead a popular informal convention is to add the epithets xiǎo (young) or lǎo (old) to the surnames. For example lǎo Máo ('Old Mao') would be a respectful but friendly way to address a person older than oneself. Young people of the same age would call each other xiǎo Zhāng, xiǎo Lóng etc. Women do not change their surnames when they marry. Formal titles always come after names. The most commonly used are xiānsheng (Mr), fūren (Mrs), xiáojie (Miss) and nǚshi (Miss or Ms). For example, Wáng xiānsheng 'Mr Wang', and Máo xiáojie 'Miss Mao'.

napkin cānjīn [tsahn-jin]
餐巾

nappy niàobù [nyow-boo]
尿布

narrow (street) zhǎi [jai]
窄

nasty (person) ràng ren tǎoyàn
[rahng run tow-yen]
让人讨厌
(weather, accident) zāotòule
[dzow-toh-lur]
糟透了

national (state) guójiā

[gwor-jyah]
国家
(nationwide) quánguó
[choo-en-gwor]
全国

nationality guójí [gwor-jee]
国籍
(for Chinese minorities) shǎoshù mínzú [show-shoo min-dzoo]
少数民族

natural zìrán [dzur-rahn]
自然

near jìn
近

near the ... lí ... hěnjìn
[hun-jin]
离 ... 很近

is it near the city centre?
lí shì zhōngxīn jìn ma? [shur joong-hsin jin mah]
离市中心近吗？

do you go near the Great Wall? nǐ zài Chángchéng fùjìn tíngchē ma? [nee dzai chahng-chung foo-jin ting-chur mah]
你在长城附近停车吗？

where is the nearest ...?
zuìjìn de ... zài nǎr? [dzway-jin dur ... dzai nar]
最近的 ... 在哪儿？

nearby fùjìn [foo-jin]
附近

nearly chàbuduō
[chah-boo-dwor]
差不多

necessary bìyào(de)
[bee-yow(-dur)]
必要（的）

neck bózi [boh-dzur]
脖子

necklace xiàngliàn
[hsyahng-lyen]
项链

necktie lǐngdài
领带

need: I need ... wǒ xūyào ...
[wor hsyew-yow]
我需要

do I need to pay? wǒ yīnggāi
fùqián ma? [foo-chyen mah]
我应该付钱吗？

needle zhēn [jun]
针

neither: neither (one) of them
liǎngge dōu bù [lyang-gur doh]
两个都不

Nepal Níbó'ěr [nee-bor-er]
尼泊尔

Nepali (adj) Níbó'ěr
尼泊尔

nephew zhízi [jur-dzur]
侄子

net (in sport) wǎng [wahng]
网

network map jiāotōngtú
[jyow-toong-too]
交通图

never (not ever) cónglái bù
[tsoong-lai]
从来不

(not yet) hái méiyou [may-yoh]
还没有

dialogue

**have you ever been to
Beijing?** nǐ qùguo Běijīng
méiyou? [chew-gwor –
may-yoh]
**no, never, I've never been
there** cónglái méiqù
[tsoong-lai may-chew]

new xīn [hsin]
新

news (radio, TV etc) xīnwén
[hsin-wun]
新闻

newspaper bào(zhǐ) [bow(-jur)]
报（纸）

New Year xīnnián [hsin-nyen]
新年

Chinese New Year chūnjié
[chun-jyeh]
春节

Happy New Year! xīnnián
hǎo! [how]
新年好

(Chinese) gōnghè xīnxǐ!
[goong-hur hsin-hshee]
恭贺新禧

Chinese New Year, or
Spring Festival, is the
biggest holiday in the

Chinese calendar, consisting of two weeks of festivities marking the beginning of a new year in the lunar calendar. Each year it falls on a different date in the Gregorian calendar, between mid-January and mid-February. China is at its most colourful at this time, with shops and houses decorated with good luck messages and stalls and shops selling paper money, drums and costumes. During the festival itself, however, is not an ideal time to be travelling – everything closes for the holiday, and much of the population goes on the move, making travel impossible or extremely crowded. The first day of the festival is marked by a family feast at which **jiǎozi** (dumplings), are eaten, sometimes with coins hidden inside, and followed by firecrackers which are supposed to frighten away demons. New Year in the cities is now a slightly more staid affair as fireworks are banned, though enterprising stall holders sell cassette tapes of explosions as a replacement. Outside the home, Spring Festival is publicly celebrated at temple fairs, which feature acrobats, drummers and gusts of smoke as the Chinese light incense sticks to placate the gods. After two weeks, the celebrations end with the lantern festival, when the streets are filled with multicoloured paper lanterns, a tradition dating from the Han Dynasty.

New Year's Eve: Chinese New Year's Eve chúxī [choo-hshee]
除夕

New Zealand Xīnxīlán [hsin-see-lahn]
新西兰

New Zealander: I'm a New Zealander wǒ shì xīnxīlánren [–run]
我是新西兰人

next xià yíge [hsyah yee-gur]
下一个

the next street on the left zuǒbiānr díyì tiáo lù [dzwor-byenr dee-yee tiao]
左边儿第一条路

at the next stop xià yízhàn [hsyah yee-jahn]
下一站

next week xià(ge) xīngqī [hsyah(-gur) hsing-chee]
下（个）星期

next to ... zài ... pángbiān [dzai ... pahng-byen]
在 ... 旁边

nice (food) hǎochī [how-chur]
好吃
(looks, view etc) hǎokàn [how-kahn]
好看

(person) hǎo [how]

好

niece zhínǚ [jin-yew]

侄女

night yè [yur]

夜

at night yèli [yur-lee]

夜里

good night wǎn ān [wahn ahn]

晚安

dialogue

do you have a single room for one night? yǒu yítiān de dānrén jiān ma? [yoh yee-tyen dur dahn-run jyen mah]

yes, madam yǒu [yoh]

how much is it per night? yìwǎn yào duōshaoqián? [yee-wahn yow dwor-show-chyen]

it's 30 yuan for one night yìwǎn yào sānshí kuài qián [sahn-shur – chyen]

thank you, I'll take it xíng [hsing]

nightclub yèzǒnghuì [yur-dzoong-hway]

夜总会

no* bù

不

I've no change wǒ méiyou líng qián [wor may-yoh – chyen]

我没有零钱

no way! bù xíng! [hsing]

不行

oh no! (upset) tiān na! [tyen nah]

天哪

nobody méirén [may-run]

没人

there's nobody there méirén zài nàr [dzai]

没人在那儿

noise zàoyīn [dzow-yin]

噪音

noisy: it's too noisy tài chǎole [chow-lur]

太吵了

non-alcoholic bù hán jiǔjīng de [hahn jyoh-jing dur]

不含酒精的

none shénme yě méiyou [shun-mur yur may-yoh]

什么也没有

noon zhōngwǔ [joong-woo]

中午

at noon zhōngwǔ

中午

no-one méirén [may-run]

没人

nor: nor do I wó yě bù [wor yur]

我也不

normal zhèngcháng(de) [jung-chahng(-dur)]

正常（的）

north běi [bay]

北

in the north běibian [bay-byen]

北边

to the north wǎng běi [wahng]

往北

north of Rome Luómǎ běi

罗马北

northeast dōngběi [doong-bay]

东北

northern běibiān [bay-byen]

北边

Northern Ireland Běi Ài'ěrlán [bay ai-er-lahn]

北爱尔兰

North Korea Běi Cháoxiǎn [bay chow-hsyen]

北朝鲜

northwest xīběi [hshee-bay]

西北

Norway Nuówēi [nwor-way]

挪威

Norwegian (adj, language) Nuówēiyǔ

挪威语

nose bízi [bee-dzur]

鼻子

not* bù

不

no, I'm not hungry wǒ búè [wor bway]

我不饿

I don't want any, thank you búyào, xièxie [boo-yow hsyeh-hsyeh]

不要谢谢

it's not necessary búbìyào

不必要

I didn't know that wǒ bù zhīdao [wor boo jur-dow]

我不知道

not that one, this one búyào nèige, yào zhèige [nay-gur yow jay-gur]

不要那个要这个

note (banknote) chāopiào [chow-pyow]

钞票

notebook bǐjìběn [bee-jee-bun]

笔记本

nothing méiyou shénme [may-yoh shun-mur]

没有什么

nothing for me, thanks wǒ shénme dōu bú yào, xièxie [wor – doh boo yow hsyeh-hsyeh]

我什么都不要谢谢

nothing else, thanks qítade búyào, xièxie [chee-tah-dur boo-yow]

其他的不要谢谢

novel (noun) xiǎoshuō [hsyow-shwor]

小说

November shíyīyuè [shur-yee-yew-eh]

十一月

now xiànzài [hsyen-dzai]

现在

number hàomǎ [how-mah]
号码
(figure) shùzì [shoo-dzur]
数字
I've got the wrong number
wó dǎcuòle [wor dah-tswor-lur]
我打错了
what is your phone number?
nǐde diànhuà hàomǎ shì
duǒshao? [nee-dur dyen-hwah
shur dwor-show]
你的电话号码是多少？
number plate chēpái [chur-pai]
车牌
nurse hùshi [hoo-shur]
护士
nut (for bolt) luósī [lwor-sur]
螺丝
nuts (chestnuts) lìzi [lee-dzur]
栗子
(hazelnuts) zhēnzi [jun-dzur]
榛子
(walnuts) hétao [hur-tow]
核桃

O

occupied (US) yǒurén [yoh-run]
有人
o'clock* diǎnzhōng
[dyen-joong]
点钟
October shíyuè [shur-yew-eh]
十月

odd (strange) qíguài [chee-gwai]
奇怪
of* de [dur]
的
off (lights, machine) guān
shangle [gwahn shahng-lur]
关上了
it's just off ... (street etc) lí ...
bùyuán [boo-ywahn]
离 ... 不远
we're off tomorrow wǒmen
míngtiān zǒu [wor-mun
ming-tyen dzoh]
我们明天走
office (place of work)
bàngōngshì [bahn-goong-shur]
办公室
often jīngcháng [jing-chahng]
经常
not often bù jīngcháng [boo
jing-chahng]
不经常
how often are the buses?
yíge zhōngtóu duōshao
qìchē? [yee-gur joong-toh
dwor-show chee-chur]
一个钟头多少汽车？
oil (for car) yóu [yoh]
油
vegetable oil càiyóu [tsai-yoh]
菜油
oily (food) yóunì [yoh-nee]
油腻
ointment yàogāo [yow-gow]
药膏

OK hǎo [how]

好

are you OK? hái hǎo ma?
[mah]

还好吗？

I feel OK hén hǎo [hun]

很好

is that OK with you? xíng bù
xíng? [hsing]

行不行？

is it OK to ...? wó kěyi ...?
[wor kur-yee]

我可以 ... ？

that's OK, thanks xíngle
xièxie [hsing-lur hsyeh-hsyeh]

行了谢谢

is this train OK for ...? zhè liè
huǒchē qù ... ma? [jer lyeh
hwor-chur chew ... mah]

这列火车去 ... 吗？

old (person) lǎo [low]

老

(thing) jiù [jyoh]

旧

dialogue

how old are you? nín duō
dà niánlíng? [dwor dah
nyen-ling]

(to an old person) nín duō dà
niánjì le? [dwor dah nyen-jee
lur]

(to a child) ni jǐsuì le?
[jee-sway lur]

I'm 25 wǒ èrshíwǔ suì
[wor – sway]

and you? nǐ ne? [nur]

old-fashioned guòshí(de)
[gwor-shur(-dur)]

过时（的）

(person) shǒujiù(de)
[shoh-jyoh(-dur)]

守旧（的）

old town (old part of town)
jiùchéng [jyoh-chung]

旧城

omelette chǎojīdàn
[chow-jee-dahn]

炒鸡蛋

on*: **on ...** (on top of) zài ...
shàngmian [dzai ...
shahng-myen]

在 ... 上面

on the street zài lùshàng

在路上

on the beach zài hǎitān
shàng

在海滩上

is it on this road?
zài zhètíaolù ma? [jur-tyow-loo
mah]

在这条路吗？

on the plane zài feījī shàng

在飞机上

on Saturday xīngqī liù [lyoh]

星期六

on television zài diànshìshang

在电视上

I haven't got it on me wǒ méi dài zài shēnshang [wor may dai dzai shun-shahng]

我没带在身上

this one's on me (drink) wǒ fùqián [wor foo-choo-en]

我付钱

the light wasn't on dēng méi kāi [dung may]

灯没开

what's on tonight? jīntiān wǎnshang yǒu shénme huódòng? [jin-tyen wahn-shahng you shun-mur hwor-dong]

今天晚上有什么活动？

once (one time) yícì [yee-tsur]

一次

at once (immediately) mǎshàng [mah-shahng]

马上

one* yī [yur]

一

the white one báisè de [bai-sur dur]

白色的

one-way ticket dānchéng piào [dahn-chung pyow]

单程票

onion yángcōng [yang-tsoong]

洋葱

only zhǐ yǒu [jur yoh]

只有

only one zhǐ yǒu yíge [yee-gur]

只有一个

it's only 6 o'clock cái liùdiǎn [tsai lyoh-dyen]

才六点

I've only just got here wǒ gāng dào le [wor gahng dow lur]

我刚到了

on/off switch kāiguān [kai-gwahn]

开关

open (adj) kāi(de) [kai(-dur)]

开（的）

(verb) kāi

开

when do you open? nǐmen shénme shíhou kāiménr? [nee-mun shun-mur shur-hoh kai-munr]

你们什么时候开门儿？

I can't get it open wǒ dǎbúkāi [wor dah-boo--kai]

我打不开

in the open air zài shìwài [dzai shur-wai]

在室外

opening times yíngyè shíjiān [ying-yur shur-jyen]

营业时间

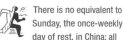

There is no equivalent to Sunday, the once-weekly day of rest, in China: all shops open every day, keeping long, late hours, especially in big cities. Banks and post offices close either on Sunday or for the whole weekend, though even this is not always the case. Museums sometimes close for one day a week, though most tourist sites or temples are open seven days a week.

opera gējù [gur-jyew]
歌剧
operation (medical) shŏushù [shoh-shoo]
手术
operator (telephone) zŏngjī [dzoong-jee]
总机
opposite: the opposite direction xiāngfǎn de fāngxiàng [hsyahng-fahn dur fahng-hsyahng]
相反的方向
the bar opposite zài duìmianr de jiǔba [dzai dway-myenr dur]
在对面儿的酒吧
opposite my hotel zài wǒ fàndiàn duìmianr
在我饭店对面儿
optician yǎnjìngdiàn [yen-jing-dyen]
眼镜店
or (in statement) huòzhě [hwor-jur]
或者
(in question) háishi [hai-shur]
还是

orange (fruit) júzi [joo-dzur]
橘子
(colour) júhuángsè [jyew-sur]
橘黄色
orange juice (fresh) xiānjúzhī [hsyen-jyew-jur]
鲜橘汁
(fizzy) júzi qìshuǐ [jyew-dzur chee-shway]
橘子汽水
(diluted) júzishuǐr [jyew-dzur-shwayr]
橘子水儿
order: can we order now? (in restaurant) wǒmen kéyi diǎncài ma? [wor-mun kur-yee dyen-tsai mah]
我们可以点菜吗？
I've already ordered, thanks yǐjing diǎn le, xièxie [yee-jing dyen lur hsyeh-hsyeh]
已经点了谢谢
I didn't order this wǒ méiyǒu diǎn zhèige cài [wor may-yoh dyen jay-gur tsai]
我没有点这个菜
out of order huàile [hwai-lur]
坏了
ordinary pǔtōng [poo-toong]
普通
other qítā [chee-tah]
其他
the other one lìng yíge [yee-gur]
另一个

the other day zuìjìn
[dzway-jin]
最近

I'm waiting for the others wǒ
děngzhe qíyúde [wor dung-jer
chee-yoo-dur]
我等着其余的

do you have any others?
(other kinds) hái yǒu biéde
ma? [yoh byeh-dur mah]
还有别的吗？

otherwise yàobùrán
[yow-boor-ahn]
要不然

our/ours* wǒmende
[wor-mun-dur]
我们的

out: he's out tā chūqule [tah
choo-chew-lur]
他出去了

three kilometres out of town
lí shìqū sān gōnglǐ [shur-chew
– goong-lee]
离市区三公里

outdoors lùtiān [loo-tyen]
露天

outside* wàimiàn
[wai-myen]
外面

can we sit outside? wǒmen
kéyǐ dào wàimiàn qù zuò
ma? [wor-mun kur-yee dow
wai-myen chew dzwor mah]
我们可以到外面去坐
吗？

oven kǎoxiāng [kow-syang]
烤箱

over: over here zài zhèr [dzai
jer]
在这儿

over there zài nàr
在那儿

over 500 wǔbǎi duō [dwor]
五百多

it's over wánle [wahn-lur]
完了

**overcharge: you've
overcharged me** nǐ
duōshōule wǒde qián
[dwor-shoh-lur wor-dur chyen]
你多收了我的钱

overland mail lùshang yóudì
[loo-shahng yoh-dee]
陆上邮递

overnight (travel) guòyè
[gwor-yur]
过夜

overtake chāoguò [chow-gwor]
超过

owe: how much do I owe you?
yígòng duōshao qián?
[yee-goong dwor-show chyen]
一共多少钱？

own: my own ... wǒ zìjǐde ...
[wor dzur-jur-dur]
我自己的 ...

are you on your own? jiù nǐ
yíge rén ma? [jyoh nee yee-gur
run mah]
就你一个人吗？

I'm on my own jiù wǒ yíge rén [jyoh wor yee-gur run]
就我一个人

P

pack (verb) shōushi [shoh-shur]
收拾

package (parcel) bāoguǒ [bow-gwor]
包裹

packed lunch héfàn [hur-fahn]
盒饭

packet: a packet of cigarettes yìbāo yān [yee-bow yen]
一包烟

paddy field dàotián [dow-tyen]
稻田

page (of book) yè [yur]
页

could you page Mr ...? nǐ néng jiào yíxia ... xiānsheng ma? [nung jyow yee-hsyah ... hsyen-shung mah]
你能叫一下 ... 先生吗？

pagoda tǎ [tah]
塔

pain téng [tung]
疼

I have a pain here wǒ zhèr téng [wor jer]
我这儿疼

painful téng
疼

painkillers zhǐténgyào [jur-tung-yow]
止疼药

painting huà [hwah]
画
(oil) yóuhuà [yoh-hwah]
油画
(Chinese) guóhuà [gwor-hwah]
国画

pair: a pair of ... yíduìr ... [yee-dwayr]
一对儿 ...

Pakistani (adj) Bājīsītǎn [bah-jee-sur-tahn]
巴基斯坦

palace gōngdiàn [goong-dyen]
宫殿

pale cāngbái [tsahng-bai]
苍白

pale blue dàn lánsè [dahn lahn-sur]
淡蓝色

panda dà xióngmāo [dah hsyoong-mow]
大熊猫

pants (underwear: men's) kùchǎ [koo-chah]
裤衩
(women's) xiǎo sānjiǎokù [hsyow sahn-jyow-koo]
小三角裤
(US: trousers) kùzi [koo-dzur]
裤子

pantyhose liánkùwà

[lyen-koo-wah]

连裤袜

paper zhǐ [jur]

纸

(newspaper) bàozhǐ [bow-jur]

报纸

a piece of paper yìzhāng zhǐ
[yee-jahng jur]

一张纸

paper handkerchiefs zhǐjīn
[jur-jin]

纸巾

parcel bāoguǒ [bow-gwor]

包裹

pardon (me)? (didn't
understand/hear) nǐ shuō
shénme? [shwor shun-mur]

你说什么？

parents fùmǔ

父母

park (noun) gōngyuán
[goong-yew-ahn]

公园

(verb) tíngchē [ting-chur]

停车

can I park here? wǒ néng zài
zhèr tíngchē ma? [wor nung
dzai-jer ting-chur mah]

我能在这儿停车吗？

parking lot tíngchē chǎng
[ting-chur chahng]

停车场

part (noun) bùfen

部分

partner (boyfriend, girlfriend etc)

bànr [bahnr]

伴儿

party (group) tuántǐ [twahn-tee]

团体

(celebration) wǎnhuì
[wahn-hway]

晚会

passenger chéngkè [chung-kur]

乘客

passport hùzhào [hoo-jow]

护照

past*: in the past guòqu
[gwor-chew]

过去

just past the information
office gāng jīngguò
wènxùnchù [gahng jing-gwor
wun-hsun-choo]

刚经过问讯处

path xiǎolù [hsyow-loo]

小路

pattern tú'àn [too-ahn]

图案

pavement rénxíng dào
[run-hsing dow]

人行道

pavilion tíngzi [ting-dzur]

亭子

pay (verb) fù qián [foo(-chyen)]

付钱

can I pay, please? suànzhàng
ba? [swahn-jahng bah]

算帐吧？

it's already paid for zhège

153

yǐjīng fùqián le [jay-gur yee-jing
foo-chyen lur]

这个已经付钱了

dialogue

who's paying? shúi
fùqián? [shway foo-chyen]
I'll pay wǒ fùqián [wor
foo-chyen]
no, you paid last time, I'll
pay bù, nǐ shì zuìhòu yícì
fùde, wǒ fùqián [shur
dzway-hoh yee-tsur foo-dur]

payphone jìfèi diànhuà [jee-fay
dyen-hwah]
计费电话
peaceful ānjìng [ahn-jing]
安静
peach táozi [tow-dzur]
桃子
peanuts huāshēng
[hwah-shung]
花生
pear lí
梨
peculiar (taste, custom) guài
[gwai]
怪
pedestrian crossing rénxíng
héngdào [run-hsing hung-dow]
人行横道
Peking Opera Jīngjù [jing-jew]
京剧

pen gāngbǐ [gahng-bee]
钢笔
pencil qiānbǐ [chyen-bee]
铅笔
penfriend bíyǒu [bee-yoh]
笔友
penicillin pánníxīlín
[pahn-nee-see-lin]
盘尼西林
penknife qiānbǐdāo
[chyen-bee-dow]
铅笔刀
pensioner lǐng yánglǎojīn de
rén [yang-low-jin dur run]
领养老金的人
people rénmín [run-min]
人民
the other people in the hotel
fàndiàn li de qítā kèrén [lee
dur chee-tah ker-run]
饭店里的其他客人
too many people rén tài duō
le [run tai dwor-lur]
人太多了
People's Republic of China
Zhōnghuá Rénmín
Gònghéguó [joong-hwah
run-min goong-hur-gwor]
中华人民共和国
pepper (spice) hújiāo
[hoo-jyow]
胡椒
(vegetable, red) shìzijiāo
[shur-dzur-jyow]
柿子椒

per: per night méi wǎn [may wahn]

每晚

how much per day? yìtiān yào duōshao qián? [yee-tyen yow dwor-show chyen]

一天要多少钱？

... per cent bǎifēn zhī ... [bai-fun jur]

百分之 ...

perfect wánměi [wahn-may]

完美

perfume xiāngshuǐr [hsyahng-shwayr]

香水儿

perhaps kěnéng [kur-nung]

可能

perhaps not kěnéng bù

可能不

period (of time) shíqī [shur-chee]

时期

(menstruation) yuèjīng [yew-eh-jing]

月经

permit (noun) xúkě zhèng [hsyew-kur jung]

许可证

person rén [run]

人

personal stereo fàngyīnjī [fahng-yin-jee]

放音机

petrol qìyóu [chee-yoh]

汽油

petrol can yóutǒng [yoh-toong]

油桶

petrol station jiāyóu zhàn [jyah-yoh jahn]

加油站

pharmacy yàodiàn [yow-dyen]

药店

 Pharmacies can help with minor injuries or ailments and large ones sometimes have a separate counter offering diagnosis and advice, though you're unlikely to find any staff who can speak anything but Chinese. The selection of reliable Asian and Western products available has improved, and it's also possible to treat yourself with herbal medicines which are effective for minor complaints.

Philippines Fēilǜbīn [fay-lew-bin]

菲律宾

phone (noun) diànhuà [dyen-hwah]

电话

(verb) dǎ diànhuà [dah]

打电话

 China's phone system is expanding and both international and domestic calls can be made with little fuss. Local calls are free and long-distance calls within China are cheap. Most big hotels offer direct dialling abroad from your room, but will add a surcharge and a minimum charge of between one and three minutes will be levied even if the call goes unanswered. International calls are best made from telecommunications offices, usually located next to or in the main post office and open 24 hours. You pay a deposit and are told to go to a particular booth. When you have finished, you pay at the desk. The minimum charge is for three minutes. Cardphones are now widely available in major cities. Cards can only be used in the province where you buy them. There's a big drawback with making an international call with one of these – as soon as the number of units left on the card drops below a certain level, you will be cut off, and left with a phonecard that can only be used to make calls within China. However, cards are the cheapest way to make long-distance calls.

phone book diànhuà bù
[dyen-hwah]
电话簿
phone box diànhuàtíng
电话亭

phonecard diànhuàkǎ
[dyen-hwah-kah]
电话卡
phone number diànhuà
hàomǎ [how-mah]
电话号码
photo zhàopiàn [jow-pyen]
照片
**could you take a photo of us,
please?** qíng géi wǒ
zhàozhāng xiàng [ching
gay-wor jow-jahng hsyahng]
请给我照张相

Common sense is required in the taking of photographs; do not photograph strategic buildings or structures such as airports and bridges. Good-quality film and fast, efficient processing are widely available.

phrasebook duìhuà shǒucè
[dway-hwah shoh-tsur]
对话手册
piano gāngqín [gahng-chin]
钢琴
pickpocket páshǒu
[pah-shoh]
扒手
**pick up: will you be there to
pick me up?** nǐ lái jiē wó hǎo
ma? [ni lai jyeh wor how mah]
你来接我好吗？

picnic (noun) yěcān [yur-tsahn]
野餐

picture (painting) huà [hwah]
画

(photo) zhàopiàn [jow-pyen]
照片

piece kuàir [kwair]
块儿

a piece of ... yíkuàir ...
[yee-kwair]
一块儿 ...

pig zhū [joo]
猪

pill bìyùnyào [bee-yewn-yow]
避孕药

I'm on the pill wǒ chī
bìyùnyào [wor chur
bee-yew-nyow]
我吃避孕药

pillow zhèntou [jun-toh]
枕头

pillow case zhěntào [jun-tow]
枕套

pin (noun) biézhēn [byeh-jun]
别针

pineapple bōluó [bor-lwor]
菠萝

pineapple juice bōluózhī
[bor-lwor-jur]
菠萝汁

pink fěnhóng [fun-hoong]
粉红

pipe (for smoking) yāndǒu
[yen-doh]
烟斗

(for water) guǎnzi [gwahn-dzur]
管子

pity: it's a pity zhēn kěxī [jun
kur-hshee]
真可惜

place (noun) dìfāng [dee-fahng]
地方

at your place zài nǐde jiā [dzai
nee-dur jyah]
在你的家

plane fēijī [fay-jee]
飞机

by plane zuò fēijī [dzwor]
坐飞机

 China has some fourteen regional airlines linking all major cities and many important sites. It's a luxury worth considering for long distances, but you'll have to offset comfort and time saved against a poor safety record, not to mention the cost – foreigners currently have to pay a hefty surcharge, making flying slightly more expensive than going soft berth on a train. You can buy tickets from CAAC (China Airlines) offices, hotel desks or tour agents.

plant zhíwù [jur-woo]
植物

plasters xiàngpí gāo
[syang-pee gow]
橡皮膏

plastic sùliào [soo-lyow]
塑料

plastic bag sùliàodài
塑料袋

plate pánzi [pahn-dzur]
盘子

platform zhàntái [jahn-tai]
站台

which platform is it for Beijing? wǎng Běijīng de huǒchē cóng jǐhào zhàntái kāichū? [wahng – dur hwor-chur tsoong jee-how jahn-tai kai-choo]
往北京的火车从几号站台开出？

play (verb) wánr [wahnr]
玩儿

(noun: in theatre) huàjù [hwah-jew]
话剧

pleasant lìngrén yúkuài [ling-run yew-kwai]
令人愉快

please qǐng [ching]
请

yes, please hǎo, xièxie [how hsyeh-hsyeh]
好谢谢

could you please ...? qǐng nín ..., hǎo ma? [mah]
请您 ... 好吗？

please don't qǐng nín bù
请您不

pleased: pleased to meet you hěn gāoxìng jiàndào nǐ [hun gow hsing jyen dow]
很高兴见到你

pleasure: my pleasure méi shìr [may shur]
没事儿

plenty: plenty of ... xǔduō ... [hsyew-dwor]
许多

there's plenty of time hǎo duō shíjian [how dwor shur-jyen]
好多时间

that's plenty, thanks gòule, xièxie [goh-lur hsyeh-hsyeh]
够了谢谢

plug (electrical) chātóu [chah-toh]
插头

(in sink) sāizi [sai-dzur]
塞子

plum lǐzi [lee-dzur]
李子

plumber guǎnzigōng [gwahn-dzur-goong]
管子工

p.m. xiàwǔ [hsyah-woo]
下午

pocket kǒudàir [koh-dair]
口袋儿

point: two point five èr diǎn wǔ [dyen]
二点五

there's no point bù zhíde [jur-dur]
不值得

poisonous yǒudúde

[yoh-doo-dur]

有毒的

police jǐngchá [jing-chah]

警察

call the police! kuài jiào jǐngchá! [kwai jyow jing-chah]

快叫警察

China is basically a police state, with the State interfering with and controlling the lives of its subjects to a degree most Westerners would find hard to tolerate, as indeed many of the Chinese do. This should not affect foreigners much, however, as the State on the whole takes a hands-off approach to visitors. As a tourist you are an obvious target for thieves. Carry your passport and money in a concealed money belt. Be wary on buses, the favoured haunt of pickpockets, and trains, particularly in hard-seat class and on overnight journeys. Hotel rooms are on the whole secure, dormitories less so. At street level, try not to be too ostentatious. Avoid eye-catching jewellery and flash watches, and try to be discreet when taking out your cash. Not looking wealthy also helps if you want to avoid being ripped off by taxi drivers, as does telling them you are a student (wǒ shì xuésheng).

If you do have anything stolen, you'll need to get the police to write up a loss report in order to claim on your insurance. If possible take a Chinese speaker with you and be prepared to pay a small fee.

The emergency number for the police is 110.

policeman jǐngchá [jing-chah]

警察

police station pàichūsuǒ [pai-choo-swor]

派出所

polish (for shoes) xiéyóu [hsyeh-yoh]

鞋油

polite kèqi [kur-chee]

客气

polluted wūrǎnle de [woo-rahn-lur dur]

污染了的

pool (for swimming) yóuyǒngchí [yoh-yoong-chur]

游泳池

poor (not rich) qióng [chyoong]

穷

(quality) lièzhì [lyeh-jur]

劣质

pop music liúxíng yīnyuè [lyoh-hsing yin-yew-eh]

流行音乐

pop singer liúxíng gēshǒu [gur-shoh]

流行歌手

159

pork zhūròu [joo-roh]

猪肉

port (for boats) gángkǒu
[gahng-koh]

港口

porter (in hotel) ménfáng
[mun-fahng]

门房

possible kěnéng [kur-nung]

可能

is it possible to ...?
kéyǐ...ma? [yoh]

可以 … 吗？

as ... as possible jǐn kěnéng

尽可能

post (noun: mail) yóujiàn
[yoh-jyen]

邮件

(verb) jì [jee]

寄

**could you post this letter for
me?** qǐng bāng wó bǎ
zhèifēng xìn jìzǒu, hǎo ma?
[ching bahng wor bah jay-fung hsin
jee-dzoh how mah]

请帮我把这封信寄走
好吗？

postal service
The Chinese postal
service is, on the whole,
reliable, with letters taking less than
a day to reach destinations in the
same city, two or more days to other
destinations in China, and up to
several weeks to destinations
abroad. Express Mail Service
operates to most countries and to
most destinations within China; the
service cuts down delivery times
and the letter or parcel is
automatically registered. Main post
offices are open seven days a week
from 8 a.m. to 6 p.m.; smaller
offices may close for a lunch hour or
be closed at weekends. As well as at
post offices, you can also post
letters in the green letterboxes,
though these are few and far
between except in the biggest cities,
or at tourist hotels, which usually
have a postbox at the front desk.
Envelopes can be scarce; try the
stationery sections of department
stores.

Poste restante services are available
in any city. A nominal fee has to be
paid to pick up mail, which will be
kept for several months, and you will
sometimes need to present ID when
collecting it. Mail is often
eccentrically filed – to cut down on
misfiling, your name should be
printed clearly at the top of the letter
and the surname underlined, but it's
still worth checking all the other
pigeonholes just in case. Have
letters addressed to you as follows:
province, town or city, GPO, c/o Poste
Restante.

postbox xìnxiāng
[hsin-hsyahng]
信箱

postcard míngxìnpiàn
[ming-hsin-pyen]
名信片

poster zhāotiē [jow-tyeh]
招贴

poste restante dàilǐng yóujiàn
[yoh-jyen]
待领邮件

post office yóujú [yoh-jew]
邮局

potato tǔdòu [too-doh]
土豆

potato chips (US) zhá
tǔdòupiànr [jah too-doh-pyenr]
炸土豆片儿

pound (money) yīngbàng
[ying-bahng]
英镑

(weight) bàng [bahng]
磅

power cut tíngdiàn [ting-dyen]
停电

power point diànyuán
chāzuò [dyen-yew-ahn
chah-dzwor]
电源插座

practise: I want to practise my
Chinese wǒ xiǎng liànxí
jiǎng Zhōngwén [wor hsyahng
lyen-hshee jyang joong-wun]
我想练习讲中文

prawn crackers xiābǐng

[hsyah-bing]
虾饼

prawns duìxiā [dway-hsyah]
对虾

prefer: I prefer ... wǒ gèng
xǐhuan ... [wor gung see-hwahn]
我更喜欢 ...

pregnant huáiyùn [hwai-yewn]
怀孕

prescription (for medicine)
yàofāng [yow-fahng]
药方

present (gift) lǐwù
礼物

president (of country) zǒngtǒng
[dzoong-toong]
总统

pretty piàoliang [pyow-lyang]
漂亮

it's pretty expensive tài guìle
[gway-lur]
太贵了

price jiàgé [jyah-gur]
价格

prime minister shǒuxiàng
[shoh-hsyahng]
首相

printed matter yìnshuāpǐn
[yin-shwah-pin]
印刷品

prison jiānyù [jyen-yew]
监狱

privacy

The Chinese have almost no concept of privacy. People will stare at each other at point-blank range and pluck letters or books out of their hands for a better look. Even toilets are built with partitions so low that you can chat with your neighbour while squatting. All activities, including visits to natural beauty spots or holy relics, are done in large, noisy groups. The desire of some Western tourists to be left alone is often interpreted as arrogance.

private sīrén(de)
[sur-run(-dur)]
私人（的）

private bathroom
sīrén(de)yùshì [–yoo-shur]
私人（的）浴室

probably dàgài [dah-gai]
大概

problem wèntí [wun-tee]
问题

no problem! méi wèntí!
[may]
没问题

programme (theatre)
jiémùdānr [jyeh-moo-dahnr]
节目单儿

**pronounce: how is this
pronounced?** zhèige zì
zěnme fāyīn? [jay-gur dzur dzun-mur fah-yin]
这个字怎么发音？

Protestant xjīnjiàotú
[hsin-jyow-too]
新教徒

public convenience gōnggòng
cèsuǒ [goong-goong tsur-swor]
公共厕所

public holiday gōngjià
[goong-jyah]
公假

There are several different kinds of holiday in the Chinese calendar when various facilities will be closed. The biggest of all, Chinese New Year or Spring Festival, **chūnjié**, is the only traditional Chinese festival marked by a holiday. It sees nearly all shops and offices closing down for three days, and a large proportion of the population off work. Even after the third day, offices such as banks may operate on restricted hours until the official end of the holiday period, eleven days later. The other traditional Chinese festivals are not marked by official holidays, though you may notice a growing tendency for businesses to operate restricted hours at these times.

There are also a number of secular public holidays which have been

Pp

celebrated since 1949, the most
important being 1 October (National
Day). Offices close on these dates,
though many shops will remain
open. Finally, there are a few other
dates, 8 March (Women's Day), 1
May (Labour Day), 1 June (Children's
Day), 1 July (Chinese Communist
Party Day) and 1 August (Army Day),
which are celebrated by parades
and festive activities by the groups
concerned, but are not general
holidays.
see **festival**

pull lā [lah]
拉

pullover tàoshān [mow-bay-hsin]
套衫

puncture (noun) pǎoqì
[pow-chee]
跑气

purple zǐ [dzur]
紫

purse (for money) qiánbāo
[chyen-bow]
钱包
(US: handbag) shǒutíbāo
[shoh-tee-bow]
手提包

push tuī [tway]
推

put fàng [fahng]
放

where can I put ...? wǒ bǎ ...

fàng zai nǎr? [wor bah – dzai]
我把 ... 放在哪儿？

**could you put us up for the
night?** wǒmen kéyi zài zhèr
guò yíyè ma? [wor-mun kur-yee
– jer gwor yee-yur mah]
我们可以在这儿过一夜
吗？

pyjamas shuìyī [shway-yee]
睡衣

Q

quality zhìliàng [jur-lyang]
质量

quarter sì fēn zhī yī [sur fun jur
yee]
四分之一

question wèntí [wun-tee]
问题

queue (noun) duì [dway]
队

quick kuài [kwai]
快

that was quick zhēn kuài
[jun]
真快

**what's the quickest way
there?** něitiáo lù zuì jìn?
[nay-tyow loo zway]
哪条路最近？

quickly hěn kuài di [hun kwai]
很快的

quiet (place, hotel) ānjìng

[ahn-jing]

安静

quite (fairly) xiāngdāng

[hsyahng-dahng]

相当

that's quite right duì jíle

[dway-jee-lur]

对极了

quite a lot xiāngdāng duō

[hsyahng-dahng dwor]

相当多

R

rabbit (meat) tùzi [too-dzur]

兔子

race (for runners, cars) bǐsài

[bee-sai]

比赛

racket (tennis, squash) qiúpāi

[chyoh-pai]

球拍

radiator (in room) nuǎnqì

[nwahn-chee]

暖器

(of car) sànrèqì

[sahn-rur-chee]

散热器

radio shōuyīnjī [shoh-yin-jee]

收音机

on the radio zài shōuyīnjīlǐ

[dzai – lee]

在收音机里

rail: by rail zuò huǒchē [dzwor

hwor-chur]

坐火车

railway tiělù [tyeh-loo]

铁路

rain (noun) yǔ [yew]

雨

in the rain zài yǔli [dzai

yew-lee]

在雨里

it's raining xià yǔ le [hsyah

yew lur]

下雨了

raincoat yǔyī [yew-yee]

雨衣

rape (noun) qiángjiān

[chyang-jyen]

强奸

rare (uncommon) xīyǒu

[hshee-yoh]

稀有

(steak) nèn diǎnr [nun dyenr]

嫩点儿

rash (on skin) pízhěn [pee-jun]

皮疹

rat láoshǔ [low-shoo]

老鼠

rate (for changing money)

duìhuànlǜ [dway-hwahn-lyew]

兑换率

rather: it's rather good búcuò

[boo-tswor]

不错

I'd rather ... wǒ nìngkě... [wor

ning-kur]

我宁可 ...

razor (wet) tìxúdāo
[tee-hsyew-dow]
剃须刀
(electric) diàntìdāo
[dyen-tee-dow]
电剃刀
razor blades tìxú dāopiàn
[tee-hsyew dow-pyen]
剃须刀片
read (book) kànshū [kahn-shoo]
看书
(newspaper) kànbào [kahn-bow]
看报
ready zhǔnbèi hǎole [jun-bay how-lur]
准备好了
are you ready? zhǔnbèi hǎole ma? [mah]
准备好了吗？
I'm not ready yet wǒ hái méi hǎo ne [wor hai may how nur]
我还没好呢

dialogue

when will it be ready?
(repair etc) shénme shíhou xiūwánle? [shun-mur shur-hoh hsyoh-wahn-lur]
it should be ready in a couple of days liǎngtiān jiù hǎole [lyang-tyen jyoh how-lur]

real (genuine) zhēn de [jun dur]
真的
really zhēnde [jun-dur]
真的
I'm really sorry zhēn duìbuqǐ
[jun dway-boo-chee]
真对不起
that's really great bàngjíle
[bahng-jee-lur]
棒极了
really? (doubt) shì ma? [shur mah]
是吗？
(polite interest) zhēnde ma?
[mah]
真的吗？
reasonable (prices etc) hélǐ
[hur-lee]
合理
receipt shōujù [shoh-jyew]
收据
recently zuìjìn [dzway-jin]
最近
reception (in hotel) fúwùtái
[foo-woo-tai]
服务台
(for guests) zhāodàihuì
[jow-dai-hway]
招待会
reception desk zǒng fúwùtái
[dzoong foo-woo-tai]
总服务台
receptionist fúwùyuán
[foo-woo-yew-ahn]
服务员

recognize rènshi [run-shur]
认识

**recommend: could you
recommend ...?** qǐng nín
tuījiàn ..., hǎo ma? [ching nin
tway-jyen ... how mah]
请您推荐 … 好吗？

red hóngsède [hoong-sur-dur]
红色的

red wine hóng pútaojiǔ [hoong
poo-tow-jyoh]
红葡萄酒

refund (noun) tuìkuǎn
[tway-kwahn]
退款

can I have a refund? qǐng nín
ba qián tuì géi wó hǎo ma?
[ching nin bah chyen tway gay wor
how mah]
请您把钱退给我好吗？

region dìqū [dee-chew]
地区

registered: by registered mail
guàhàoxìn [gwah-how-hsin]
挂号信

registration number chēhào
[chur-how]
车号

religion zōngjiào [dzoong-jyow]
宗教

remember: I don't remember
wǒ jìbudé le [wor jee-boo-dur
lur]
我记不得了

I remember wǒ jìdé [wor

jee-dur]
我记得

do you remember? nǐ jìde
ma? [nee jee-dur mah]
你记得吗？

rent (noun: for apartment etc)
fángzū [fahng-dzoo]
房租
(verb: car etc) chūzū [choo-dzoo]
出租

to rent chūzū
出租

I'd like to rent a bike wó
xiǎng zū yīliàng zìxíng chē
[wor hsyahng dzoo yee-lyang
dzur-hsing chur]
我想租一辆自行车

repair (verb) xiūlǐ [hsyoh-lee]
修理

can you repair it? nǐ kéyi
xiūxiu ma? [kur-yee
hsyoh-hsyoh mah]
你可以修修吗？

repeat chóngfù [choong-foo]
重复

could you repeat that? qǐng
nǐ zài shuō yíbiàn, hǎo ma?
[ching nee dzai shwor yee-byen how
mah]
请你再说一遍好吗？

reservation yùdìng [yew-ding]
预订

**I'd like to make a reservation
for a train ticket** wó xiǎng
yùdìng huǒchēpiào [wor

hsyahng yew-ding
hwor-chur-pyow]
我想预订火车票

dialogue

I have a reservation wó
yǐjīng yùdìng le [yee-jing
–lur]
**yes sir, what name,
please?** hǎo, nín guì xìng?
[how nin gway hsing]

reserve (verb) yùdìng
[yew-ding]
预订

dialogue

**can I reserve a table for
tonight?** wǒ kéyi dìng ge
jīntian wǎnshang de zuò
ma? [kur-yee ding gur jin-tyen
wah-shahng dur dzwor mah]
**yes madam, for how many
people?** hǎo, yígòng jǐge
rén? [how yee-goong jee-gur
run]
for two liǎngge rén
[lyang-gur run]
and for what time? jǐdiǎn
zhōng? [jee-dyen joong]
for eight o'clock bā diǎn
zhōng [bah dyen]
and could I have your

name, please? hǎo, nín
guì xìng? [how nin gway
hsing]

rest: I need a rest wǒ xūyào
xiūxi yíxià [wor hsyew-yow
hsyoh-hshee yee-hsyah]
我需要休息一下
the rest of the group tāmen
biéde rén [tah-mun byeh-dur]
他们别的人
restaurant cāntīng [tsahn-ting]
餐厅
(big) fàndiàn [fahn-dyen]
饭店
(small) fànguǎnr [fahn-gwahnr]
饭馆儿
(Western-style) xīcāntīng
[hshee-tsahn-ting]
西餐厅

 Small noodle shops and
food-stalls around train
and bus stations have
flexible hours, but restaurant
opening times, outside the big cities,
tend to be early and short. By 6 a.m.
breakfast is usually well under way,
and by 9 a.m. the noodle soups,
buns, dumplings and rice porridge
will have run out. Get up late and
you'll have to join the first sitting for
lunch at 11 a.m. or so, leaving you
plenty of time to work up an appetite
for the evening meal at 5 p.m. An

hour later you'd be lucky to get a table in some places, and by 9 p.m. the staff will be sweeping the debris off the tables and from around your ankles.

Standard restaurants are often divided into two or three floors. The first will offer a limited choice, usually scrawled illegibly on strips of paper or a board hung on the wall. You buy chits from a cashier for what you want, which you exchange at the kitchen hatch for your food and sit down at large communal tables or benches. Upstairs will be pricier and have waitress service and a written menu, while further floors are generally reserved for banquet parties or foreign tour groups. There is now a big selection of foreign cuisine in the major cities, especially in the best hotels. Western-style fast-food outlets such as McDonald's and Kentucky Fried Chicken are mushrooming throughout the big cities of China. There are also some Chinese fast-food restaurants. However, Chinese food is by nature fast food so it is as well to go to proper restaurants. Getting fed is never difficult as everyone wants your custom. Walk past anywhere that sells cooked food and you'll be hailed by

cries of **chī fàn** – basically, 'come and eat!' Pointing is all that's required at street stalls and small restaurants. In bigger places you'll sometimes be escorted through to the kitchen to make your choice. Menus, where available, are often more of an indication of what's on offer than a definitive list.

When you enter a proper restaurant you'll be quickly escorted to a table – standing around dithering is impolite, so avoid it. In all but the cheapest places, tea, pickles and nuts immediately follow, to take the edge off your hunger while you order. The only tableware provided is a spoon, bowl, and a pair or chopsticks, and at this point the Chinese will ask for a flask of boiling water and a bowl to wash it all in – not usually necessary, but something of a ritual.

Dishes are generally all served at once, placed in the middle of the table for diners to share.

Soup is generally fairly bland and is consumed last to wash the meal down, the liquid slurped from a spoon or the bowl once the noodles, vegetables or meat in it have been eaten. When you've finished your meal, rest your chopsticks together across the top of your bowl.

restaurant car cānchē
[tsahn-chur]
餐车

rest room cèsuǒ [tsur-swor]
厕所

retired: I'm retired wǒ tuìxiūle
[wor tway-hsyoh-lur]
我退休了

return: a return to ... dào ... de
láihuí piào [dow ... dur lai-hway
pyow]
到 ... 的来回票

return ticket láihuí piào
来回票
see ticket

reverse charge call duìfāng
fùkuǎn [dway-fahng foo-kwahn]
对方付款

revolting ràng rén ěxīn [rahng
run ur-hsin]
让人恶心

rice (cooked) mǐfàn [mee-fahn]
米饭
(uncooked) dàmǐ [dah-mee]
大米

rice bowl fànwǎn [fahn-wahn]
饭碗

rice field dàotián [dow-tyen]
稻田

rice wine mǐjiǔ [mee-jyoh]
米酒

rich (person) yǒuqián
[yoh-chyen]
有钱

ridiculous kěxiàode

[kur-hsyow-dur]
可笑的

right (correct) duì [dway]
对
(not left) yòu(biānr)
[yoh(-byenr)]
右（边儿）

you were right nǐ duìle [nee
dway-lur]
你对了

that's right duì le
对了

this can't be right zhè búduì
[jur boo-dway]
这不对

right! duì!
对

is this the right road for ...?
qù ..., zhème zǒu duì ma?
[chew ... jur-mur dzoh dway mah]
去 ... 这么走对吗？

on the right zài yòubiānr
[dzai]
在右边儿

turn right wǎng yòu guǎi
[wahng yoh gwai]
往右拐

ring (on finger) jièzhi [jyeh-jur]
戒指

I'll ring you wó géi ní dǎ
diànhuà [wor gay nee dah
dyen-hwah]
我给你打电话

ring back zài dǎ diànhuà [dzai]
再打电话

169

ripe (fruit) shú [shoo]

熟

rip-off: it's a rip-off zhè shì qiāozhúgàng [jur shur chyow-joo-gahng]

这是敲竹杠

rip-off prices qiāozhúgàng de jiàr [chyow-joo-gahng dur jyahr]

敲竹杠的价儿

risky màoxiǎn [mow-hsyen]

冒险

river hé [hur]

河

RMB rénmínbì [run-min-bee]

人民币

road lù

路

is this the road for ...? zhèi tiáo lù wǎng ... qù? [jay tyow loo wahng ... chew]

这条路往 … 去？

rob: I've been robbed wǒ bèi rén qiǎngle [wor bay run chyang-lur]

我被人抢了

rock yánshí [yen-shur]

岩石

(music) yáogǔn yuè [yow-gun yew-eh]

摇滚乐

on the rocks (with ice) jiā bīngkuàir [jyah bing-kwair]

加冰块儿

roll (bread) miànbāo juǎnr

[myen-bow jyew-ahnr]

面包卷儿

roof fángdǐng [fahng-ding]

房顶

room (hotel) fángjiān [fahng-jyen]

房间

(space) kōngjiān [koong-jyen]

空间

in my room zài wǒ fángjiānli [dzai]

在我房间里

dialogue

do you have any rooms? yǒu fángjiān ma? [yoh – mah]

for how many people? jǐge rén? [jee-gur run]

for one/for two yí/liǎngge [yee/lyang-gur]

yes, we have rooms free yǒu fángjiān

for how many nights will it be? jǐtiān? [jee-tyen]

just for one night yìtiān [yee-tyen]

how much is it? duōshao qián? [dwor-show chyen]

... yuan with bathroom, and ... yuan without bathroom yǒu yùshì de fángjiān yào ... kuài, méiyou yùshì de yào ...

kuài [yoh yoo-shee dur fahng-jyen yow ... kwai may-yoh yoo-shur]

can I see a room with bathroom? wó xiǎng kàn yìjian yǒu yùshìde fángjiān [wor hsyang kahn yee-jyen yoh yoo-shur-dur]

OK, I'll take it hǎo, xíngle [how hsing-lur]

room service sòng fàn fúwù [soong fahn foo-woo]
送饭服务

rope shéngzi [shung-dzur]
绳子

roughly (approximately) dàyuē [dah-yew-eh]
大约

round: it's my round gāi wó mǎi le [gai wor mai lur]
该我买了

round trip ticket láihuí piào [lai-hway pyow]
来回票

route lùxiàn [loo-hsyen]
路线

what's the best route? něitiáo lùxiàn zuì hǎo? [nay-tyow loo-hsyen dzway how]
哪条路线最好？

rubber (material) xiàngjiāo [hsyang-jyow]
橡胶
(eraser) xiàngpí

[hsyahng-pee]
橡皮

rubbish (waste) lājī [lah-jee]
垃圾
(poor-quality goods) fèiwù [fay-woo]
废物

rubbish! (nonsense) fèihuà! [fay-hwah]
废话

rucksack bèibāo [bay-bow]
背包

rude bù lǐmào [lee-mow]
不礼貌

ruins fèixū [fay-hsyew]
废墟

rum lángmújiǔ [lahng-moo-jyoh]
朗姆酒

rum and Coke® kékoukělè jiā lángmújiǔ [kur-koh-kur-lur jyah lahng-moo-jyoh]
可口可乐加朗姆酒

run (verb: person) pǎo [pow]
跑

how often do the buses run? gōnggòng qìchē duócháng shíjian yítàng? [goong-goong chee-chur dwor-chahng shur-jyen yee-tahng]
公共汽车多长时间一趟？

Russia Éguó [ur-gwor]
俄国

Russian (adj) Éguó
俄国

S

saddle (for horse) ānzi
[ahn- dzur]
鞍子

safe (not in danger) píng'ān
平安
(not dangerous) ānquán
[ahn-choo-en]
安全

safety pin biézhēn [byeh-jun]
别针

sail (noun) fān [fahn]
帆

salad shālà [shah-lah]
沙拉

salad dressing shālà yóu [yoh]
沙拉油

sale: for sale chūshòu
[choo-shoh]
出售

salt yán [yahn]
盐

same: the same yíyàng
[yee-yang]
一样
the same as this gēn zhèige
yíyàng [gun jay-gur yee-yang]
跟这个一样
the same again, please qǐng
zài lái yíge [ching dzai lai
yee-gur]
请再来一个
it's all the same to me wǒ

wú suǒwèi [wor woo swor-way]
我无所谓

sandals liángxié [lyang-hsyeh]
凉鞋

sandwich sānmíngzhì
[sahn-ming-jur]
三明治

sanitary napkins/towels
wèishēngjīn [way-shung-jin]
卫生巾

Saturday xīngqiliù
[hsing-chee-lyoh]
星期六

say (verb) shuō [shwor]
说
how do you say ... in
Chinese? yòng Zhōngwén
zěnme shuō ...? [yoong
joong-wun dzun-mur shwor]
用中文怎么说 ... ?
what did he say? tā shuō
shénme? [tah – shun-mur]
他说什么 ?
he said tā shuō [tah]
他说
could you say that again?
qǐng zài shuō yíbiān [ching
dzai – yee-byen]
请再说一遍

scarf (for neck) wéijīn [way-jin]
围巾
(for head) tóujīn [toh-jin]
头巾

scenery fēngjǐng [fung-jing]
风景

schedule (US: train) lièchē
shíkè biǎo [lyeh-chur shur-kur
byow]

列车时刻表

scheduled flight bānjī
[bahn-jee]

班机

school xuéxiào
[hsyew-eh-hsyow]

学校

scissors: a pair of scissors
yìbǎ jiǎnzi [yee-bah jyen-dʒɪr]

一把剪子

scotch wēishìjì [way-shur-jee]

威士忌

Scotch tape® tòumíng
jiāodài [toh-ming jyow-dai]

透明胶带

Scotland Sūgélán

苏格兰

Scottish Sūgélán [soo-gur-lahn]

苏格兰

I'm Scottish wǒ shi
Sūgélánren [wor shur –run]

我是苏格兰人

scrambled eggs chǎo jīdàn
[chow jee-dahn]

炒鸡蛋

sea hǎi

海

by the sea zài hǎibiānr [dzai
hai-byenr]

在海边儿

seafood hǎiwèi [hai-way]

海味

seal (for printing name) túzhāng
[too-jahng]

图章

seasick: I feel seasick wǒ
yūnchuánle [wor
yewn-chwahn-lur]

我晕船了

I get seasick wǒ yūnchuán
[wor yewn-chwahn]

我晕船

seat zuòwei [dzwor-way]

座位

is this seat taken? yǒu rén
ma? [yoh run mah]

有人吗？

second (adj) dìerge [dee-er-gur]

第二个

(of time) miǎo [myow]

秒

just a second! zhè jiù dé! [jur
jyoh dur]

这就得

second class (travel etc) èr
děng [er dung]

二等

(hard sleeper) yìngwò
[ying-wor]

硬卧

see **train**

second-hand jiù(de)
[jyoh(-dur)]

旧（的）

see kànjian [kahn-jyen]

看见

can I see? wó kéyi kànkan

173

ma? [wor kur-yee kahn-kahn mah]

我可以看看吗？

have you seen ...? nǐ
kàndàole ... ma? [kahn-dow-lur
mah]

你看到了 ... 吗？

I saw him this morning wǒ
jīntian zǎoshang kànjian tā le
[wor jin-tyen dzow-shahng
kahn-jyen tah lur]

我今天早上看见他了

see you! zàijiàn! [dzai-jyen]

再见

I see (I understand) wǒ
míngbai le [wor ming-bai lur]

我明白了

self-service zìzhù [dzur-joo]

自助

sell mài

卖

do you sell ...? nǐ mài bu
mài ...?

你卖不卖 ... ？

Sellotape® tòumíng jiāobù
[toh-ming jyow-boo]

透明胶布

send sòng [soong]

送

(by post) jì

寄

I want to send this to England
wó xiǎng ba zhèige jì dào
Yīngguó qù [wor syahng bah
jay-gur jee dow ying-gwor chew]

我想把这个寄到英国去

senior citizen lǎoniánren
[low-nyen-run]

老年人

separate fēnkāi [fun-kai]

分开

separately (pay, travel) fēnkāi
de

分开地

September jiǔyuè
[jyoh-yew-eh]

九月

serious (problem, illness)
yánzhòng(de) [yen-joong(-dur)]

严重（的）

service charge (in restaurant)
xiǎofèi [hsyow-fay]

小费

serviette cānjīn [tsahn-jin]

餐巾

set menu fènrfàn [funr-fahn]

份儿饭

several jǐge [jee-gur]

几个

sew fèng [fung]

缝

**could you sew this ... back
on?** qíng nǐn bāng wó bǎ
zhèige ... fénghuíqu, hǎo
ma? [ching nin bahng wor bah jay-
gur ... fung-hway-chew how mah]

请您帮我把这个 ... 缝回
去好吗？

sex (male/female) xìngbié
[hsing-byeh]

性别

se

sexy xìnggǎn [hsing-gahn]
性感

shade: in the shade zài
yīnliáng chù [dzai yin-lyang]
在阴凉处

shake: let's shake hands
wǒmen wòwo shǒu ba
[wor-mun wor-wor shoh bah]
我们握握手吧

shallow (water) qiǎn [chyen]
浅

shame: what a shame! zhēn
kěxī! [jun kur-hshee]
真可惜

shampoo (noun) xǐfàqì
[hshee-fah-chee]
洗发剂

share (verb: room, table etc)
héyòng [hur-yoong]
合用

sharp (knife) jiānruì
[jyen-rway]
尖锐

(pain) ruì [rway]
锐

shaver diàndòng tìxū dāo
[dyen-doong tee-hsyew dow]
电动剃须刀

shaving foam guā hú pàomò
[gwah hoo pow-mor]
刮胡泡沫

shaving point diàntìdāo
chāxiāo [dyen-tee-dow
chah-hsyow]
电剃刀插销

she* tā [tah]
她

is she here? tā zài ma? [dzai
mah]
她在吗？

sheet (for bed) bèidān [bei-dahn]
被单

shelf jiàzi [jyah-dzur]
架子

shellfish bèilèi [bay-lay]
贝类

ship chuán [chwahn]
船

by ship zuò chuán [dzwor]
坐船

shirt chènyī [chun-yee]
衬衣

shock: I got an electric shock
from the ... wǒ pèngzhe... ér
chùdiàn [wor pung-jur – dyen]
我碰着 ... 而触电

shocking jīngrénde
[jing-run-dur]
惊人的

shoe xié [hsyeh]
鞋

a pair of shoes yìshuāng xié
[yee-shwahng]
一双鞋

shoelaces xiédài [hsyeh-dai]
鞋带

shoe polish xiéyóu
[hsyeh-yoh]
鞋油

shoe repairer xiūxiéjiàng

[hsyoh-hsyeh-jyang]

修鞋匠

shop shāngdiàn [shahng-dyen]

商店

see **opening times**

shopping: I'm going shopping
wǒ qù mǎi dōngxi [wor chew
mai doong-hshee]

我去买东西

shore (of sea, lake) àn [ahn]

岸

short (person) ǎi

矮

(time, journey) duǎn [dwahn]

短

shorts duǎnkù [dwahn-koo]

短裤

should: what should I do? wǒ
gāi zěnme bàn? [wor gai
dzun-mur bahn]

我该怎么办？

you should ... nǐ
yīnggāi ... [ying-gai]

你应该 ...

you shouldn't ... nǐ bù
yīnggāi ...

你不应该 ...

he should be back soon guò
yíhuìr, tā yīng zài huílai [gwor
yee-hwayr tah ying dzai hway-lai]

过一回儿他应再回来

shoulder jiānbǎng [jyen-bahng]

肩膀

shout (verb) hǎn [hahn]

喊

show (in theatre) biáoyǎn
[byow-yahn]

表演

could you show me? nǐ néng
ràng wǒ kànkan ma? [nung
rahng wor kahn-kahn mah]

你能让我看看吗？

shower (of rain) zhènyǔ
[jun-yew]

阵雨

(in bathroom) línyù [lin-yew]

淋浴

with shower dài línyù

带淋浴

shrine shénkān [shun-kahn]

神龛

shut (verb) guān [gwahn]

关

when do you shut? nǐmen
jídiǎn guānménr? [nee-mun
jee-dyen gwahn-munr]

你们几点关门儿？

when does it shut? jídiǎn
guānménr? [jee-dyen]

几点关门儿？

they're shut guānménr le
[lur]

关门儿了

I've shut myself out wó bǎ
zìjǐ guān zài wàitou le [wor
bah dzur-jee gwahn dzai wai-toh
lur]

我把自己关在外头了

shut up! zhù zuǐ! [joo dzway]

住嘴

English → Chinese

shy hàixiū [hai-hsyoh]
害羞
sick (ill) yǒubìng [yoh-bing]
有病
I'm going to be sick (vomit)
wǒ yào ǒutù [wor yow oh-too]
我要呕吐
**side: the other side of the
street** zài jiē duìmian [dzai
jyeh dway-myen]
在街对面
sidewalk rénxíng dào
[run-hsing dow]
人行道
sight: the sights of ... ... de
fēngjǐng [fung-jing]
... 的风景
**sightseeing: we're going
sightseeing** wǒmen qù
yóulǎn [wor-mun chew yoh-lahn]
我们去游览
silk sīchóu [sur-choh]
丝绸
Silk Road sīchóu zhī lù [jur]
丝绸之路
silly chǔn
蠢
silver (noun) yín(zi) [yin-dzur]
银（子）
similar xiāngjìn de [hsyahng-jin
dur]
相近
simple (easy) jiǎndān [jyen-dahn]
简单
since: since last week zìcóng

shàngge xīngqī yǐlái
[dzur-tsoong shahng-gur hsing-chee
yee-lai]
自从上个星期以来
since I got here zìcóng wǒ
lái yǐhòu [dzur-tsoong wor lai
yee-hoh]
自从我来以后
sing chànggē [chahng-gur]
唱歌
Singapore Xīnjiāpō
[hsin-jyah-por]
新加坡
singer gēchàngjiā
[gur-chahng-jyah]
歌唱家
single: a single to ... yìzhāng
qù ... de dānchéngpiào
[yee-jahng chew ... dur
dahn-chung-pyow]
一张去 ... 的单程票
I'm single wǒ shì dúshēn
[wor shur dahn-shun]
我是独身
single bed dānrén chuáng
[dahn-run chwahng]
单人床
single room dānrén jiān [jyen]
单人间
single ticket (dānchéng) piào
[pyow]
（单程）票
sink (in kitchen) shuǐchí
[shway-chur]
水池

177

sister (elder) jiějie [jyeh-jyeh]
姐姐
(younger) mèimei [may-may]
妹妹
sit: can I sit here? wǒ kéyi zuò zhèr ma? [wor kur-yee dzwor jer mah]
我可以坐这儿吗？
is anyone sitting here? yǒu rén zài zhèr ma? [yoh run]
有人在这儿吗？
sit down zuòxià [dzwor-hsyah]
坐下
sit down! qǐng zuò! [ching]
请坐
size chǐcùn [chur-tsun]
尺寸
skin (human) pífu
皮肤
(animal) pí
皮
skinny shòu [shoh]
瘦
skirt qúnzi [chewn-dzur]
裙子
sky tiān [tyen]
天
sleep (verb) shuìjiào [shway-jyow]
睡觉
did you sleep well? nǐ shuì de hǎo ma? [shway dur how mah]
你睡得好吗？
sleeper (on train) wòpù

[wor-poo]
卧铺
(soft) ruǎnwò [rwahn-wor]
软卧
(hard) yìngwò [ying-wor]
硬卧
sleeping bag shuìdài [shway-dai]
睡袋
sleeping car wòpù chēxiāng [wor-poo chur-hsyahng]
卧铺车厢
sleeve xiùzi [hsyoh-dzur]
袖子
slide (photographic) huàndēngpiānr [hwahn-dung-pyenr]
幻灯片儿
slip (garment) chènqún [chun-chewn]
衬裙
slow màn [mahn]
慢
slow down! màn diǎnr! [dyenr]
慢点儿
slowly màn
慢
very slowly hěn màn [hun]
很慢
small xiǎo [hsyow]
小
smell: it smells (bad) yǒu wèir le [yoh wayr lur]
有味儿了

smile (verb) xiào [hsyow]
笑

smoke (noun) yān [yahn]
烟

do you mind if I smoke? wǒ kéyi zài zhèr chōu yān ma? [wor kur-yee dzai jer choh yahn mah]
我可以在这儿抽烟吗？

I don't smoke wǒ bú huì chōu yān [hway]
我不会抽烟

do you smoke? nǐ chōu yān ma?
你抽烟吗？

see **cigarette**

snack diǎnxīn [dyen-hsln]
点心

sneeze (noun) dǎ pēntì [da pun-tee]
打喷嚏

snow (noun) xuě [hsyew-eh]
雪

so: it's so good nàme [nah-mur]
那么好

it's so expensive nàme guì
那么贵

not so much méi nàme duō [may – dwor]
没那么多

not so bad méi nàme huài
没那么坏

so-so búguò rúcǐ [boo-gwor roo-tsur]
不过如此

soap féizào [fay-dzow]
肥皂

soap powder xǐyīfěn [hshee-yee-fun]
洗衣粉

sock duǎnwà [dwahn-wah]
短袜

socket chāzuò [chah-dzwor]
插座

soda (water) sūdá [soo-dah]
苏打

sofa shāfā [shah-fah]
沙发

soft (material etc) ruǎn [rwahn]
软

soft drink qìshuǐr [chee-shwayr]
汽水儿

 Canned drinks, usually sold unchilled, include various lemonades and colas, such as Coca-Cola, and the national sporting drink Jianlibao, an orange and honey confection which most foreigners find too sweet. Fruit juices can be unusual and refreshing, however, as they are often flavoured with chunks of lychee, lotus and water chestnuts. Sweetened yoghurt drinks, available all over the country in little packs of six, are a popular treat for children.

soft seat ruǎnzuò

【rwahn-dzwor】

软座

see train

sole (of shoe) xiédǐ 【hsyeh-dee】

鞋底

(of foot) jiǎodǐ 【jyow-dee】

脚底

could you put new soles on these? qǐng nín huàn shuāng xīn xiédǐ, hǎo ma? 【ching nin hwahn shwahng hsin – how mah】

请你换双新鞋底好吗？

some: can I have some water? qǐng lái yídiǎnr shuǐ, hǎo ma? 【ching lai yee-dyenr – how mah】

请来一点儿水好吗？

can I have some apples? qǐng lái yíxiē píngguǒ, hǎo ma? 【yee-hsyeh】

请来一些苹果好吗？

somebody, someone mǒurén 【moh-run】

某人

something mǒushì 【moh-shur】

某事

I want something to eat wǒ xiǎng chī diǎn dōngxī 【wor hsyahng chur dyen doong-hshee】

我想吃点东西

sometimes yǒushíhhou 【yoh-shur-hoh】

有时候

somewhere mǒudì 【moh-dee】

某地

I need somewhere to stay wǒ yào zhǎoge zhùchù 【wor yow jow-gur】

我要找个住处

son érzi 【er-dzur】

儿子

song gē 【gur】

歌

son-in-law nǚxu 【nyoo-hsoo】

女婿

soon (after a while) yìhtǐr 【yee-hwayr】

一会儿

(quickly) kuài 【kwai】

快

I'll be back soon wǒ yìhuǐr jiù huílai 【wor yee-hwayr jyoh hway-lai】

我一会儿就回来

as soon as possible yuè kuài yuè hǎo 【yew-eh – how】

越快越好

sore: it's sore téng 【tung】

疼

sore throat sǎngziténg 【sahng-dzur-tung】

嗓子疼

sorry: (I'm) sorry duìbuqǐ 【dway-boo-chee】

对不起

sorry? (didn't understand) nǐ shuō shénme? 【shwor shun-mur】

你说什么？

sort: what sort of ...? shénme

yàng de ...? [dur]

什么样的 ... ?

soup tāng [tahng]

汤

sour (taste) suān [swahn]

酸

south nán [nahn]

南

in the south nánfāng

[nahn-fahng]

南方

South Africa Nánfēi [nahn-fay]

南非

South African (adj) Nánfēi

南非

I'm South African wǒ shì

Nánfēirén [wor shur –run]

我是南非人

South China Sea Nánhǎi

[nahn-hai]

南海

southeast dōngnán

[doong-nahn]

东南

southern nánde [nahn-dur]

南的

South Korea nán Cháoxiān

[nahn chow-hsyen]

南朝鲜

southwest xīnán [hsin-ahn]

西南

souvenir jìniànpǐn

[jin-yen-pin]

纪念品

soy sauce jiàngyóu

[jyahn-gyoh]

酱油

Spain Xībānyá

[hshee-bahn-yah]

西班牙

Spanish (adj) Xībānyáde

[hshee-bahn-yah-dur]

西班牙的

speak: do you speak English?

nín huì jiǎng Yīngyǔ ma?

[hway jyang ying-yew mah]

您会讲英语吗 ?

I don't speak ... wǒ búhuì

jiǎng ... [wor boo-hway]

我不会讲 ...

can I speak to ...? (in person)

máfan nín zhǎo yíxia ... hǎo

ma? [mah-fahn nin jow

yee-hsyah ... how]

麻烦您找一下 ... 好吗 ?

dialogue

can I speak to Mr Wang?

Wáng xiānsheng

zàibúzài? [hsyahng-shung

dzai-boo-dzai]

who's calling? nǐ shì

nǎwéi? [shur nar-way]

it's Patricia wǒ shì Patricia

[wor]

I'm sorry, he's not in, can I

take a message? duìbuqǐ,

tā búzài, yàobúyào liú

gexìn? [dway-boo-chee tah

boo-dzai yow-boo-yow lyoh
gur-hsin]
**no thanks, I'll call back
later** xièxie, guò yìhuìr
wǒ zài dǎ [hsyeh-hsyeh gwor
yee-hwayr wor dzai dah]
please tell him I called
qǐng gàosu tā wǒ dǎ le
diànhuà [ching gow-soo tah
wor dah lur dyen-hwah]

spectacles yǎnjìng [yenjing]
眼镜
spend huāfèi [hwah-fay]
花费

spirits
In Chinese the word **jiǔ**,
loosely translated as
'wine', is used to refer to all
alcoholic drinks, including spirits,
wine and beer. The favourite drink is
báijiǔ ('white alcohol'), a clear
vodka-like spirit made from rice or
millet and nauseatingly strong for
the uninitiated. A lot of male bonding
takes place over glasses of báijiǔ,
normally drunk neat during
banquets from small glasses, and in
single gulps. Local home-made
varieties can be quite good, but the
mainstream brands – especially the
nationally famous **Maotai** – are
pretty vile to the Western palate.

Imported spirits, particularly
whiskies, are sold in large
department stores and in tourist
hotel bars, but are always very
expensive.
Wine is far less common, though
some very palatable wines are
produced locally and can be found in
tourist centres.

spitting
Spitting, as a means of
clearing the throat, is
normal practice in mainland China
and takes place not only in the
street but also inside trains,
restaurants, school classrooms and
even people's homes. There are now
government-led campaigns to
restrict the unhygienic habit, but in
the meantime it would still not be
considered disrespectful, for
example, to spit powerfully onto the
floor during conversation with
guests or strangers.

spoke (in wheel) fútiáo
[foo-tyow]
辐条
spoon sháozi [show-dzur]
勺子
sport yùndòng [yewn-doong]
运动
**sprain: I've sprained
my ...** wǒde ...niǔ le

[wor-dur ... nyoh lur]

我的 ... 扭了

spring (season) chūntiān

[chun-tyen]

春天

in the spring chūntiān

春天

square (in town) guángchǎng

[gwahng-chahng]

广场

stairs lóutī [loh-tee]

楼梯

stamp (noun) yóupiào

[yoh-pyow]

邮票

dialogue

a stamp for England,
please mǎi yìzhāng jì
Yīngguó de yóupiào [mai
yee-jahng jee ying-gwor dur]

what are you sending? nǐ
jì shénme? [shun-mur]

this postcard zhèizhāng
míngxìnpiàn [jay-jahng
ming-hsin-pyen]

star xīngxing [hsing-hsing]

星星

start kāishǐ [kai-shur]

开始

when does it start? jǐdiǎn
kāishǐ? [jee-dyen]

几点开始 ？

the car won't start chē
fādòngbùqǐlái [chur
fah-doong-boo-chee-lai]

车发动不起来

starter (food) lěngpánr

[lung-pahnr]

冷盘儿

station (train) huǒchē zhàn

[hwor-chur jahn]

火车站

(city bus) qìchē zǒng zhàn

[chee-chur dzoong]

汽车总站

(long-distance bus) chángtú
qìchēzhàn [chahng-too chee-
chur-jahn]

长途汽车站

(underground) dì tiě zhàn [tyeh
jahn]

地铁站

statue sùxiàng [soo-hsyahng]

塑像

stay: where are you staying?
nǐmen zhù zài nǎr? [nee-mun
joo dzai nar]

你们住在哪儿 ？

I'm staying at ... wǒ zhù
zài ... [wor joo dzai]

我住在 ...

**I'd like to stay another two
nights** wó xiǎng zài zhù
liǎng tiān [syahng dzai joo]

我想再住两天

steak niúpái [nyoh-pai]

牛排

steal tōu [toh]

偷

my bag has been stolen
wǒde bāo bèi tōule [wor-dur
bow bay toh-lur]

我的包被偷了

steamed zhēng [jung]

蒸

steamed roll huājuǎnr
[hwah-jwahnr]

花卷儿

steep (hill) dǒu [doh]

陡

step: on the steps zài táijiē
shang [dzai tai-jyeh shahng]

在台阶上

stereo lìtǐshēng [lee-tee-shung]

立体声

Sterling yīngbàng [ying-bahng]

英镑

steward (on plane) fúwùyuán
[nahn foo-woo-yew-ahn]

服务员

stewardess kōngzhōng
xiǎojiě [koong-joong hsyow-jyeh]

空中小姐

still: I'm still here wǒ hái zài
[wor hai dzai]

我还在

is he still there? tā hái zài
ma? [tah – mah]

他还在吗？

keep still! bié dòng! [byeh
doong]

别动

sting: I've been stung wó gěi
zhēle [wor gay jur-lur]

我给螫了

stockings chángtǒngwà
[chahng-toong-wah]

长统袜

stomach wèi [way]

胃

stomach ache wèiténg
[way-tung]

胃疼

stone (rock) shítou [shur-toh]

石头

stop (verb) tíng

停

please, stop here (to taxi driver
etc) qǐng tíng zài zhèr [ching
ting dzai jer]

请停在这儿

do you stop near ...?
zài ... fùjìn tíng ma? [mah]

在 ... 附近停吗？

stop it! tíngzhǐ! [ting-jur]

停止

storm bàofēngyǔ
[bow-fung-yew]

暴风雨

straight (whisky etc) chún

纯

it's straight ahead yìzhí
cháoqián [yee-jur chow-chyen]

一直朝前

straightaway mǎshàng
[mah-shahng]

马上

strange (odd) qíguài de
[chee-gwai dur]
奇怪的

stranger shēngrén [shun-grun]
生人

strap dàir
带儿

strawberry cǎoméi [tsow-may]
草莓

stream xiǎoxī [hsyow-hshee]
小溪

street jiē(dào) [jyeh(-dow)]
街（道）

on the street zài jiēshang
[dzai jyeh-shahng]
在街上

streetmap jiāotōngtú
[jyow-toong-too]
交通图

string shéngzi [shung-dzur]
绳子

strong (person)
qiángzhuàng [chyang-jwahng]
强壮
(material) jiēshi [jyeh-shur]
结实
(drink, taste) nóng [noong]
浓

stuck: it's stuck kǎle [kah-lur]
卡了

student xuésheng
[hsyew-eh-shung]
学生

stupid bèn [bun]
笨

suburb jiāoqū [jyow-chew]
郊区

subway (US) dìtiě [dee-tyeh]
地铁

suddenly tūrán [too-rahn]
突然

sugar táng [tahng]
糖

suit (noun) tàozhuāng
[tow-jwahng]
套装
it doesn't suit me (jacket etc)
wǒ chuān bù héshì [wor
chwahn boo hur-shur]
我穿不合适
it suits you nǐ chuān
héshì
你穿合适

suitcase shǒutíxiāng
[shoh-tee-hsyahng]
手提箱

summer xiàtiān [hsyah-tyen]
夏天
in the summer xiàtiān
夏天

sun tàiyáng
太阳

sunbathe shài tàiyáng
晒太阳

sunblock (cream) fángshàirǔ
[fahng-shai-roo]
防晒乳

sunburn rìzhì [rur-shur]
日炙

Sunday xīngqītiān

[hsing-chee-tyen]

星期天

sunglasses tàiyángjìng
[tai-yang-jing]

太阳镜

sunny: it's sunny yángguāng
chōngzú [yang-gwahng
choong-dzoo]

阳光充足

sunset rìluò [rur-lwor]

日落

sunshine yángguāng
[yang-gwahng]

阳光

sunstroke zhòngshǔ
[joong-shoo]

中暑

suntan lotion fángshài jì
[fahng-shai]

防晒剂

suntan oil fángshàiyóu [–yoh]

防晒油

super hǎojíle [how-jee-lur]

好极了

supermarket chāojí shìchǎng
[chow-jee shur-chahng]

超级市场

supper wǎnfàn [wahn-fahn]

晚饭

supplement (extra charge)
fùjiāfèi [foo-jyah-fay]

附加费

sure: are you sure? zhēnde
ma? [jun dur mah]

真的吗？

sure! dāngrán! [dahn-grahn]

当然

surname xìng [hsing]

姓

swearword zāngzìr
[dzahng-dzur]

脏字儿

sweater máoyī [mow-yee]

毛衣

sweatshirt (chángxiù)
hànshān [chahng-hsyoh
hahn-shahn]

（长袖）汗衫

Sweden Ruìdiǎn [rway-dyen]

瑞典

Swedish (adj) Ruìdiǎnyǔ

瑞典语

sweet (taste) tián [tyen]

甜

(noun: dessert) tiánshí
[tyen-shur]

甜食

sweets tángguǒ [tahng-gwor]

糖果

swim (verb) yóuyǒng
[yoh-yoong]

游泳

I'm going for a swim wǒ qù
yóuyǒng [wor chew
yoh-yoong]

我去游泳

let's go for a swim zánmen
qù bayóuyǒng ba
[zahn-mun]

咱们去游泳吧

swimming costume
yóuyǒngyī [yoh-yoong-yee]
游泳衣

swimming pool yóuyǒng chí
[chur]
游泳池

swimming trunks yóuyǒngkù
[yoh-yoong-koo]
游泳裤

switch (noun) kāiguān
[kai-gwahn]
开关

switch off guān [gwahn]
关

switch on kāi [kai]
开

swollen zhǒng [joong]
肿

T

table zhuōzi [jwor-dzur]
桌子

a table for two liǎngrén zhuō
[lyang-run]
两人桌

tablecloth zhuōbù
[jwor-boo]
桌布

table tennis pīngpāngqiú
[ping-pahng-chyoh]
乒乓球

tailor cáifeng [tsai-fung]
裁缝

Taiwan Táiwān [tai-wahn]
台湾

Taiwanese (adj) Táiwān(de)
[–dur]
台湾（的）

take ná [nah]
拿

(somebody somewhere) lǐng
领

(something somewhere) dài
带

(accept) jiēshòu [jych-shoh]
接受

can you take me to the ...?
qǐng dài wǒ dào ...? [ching dai
wor dow]
请带我到 … ?

do you take credit cards? nǐ
shòu xìnyòngkǎ ma? [shoh
hsin-yoong-kah mah]
你受信用卡吗 ?

fine, I'll take it hǎo, xíngle
[how hsing-lur]
好行了

can I take this? (leaflet etc)
kéyi ná ma? [kur-yee nah]
可以拿吗 ?

how long does it take? yào
duōcháng shíjiān? [yow
dwor-chahng shur-jyen]
要多长时间 ?

it takes three hours yào
sānge zhōngtóu [yow
sahng-gur joong-toh]
要三个钟头

is this seat taken? zhèr yǒu rén ma? [jer yoh run mah]

这儿有人吗？

talk (verb) shuōhuà [shwor-hwah]

说话

tall gāo [gow]

高

tampons wèishēngjīn [way-shung-jin]

卫生巾

tap shuǐlóng tóu [shway-loong toh]

水龙头

tape (cassette) cídài [tsur-dai]

磁带

taste (noun) wèir [wayr]

味儿

can I taste it? kéyi chángchang ma? [kur-yee chahng-chahng mah]

可以尝尝吗？

taxi chūzū qìchē [choo-dzoo chee-chur]

出租汽车

will you get me a taxi? qíng nǐn bāng wǒ jiào liàng chūzūchē, hǎo ma? [ching nin bahng wor jyow lyang choo-dzoo-chur how mah]

请您帮我叫辆出租车好吗？

where can I find a taxi? zài nǎr kéyi zhǎodao chūzū qìchē? [dzai nar kur-yee jow-dow]

在哪儿可以找到出租汽车？

dialogue

to the airport/to the Xian Hotel, please qíng dài wǒ dào fēijīcháng/Xīān fàndiàn [dow – fay-jee-chahng]

how much will it be? duōshao qián? [dwor-show chyen]

30 yuan sānshí kuài qián [sahn-shur kwai]

that's fine right here, thanks jiù zài zhèr, xièxie [jyoh dzai jer hsyeh-hsyeh]

A taxi in China can be a car, a minivan, a motorbike or a three-wheeled rickshaw (**sānlún chē**) with pedals or a motor. For anything smaller than a car, you have to negotiate your fare in advance and at the very least foreigners will be expected to pay two or three times the local rate. By international standards, taxi cars are cheap: in major cities, taxis have meters and the rates (which increase in proportion to the size of the car) are displayed on the side window. To avoid being taken on unnecessary detours, sit in the front seat ostentatiously consulting a map. Late at night, meters will not be used, so, if at all possible, a price should be negotiated. You'll find taxis of all kinds outside just about every mainland bus and train station.

taxi driver chūzū sījī [choo-dzoo sur-jee]
出租司机

taxi rank chūzūchē diǎnr [dyenr]
出租车点儿

tea (drink) chá [chah]
茶

tea for one/two, please qǐng lái yí/liǎngge rén de chá [ching – run dur]
请来一／两个人的茶

Chinese tea comes in black, red, green and flower-scented varieties. Some regional kinds, such as **pú'ěr** from Yunnan and oolong (**wūlóng**) from the east, are highly sought after. Though always drunk without milk and only very rarely with sugar, the method of serving tea varies from place to place: sometimes it comes in huge mugs with a lid, elsewhere in dainty cups served

from a miniature pot. When drinking in company, it's polite to top up others' cups before your own, whenever they become empty; if somebody does this for you, lightly tap your first two fingers on the table to show your thanks. In a restaurant, take the lid off or turn it over if you want the pot refilled during the meal; if you've had enough, leave your cup full.

teach: could you teach me?
nín kéyi jiāojiao wǒ ma? [kur-yee jyow-jyow wor mah]
您可以教教我吗？

teacher lǎoshī [low-shur]
老师

team duì [dway]
队

teaspoon cháchí [chah-chur]
茶匙

tea towel cāwǎnbù [tsah-wahn-boo]
擦碗布

teenager qīngshàonián [ching-show-nyen]
青少年

telegram diànbào [dyen-bow]
电报

telephone diànhuà [dyen-hwah]
电话
see **phone**

television diànshì [dyen-shur]
电视

tell: could you tell him ...?
qǐng nǐn gàosu tā ..., hǎo
ma? [ching nin gow-soo tah ... how
mah]

请您告诉他 ... 好吗 ？

temperature (weather) qìwēn
[chee-wun]

气温

(fever) fāshāo [fah-show]

发烧

temple (Buddhist) sì [sur]

寺

(Taoist) guàn [gwahn]

观

tennis wǎngqiú [wahng-chyoh]

网球

term (at university, school) xuéqī
[hsyew-eh-chee]

学期

terminus (rail) zhōngdiǎnzhàn
[joong-dyen-jahn]

终点站

terrible zāogāo [dzow-gow]

糟糕

that's terrible tài zāogāo le
[lur]

太糟糕了

terrific bàngjíle [bahng-jee-lur]

棒极了

Thailand Tàiguó [tai-gwor]

泰国

than* bǐ

比

even

more ... than ... bǐ ... gèngdu

ō [gung ... dwor]

比 ... 更多

smaller than bǐ ... xiǎo [hsyow]

比 ... 小

thank: thank you xièxie
[hsyeh-hsyeh]

谢谢

thank you very much
fēicháng gǎnxiè [fay-chahng
gahn-hsyeh]

非常感谢

thanks for the lift xièxie nǐn
ràng wǒ dāle chē [rahng wor
dah-lur chur]

谢谢您让我搭了车

no, thanks xièxie, wǒ bú yào
[boo yow]

谢谢我不要

dialogue

> thanks xièxie
> that's OK, don't mention it
> bú kèqi [kur chee]

that* nèige [nay-gur]

那个

that one nèi yíge [yee-gur]

那一个

I hope that ... wǒ
xīwàng ... [wor hshee-wahng]

我希望 ...

that's nice nà zhèng hǎo
[nah jung-how]

那正好

is that ...? nà shì ... ma?
[shur ... mah]
那是 ... 吗？

that's it (that's right) duìle
[dway-lur]
对了

the*

theatre jùyuàn
[jyew-yew-ahn]
剧院

their/theirs* tāmende
[tah-mun-dur]
他们的

them* tāmen [tah-mun]
他们

then (at that time) nèi shíhou
[nay shur-hoh]
那时候
(after that) ránhòu [rahn-hoh]
然后

there nàr
那儿

over there zài nàr [dzai]
在那儿

up there zài shàngtou [dzai
shahng-toh]
在上头

is/are there ...? yǒu ... ma?
[yoh ... mah]
有 ... 吗？

there is/are ... yǒu ...
有 ...

there you are (giving something)
géi nǐ [gay]
给你

Thermos® flask rèshuǐpíng
[rush-way-ping]
热水瓶

these* zhèixie [jay-hsyeh]
这些

they* tāmen [tahmun]
他们

thick hòu [hoh]
厚
(stupid) bèn [bun]
笨

thief zéi [dzay]
贼

thigh dàtuǐ [dah-tway]
大腿

thin (person) shòu [shoh]
瘦
(object) xì [hshee]
细

thing (matter) shìr [shur]
事儿
(object) dōngxi [doong-hshee]
东西

my things wǒde dōngxi
我的东西

think xiǎng [hsyahng]
想

I think so wó xiǎng shì
zhèiyang [wor hsyahng shur
jay-yang]
我想是这样

I don't think so wǒ bú
zhèiyang xiǎng [jay-yang]
我不这样想

I'll think about it wó kǎolǜ

yíxia [kow-lyew yee-hsyah]
我考虑一下
third class sānděng [sahn-dung]
三等
(hard seat) yìngzuò
[ying-dzwor]
硬座
see **train**
thirsty: I'm thirsty wǒ kóukě
[wor koh-kur]
我口渴
this* zhèige [jay-gur]
这个
this one zhèige
这个
this is my wife zhè shì wǒ
qīzi [jur shur wor chee-dzur]
这是我妻子
is this ...? zhèi shìbúshì ...?
[shur-boo-shur]
这是不是 … ?
those* nèixie [nay-hsyeh]
那些
thread (noun) xiàn [hsyen]
线
throat sǎngzi [sahng-dzur]
嗓子
throat lozenges rùnhóu piàn
[run-hoh pyen]
润喉片
through jīngguò [jing-gwor]
经过
does it go through ...? (train,
bus) jīngguò ... ma? [mah]
经过 … 吗 ?

Th

throw/throw away rēng [rung]
扔
thumb dàmúzhǐ [dah-moo-jur]
大拇指
thunderstorm léiyǔ [lay-yew]
雷雨
Thursday xīngqīsì
[hsing-chee-sur]
星期四
Tibet Xīzàng [hshee-dzahng]
西藏
Tibetan (adj) Xīzàngde
[hshee-dzahng]
西藏的
ticket piào [pyow]
票

dialogue

a return to Xian wǎng
Xiān de láihuí piào [wahng
– dur lai-hway]
coming back when?
nèitiān yào huílái? [shur
nay-tyen yow]
today/next Tuesday
jīntian/xiàge xīngqīèr
that will be 30 yuan sānshí
kuài qián [chyen]

ticket office (bus, rail)
shòupiàochù [shoh-pyow-choo]
售票处
tie (necktie) lǐngdài
领带

tight (clothes etc) xiǎo [hsyow]

小

　it's too tight tài xiǎo le [lur]

太小了

tights liánkùwà [lyen-koo-wah]

连裤袜

time* shíjiān [shur-jyen]

时间

　what's the time? jǐdiǎn le?
　[jee-dyen lur]

几点了？

this time zhèicì [jay-tsur]

这次

last time shàngcì [shahng-tsur]

上次

next time xiàcì [hsyah]

下次

three times sāncì

三次

timetable (train) lièchē shíkè
biǎo [lyeh-chur shur-kur byow]

列车时刻表

tin (can) guàntou [gwahn-toh]

罐头

tinfoil xīzhǐ [hshee-jur]

锡纸

tin-opener guàntou qǐzi
[gwahn-toh chee-dzur]

罐头起子

tiny yìdiánrdiǎnr [yee-dyenr-
dyenr]

一点儿点儿

tip (to waiter etc) xiǎo fèi [hsyow
fay]

小费

Tipping is expected in
larger hotels and
restaurants – the amount
is up to you, but you are not
expected to tip taxi drivers.

tire (US) lúntāi [lun-tai]

轮胎

tired lèi [lay]

累

　I'm tired wǒ lèi le [wor lay lur]

我累了

tissues zhǐjīn [jur-jin]

纸巾

to*: to Shanghai/London dào
Shànghǎi/Lúndūn [dow]

到上海／伦敦

to China/England qù
Zhōngguó/Yīnggélán [chew]

去中国／英格兰

to the post office qù yóujú

去邮局

toast (bread) kǎo miànbāo
[kow myen-bow]

烤面包

today jīntian [jin-tyen]

今天

toe jiǎozhǐtou [jyow-jur-toh]

脚指头

together yìqǐ [yee-chee]

一起

　we're together (in shop etc)
　wǒmen shì yíkuàir de
　[wor-mun shur yee-kwair dur]

我们是一块儿的

toilet cèsuǒ [tsur-swor]

厕所

where is the toilet? cèsuǒ zài nǎr? [dzai]

厕所在哪儿？

I have to go to the toilet wó děi qù fāngbian fāngbian [wor day chew fahng-byen]

我得去方便方便

There are public toilets everywhere in China. In the more remote towns and villages they can be fairly stomach-churning. Public toilets are always of the squatting variety and consist of a hole in the ground. You should bring your own toilet paper. The contents of public toilets are collected for fertilizer, known as 'night soil'.

toilet paper wèishēngzhǐ [way-shung-jee]

卫生纸

tomato xīhóngshì [hshee-hoong-shur]

西红柿

tomato juice fānqié zhī [fahn-chyeh jur]

番茄汁

tomorrow míngtian [ming-tyen]

明天

tomorrow morning míngtian

zǎoshang [dzow-shahng]

明天早上

the day after tomorrow hòutian [hoh-tyen]

后天

tongue shétou [shur-toh]

舌头

tonic (water) kuàngquánshuǐ [kwahng-choo-en-shway]

矿泉水

tonight jīntian wǎnshang [jin-tyen wahn-shahng]

今天晚上

too (also) yě [yur]

也

(excessively) tài

太

too hot tài rè [rur]

太热

too much tài duō [dwor]

太多

me too wó yě [wor]

我也

tooth yá [yah]

牙

toothache yáténg [yah-tung]

牙疼

toothbrush yáshuā [yah-shwah]

牙刷

toothpaste yágāo [yah-gow]

牙膏

top: on top of ... zài ... shàngtou [dzai ... shahng-toh]

在 ...上头

at the top zài dǐngshang

[ding-shahng]

在顶上

torch shǒudiàntǒng

[shoh-dyen-toong]

手电筒

total (noun) zǒnggòng

[dzoong-goong]

总共

tour (noun) lǚxíng [lyew-hsing]

旅行

is there a tour of ...? yǒu
méiyou wǎng ... de lǚxíng?

[yoh may-yoh wahng ... dur]

有没有往 ... 的旅行 ？

tour guide dǎoyóu [dow-yoh]

导游

tourist lǚyóu zhě [lyew-yoh jur]

旅游者

**tourist information
office**

Inside the People's
Republic, there is no such thing as a
tourist information office. CITS, the
state tour operator with a special
responsibility for foreigners, is just
one of a large number of operators
who have no function other than
selling tours and tickets, and renting
cars. However, it may still be
worthwhile dropping in on the local
branch of CITS, or an affiliated
organization, especially in out-of-
the-way places, as sometimes it is
here that you will find the only

person in town who can speak
English. As for handouts, in the form
of leaflets, brochures or maps, these
are never free in China. Other
sources of information are your
hotel staff (in upmarket places) and,
in certain tourist centres, restaurant
proprietors, who give advice in
exchange for custom.

tour operator lǚxíng shè

[lyew-hsing shur]

旅行社

towards cháozhe [chow-jur]

朝着

towel máojīn [mow-jin]

毛巾

town chéngzhèn [chung-jun]

城镇

in town (zài) chéngli [(dzai)
chung-lee]

（在）城里

out of town (zài) chéngwài
[chung-wai]

（在）城外

town centre shì zhōngxīn

[shur joong-hsin]

市中心

town hall shì zhèngfǔ dàlóu

[shur-jung-foo]

市政府大楼

toy wánjù [wahn-jyew]

玩具

track (US) zhàntái [jahn-tai]

站台

tracksuit yùndòngfú
〔yewn-doong-foo〕
运动服
traditional chuántǒng
〔chwahn-toong〕
传统
train huǒchē 〔hwor-chur〕
火车
by train zuò huǒchē 〔dzwor hwor-chur〕
坐火车

China's rail network is vast, efficient, and definitely the safest, most reliable way to travel through the country, even though getting hold of a seat can be difficult. There is an incredible demand for train tickets and you'll need to buy one well in advance. Theoretically, tickets are sold up to three days in advance, and stations in most big cities have foreigners' ticket offices which makes buying what's available fairly straightforward.

There are four train classes. The best is **ruǎnwò** (soft berth), roughly the same price as flying, and generally patronized by foreigners, party officials, and successful entrepreneurs. It's a pleasant experience; there's a plush waiting room at the station, and on the train itself, you get a wood-panelled four-berth compartment with a soft mattress, fan, optional radio, and a choice of Western or Chinese-style toilets. There's an attendant on hand, too, and meals – though good in all classes – are more varied and taken separately from the other passengers. If you've a long way to travel and can afford it, soft berth is well worth the money.

Yìngwò (hard berth) is about half the price of ruǎnwò, is favoured by China's emerging middle class and money-conscious foreigners, and hence is the most difficult to book in advance. Unreserved hard travel can be hellishly crowded; reserved hard travel, however, is perfectly comfortable if you book a sleeper: clean sheets and blankets are supplied, and constant supplies of hot water are available. Carriages are divided into twenty rows of three bunks each. To every six bunks is allocated a Thermos flask of boiled water (topped up from the huge urn at the end of each carriage), and you bring your own mugs and beverage. Polystyrene boxes of rice and stir-fries are wheeled around from time to time, or you can use the restaurant car. Every carriage also has a toilet and washbasin.

For the really impecunious there's **yìngzuò** (hard seat), sometimes the only advance ticket available. Much rarer is the more upmarket **ruǎnzuò** (soft seat), only found on short-haul trains. Hard-seat train travel is cheaper and faster than bus travel, though on long journeys the discomfort can be excruciating, especially as the air is thick with cigarette smoke and every available inch of floor space is crammed with travellers who were unable to book a seat.

There are three types of train in China, and not all have the three main classes. Express trains do – they're identified by a number between 1 and 90, and you pay a small supplement to the standard fare. Trains numbered 100–350 or so are marginally cheaper, but make more stops, and have fewer berths. Anything marked 400 or above will stop whenever possible and have seats only, and should be avoided if possible.

Chinese train travellers nearly all bring slippers, a facecloth, a jam jar with a lid (to drink from) and tea leaves, as well as large quantities of food. Music and news is played incessantly over loudspeakers up and down the train.

dialogue

is this the train for Shanghai? zhèliè huǒchē qù Shànghǎi ma? [jur-lyeh hwor-chur chew – mah]
sure qù [chew]
no, you want that platform there búqù, nǐ yào dào nèige zhàntái qù [boo-chew nee yow dow nay-gur jahn-tai]

trainers (shoes) lǚyóuxié [lyew-yoh-hsyeh]
旅游鞋
train station huǒchēzhàn [hwor-chur-jahn]
火车站
tram yóuguǐ diànchē [yoh-gway dyen-chur]
有轨电车
translate fānyì [fahn-yee]
翻译
could you translate that? qǐng nín fānyì yíxia, hǎo ma? [ching nin fahn-yee yee-hsyah how mah]
请您翻译一下好吗？
translator fānyì [fahn-yee]
翻译
trash lājī [lah-jee]
垃圾
travel lǚxíng [lyew-hsing]
旅行
we're travelling around

wǒmen zài lǚxíng [wor-mun dzai]

我们在旅行

travel agent's lǚxíngshè [lyew-hsing-shur]

旅行社

traveller's cheque lǚxíng zhīpiào [lyew-hsing jur-pyow]

旅行支票

 Traveller's cheques, available through banks and travel agents, are the best way to carry your funds around; their exchange rate in China is fixed and better than for cash. However, in mainland China they can only be cashed at major branches of the Bank of China and tourist hotels and the process always involves lengthy paperwork. Stick to well-known names such as Thomas Cook or American Express. Charges for transactions are variable. In case you find yourself in difficulties, it's also worth taking along a small supply of foreign currency such as US dollars or British sterling, which are more widely exchangeable. There's a low-key black market in China for foreign currency, but the small profits you'll make and the risks of getting ripped off or attracting police attention don't make it worthwhile.

tray chápán [chah-pahn]

茶盘

tree shù [shoo]

树

trim: just a trim, please (to hairdresser) qíng zhǐ xiūxiu biānr [ching jur hsyoh-hsyoh byenr]

请只修修边儿

trip: I'd like to go on a trip to ... wó xiǎng dào ... qù [wor hsyahng dow ... chew]

我想到 ... 去

trouble (noun) máfan [mah-fahn]

麻烦

I'm having trouble with ... wǒde ... yùdàole diǎnr máfan [wor-duh ... yew-dow-lur dyenr]

我的 ... 遇到了点儿麻烦

trousers kùzi [koo-dzur]

裤子

true zhēnde [jun-dur]

真的

that's not true bú duì [dway]

不对

trunk (US: of car) xínglixiāng [hsing-lee-hsyahng]

行李箱

trunks (swimming) yóuyǒngkù [yoh-yoong-koo]

游泳裤

try (verb) shì [shur]

试

can I try it? kéyi shìyishì ma?

[kur-yee shur-yee-shur mah]

可以试一试吗？

try on: can I try it on? kéyi shìyishì ma?

可以试一试吗？

T-shirt T xùshān [tee hsoo shahn]

T 恤衫

Tuesday xīngqièr [hsing-chee-er]

星期二

tunnel suìdào [sway-dow]

隧道

turn: turn left wǎng zuó guǎi [wahng dzwor gwai]

往左拐

turn right wǎng yòu guǎi

往右拐

turn off: where do I turn off? wó děi zài nǎr guǎiwān? [wor day dzai nar gwai-wahn]

我得在哪儿拐弯？

can you turn the heating off? qǐng ba nuǎnqì guānshang [ching bah nwahn-chee-gwahn-shahng]

请把暖器关上？

turn on: can you turn the heating on? qǐng ba nuǎnqì dǎkāi yíxià [dah-kai yee-hsyah]

请把暖器打开一下？

turning (in road) zhuǎnwānr [jwahn-wahnr]

转弯儿

TV diànshì [dyen-shur]

电视

twice liǎngcì [lyang-tsur]

两次

twice as much duō yíbèi [dwor yee-bay]

多一倍

twin beds liǎngge dānrénchuáng [lyang-gur dahn-run-chwahng]

两个单人床

twin room shuāngrén fángjiān [shwahng-run fahng-jyen]

双人房间

twist: I've twisted my ankle wǒde jiǎobózi niǔle [wor-dur jyow-bor-dzur nyoh-lur]

我的脚脖子扭了

type (noun) zhǒng [joong]

种

another type of ... lìng yìzhǒng ... [ling yee-joong]

另一种 ...

typical diǎnxíng [dyen-hsing]

典型

tyre lúntāi

轮胎

U

ugly nánkàn [nahn-kahn]

难看

UK Yīngguó [ying-gwor]

英国

umbrella yúsǎn [yew-sahn]
雨伞
uncle (father's elder brother) bófù
伯父
(father's younger brother) shūshu
[shoo-shoo]
叔叔
(mother's brother) jiùjiu
[jyoh-jyoh]
舅舅
under ... (in position) zài ... xià
[dzai ... hsyah]
在 ... 下
(less than) shǎoyú ... [show-yew]
... 少于
underdone (meat) bàn shēng
bù shú [bahn shung boo shoo]
半生不熟
underground (railway) dìtiě
[dee-tyeh]
地铁
see **bus**
underpants kùchǎ [koo-chah]
裤衩
understand: I understand wó
dǒng le [wor doong lur]
我懂了
I don't understand wǒ bù
dǒng
我不懂
do you understand? ní
dǒngle, ma?
你懂了吗？
unemployed shīyè [shur-yur]
失业

unfashionable bù shímáo [boo
shur-mow]
不时髦
United States Měiguó
[may-gwor]
美国
university dàxué
[dah-hsyew-eh]
大学
unlock kāi
开
unpack dǎkāi [dah-kai]
打开
until ... zhǐdào ... wéizhǐ
[jur-dow ... way-jur]
只到 ... 为止
unusual bù chángjiàn(de)
[chahng-jyen(-dur)]
不常见（的）
up shàng [shahng]
上
up there zài nàr [dzai]
在那儿
he's not up yet tā hái méi
qǐlai [tah hai may chee-lai]
他还没起来
what's up? zěnme huí shìr?
[dzun-mur hway shur]
怎么回事儿？
upmarket gāojí [gow-jee]
高级
upset stomach wèi bù shūfu
[way boo shoo-foo]
胃不舒服
upside down dàoguolai

[dow-gwor-lai]

倒过来

upstairs lóushàng

[loh-shahng]

楼上

urgent jǐnjí(de) [jin-jee(-dur)]

紧急（的）

us* wǒmen [wor-mun]

我们

with us gēn wǒmen yìqǐ [gun – yee-chee]

跟我们一起

for us wéi wǒmen [wei]

为我们

use (verb) yòng [yoong]

用

may I use ...? wǒ kéyi yòng yíxia... ma? [wor kur-yee yoong yee-hsyah ... mah]

我可以用一下 ... 吗？

useful yǒuyòng [yoh-yoong]

有用

usual (normal) píngcháng [ping-chahng]

平常

(habitual) yuánlái de [yew-ahn-lai dur]

原来的

V

vacancy: do you have any vacancies? (hotel) zhèr yǒu kòng fángjiān ma? [jer yoh koong fahng-jyen mah]

这儿有空房间吗？

see **room**

vacation (holiday) jiàqī [jyah-chee]

假期

on vacation xiūjià [hsyoh-jyah]

休假

vacuum cleaner xīchénqì [hshee-chun-chee]

吸尘器

valid (ticket etc) yǒuxiào [yoh-hsyow]

有效

how long is it valid for? duō cháng shíjiānnei yǒuxiào? [dwor chahng shur-jyen nay yoh-hsyow]

多长时间内有效？

valley shāngǔ [shahn-goo]

山谷

valuable (adj) bǎoguì(de) [bow-gway(-dur)]

宝贵（的）

can I leave my valuables here? wǒ kéyi bǎ guìzhòng de dōngxi fàng zài zhèr ma? [wor kur-yee bah gway-joong dur doong-hshee fahng dzai jer mah]

我可以把贵重的东西放在这儿吗？

van huòchē [hwor-chur]

货车

vary: it varies jīngcháng biàn

201

[jing-chahng byen]

经常变

vase huāpíng [hwah-ping]

花瓶

vegetables shūcài [shoo-tsai]

蔬菜

vegetarian (noun) chīsùde

[chur-soo-dur]

吃素的

Vegetarianism has been practised for almost two thousand years in China for both religious and philosophical reasons. Vegetarian cooking takes at least three recognized forms: plain vegetable dishes, commonly served at home or in ordinary restaurants; imitation meat dishes, derived from Qing court cuisine, which use gluten, beancurd, and potato to mimic meat, fowl and fish; and Buddhist cooking, which avoids onions, ginger, garlic and other spices considered stimulating.

Having said all this, strict vegetarians visiting China will find their options limited. Vegetables might be considered intrinsically healthy, but the Chinese also believe that they lack any fortifying properties, and vegetarian diets are unusual except for religious reasons. There's also a stigma of poverty attached to not eating meat.

Although you can get vegetable dishes everywhere, be aware that cooking fat and stocks in the average dining room are of animal origins.

very fēicháng [fay-chahng]

非常

very little hén xiǎo [hun hsyow]

很小

I like it very much wǒ hén xǐhuan [wor hun hshee-hwahn]

我很喜欢

via tújīng [toojing]

途经

Vietnam Yuènán [yew-eh-nahn]

越南

view jǐng

景

village cūnzi [tsun-dzur]

村子

vinegar cù [tsoo]

醋

visa qiānzhèng [chyen-jung]

签证

All foreign nationals require a visa to enter China. Single entry tourist visas must be used within three months of date of issue: they are usually valid for thirty days from your date of entry into China, but regulations vary to control tourist traffic. Visas are available worldwide from Chinese embassies and consulates and through specialist tour operators and visa agents; if you are planning to enter China through Hong Kong, you'll find this is probably the best place to buy your visa.

Visa extensions are handled by the Foreign Affairs section of the Public Security Bureau (PSB), so you can apply for one in any reasonably-sized town. The amount of money you'll pay for this, and the amount of hassle you'll have, will vary greatly depending where you are. A first extension, valid for a month, is not usually difficult to obtain. A second extension is much harder to get, though not impossible. If the PSB refuse to grant an extension they may be able to point you in the direction of a private office which can.

visit (verb: person) qù kàn [chew kahn]
去看
(place) cānguān [tsahn-gwahn]
参观
I'd like to visit ... wó xiǎng cānguān ... [wor hsyahng]
我想参观 ...
voice shēngyīn [shung-yin]
声音

voltage diànyā [dyen-yah]
电压

 Voltage is 220V, 50Hz AC. Sockets are generally two-pin so bring an adaptor with you. Certain parts of China have frequent power cuts.

vomit ǒutù [oh-too]
呕吐

W

waist yāo [yow]
腰
wait děng [dung]
等
wait for me děngdeng wǒ [wor]
等等我
don't wait for me búyòng déng wǒ [boo-yoong]
不用等我
can I wait until my wife gets here? wǒ néng děngdào wǒ qīzi lái ma? [nung dung-dow wor chee-dzur lai mah]
我能等到我妻子来吗？
can you do it while I wait? shìbúshì lìděng kéqǔ? [shur-boo-shur lee-dung kur-chew]
是不是立等可取？

could you wait here for me? qǐng zài zhèr děng hǎo ma? [ching dzai jer dung how mah]

请在这儿等好吗？

waiter/waitress fúwùyuán [foo-woo-yew-ahn]

服务员

waiter!/waitress! fúwùyuán!

服务员

wake: can you wake me up at 5.30? qǐng zài wǔdiǎnbàn jiàoxíng wǒ, hǎo ma? [ching dzai – jyow-hsing wor]

请在五点半叫醒我好吗？

Wales Wēiěrshì [way-er-shur]

威尔士

walk: is it a long walk? yào zǒu hén yuǎn ma? [yow dzoh hun yew-ahn mah]

要走很远吗？

it's only a short walk zhǐ shì liūdaliūda [jur shur lyoh-dah-]

只是溜达溜达

I'll walk wǒ zǒuzhe qù [wor dzoh-jur chew]

我走着去

I'm going for a walk wǒ chūqu sànsan bù [choo-chew sahn-sahn]

我出去散散步

wall qiáng [chyang]

墙

the Great Wall of China Chángchéng [chahng-chung]

长城

wallet qiánbāo [chyen-bow]

钱包

want: I want a ... wǒ yào yíge ... [wor yow yee-gur]

我要一个

I don't want any ... wǒ bú yào ...

我不要

I want to go home wǒ yào huíjiā [hway-jyah]

我要回家

I don't want to wǒ bú yào

我不要

he wants to ... tā xiǎng ... [tah hsyahng]

他想 ...

what do you want? nǐ yào shénme? [shun-mur]

你要什么？

ward (in hospital) bìngfáng [bing-fahng]

病房

warm nuǎnhuo [nwahn-hwor]

暖和

was*: he/she was tā yǐqián shì [tah yee-chyen shur]

他／她以前是

it was shì

是

wash (verb) xǐ [hshee]

洗

can you wash these? qǐng

xǐxi zhèixie, hǎo ma? [ching
hshee-hshee jay-hsyeh how mah]

请洗洗这些好吗？

washhand basin liǎnpén
[lyen-pun]

脸盆

washing (dirty clothes) dài xǐ de
yīfu [yow hshee dur yee-foo]

待洗的衣服

(clean clothes) yíxǐ de yīfu
[yee-hshee-how]

已洗的衣服

washing machine xǐyījī
[hshee-yee-jee]

洗衣机

washing powder xǐyīfěn [–fun]

洗衣粉

wasp huángfēng [hwahng-fung]

黄蜂

watch (wristwatch) shóubiāo
[shoh-byow]

手表

water shuǐ [shway]

水

may I have some water? qǐng
lái diánr shuǐ, hǎo ma? [ching
lai dyenr shway how mah]

请来点儿水好吗？

 It's best not to drink what
comes out of the tap;
however tap water should
be OK for brushing your teeth if you
don't swallow it. Hotels provide a
Thermos of drinkable water that can

be refilled any time by the floor
attendant. On trains, hot water is
provided by an urn in each carriage.
Boiled water is available just about
everywhere; bottled spring water is
widely available.

water melon xīguā
[hshee-gwah]

西瓜

waterproof (adj) fángshuǐ
[fahng-shway]

防水

way: it's this way shì zhèitiáo
lù [shur jay-tyow]

是这条路

it's that way shì nèitiáo lù
[nay-tyow]

是那条路

is it a long way to ...?
dào ... yuǎn ma? [dow ... chew
yew-ahn mah]

到 ... 远吗？

no way! bù kěnéng!
[kur-nung]

不可能

dialogue

**could you tell me the way
to ...?** qǐng nín gàosu wǒ,
dào ... zěnme zǒu, hǎo
ma? [ching nin gow-soo wor
dow ... dzun-mur dzoh how mah]
go straight on until you

reach the traffic lights
yìzhí zǒu hónglùdēng
[yee-jur dzoh hoong-loo-dung]
turn left wǎng zuǒ guǎi
[wahng dzwor gwai]
take the first on the right
yào yòubiānr dì yízhuǎn
[yow yoh-byenr dee
yee-jwahn]
see where

we* wǒmen [wor-mun]
我们
weak (person) ruò [rwor]
弱
(drink) dàn [dahn]
淡
weather tiānqi [tyen-chee]
天气
wedding hūnlǐ [hun-lee]
婚礼
wedding ring jiéhūn jièzhǐ
[jyeh-hun jyeh-jur]
结婚戒指
Wednesday xīngqīsān
[hsing-chee-sahn]
星期三
week xīngqī [hsing-chee]
星期
a week (from) today xiàge
xīngqī de jīntian [hsyah-gur –
dur jin-tyen]
下个星期的今天
a week (from) tomorrow xiàge
xīngqi de míngtian

[ming-tyen]
下个星期的明天
weekend zhōumò [joh-mor]
周末
at the weekend zhōumò
周末
weight zhòngliàng [joong-lyang]
重量
**welcome: welcome
to ...** huānyíng
dào ... [hwahn-ying dow]
欢迎到 ...
you're welcome (don't mention
it) búyòng xiè [boo-yoong
hsyeh]
不用谢
well: I don't feel well wǒ bù
shūfu [wor boo shoo-foo]
我不舒服
she's not well tā bù shūfu
[tah]
她不舒服
you speak English very well
nǐ Yīngyǔ jiǎngde hén hǎo
[ying-yew jyang-dur hun how]
你英语讲得很好
well done! tài hǎole!
[how-lur]
太好了
I would like this one as well
zhèige wǒ yě yào [jay-gur wor
yeh yow]
这个我也要
well well! āiyā! [ai-yah]
哎呀

dialogue

how are you? nǐn hǎo ma?
[how mah]

very well, thanks, and you?
hén hǎo xièxie, nǐ ne?
[hun how hsych-hsyeh nee-neh]

well-done (meat) lànshú [lahn-shoo]
烂熟

Welsh Wēi'ěrshì [way-er-shur]
威尔士

I'm Welsh wǒ shì
Wēi'ěrshìrén [wor shur –run]
我是威尔士人

were*: we were wǒmen
yǐqián shì [wor-mun yee-chyen shur]
我们以前是

you were nǐmen shì
[nee-mun]
你们是

west xī [hshee]
西

in the west xībiānr
[hshee-byenr]
西边儿

West (European etc) Xīfāng
[hshee-fahng]
西方

in the West Xīfāng
西方

western (adj) xī [hshee]
西

Western (adj: European etc)
xīfāng de [hshee-fahng dur]
西方的

Western-style xīshì
[hshee-shur]
西式

Western-style food xīcān
[hshee-tsahn]
西餐

West Indian (adj) Xī Yìndù
qúndǎo rén [hshee yin-doo
chun-dow run]
西印度群岛人

wet shī [shur]
湿

what? shénme? [shun-mur]
什么？

what's that? nà shì shénme?
[nah shur]
那是什么？

what should I do? wǒ
yīnggāi zuò shénme? [wor
ying-gai dzwor]
我应该作什么？

what a view! kàn zhè jǐngr!
[kahn jur]
看这景儿

what bus do I take? wǒ gāi
zuò nèilù chē? [wor gai dzwor
nay-loo chur]
我该坐哪路车？

wheel lúnzi [lun-dzur]
轮子

wheelchair lúnyǐ [lun-yee]
轮椅

when? shénme shíhou?
[shun-mur shur-hoh]

什么时侯？

when we get back wǒmen
huílai de shíhou [wor-mun
hway-lai dur]

我们回来的时侯

when's the train/ferry?
huǒchē/dùchuán jídiǎn kāi?
[hwor-chur/doo-chwahn jee-dyen]

火车／渡船几点开？

where? nǎr?

哪儿？

I don't know where it is wǒ
bù zhīdao zài nàr [wor boo
jur-dow dzai nar]

我不知道在那儿

dialogue

**where is the Dragon
temple?** lóng miào zài
nǎr? [dzai]

it's over there jiù zài nàr
[jyoh]

**could you show me where
it is on the map?** qǐng zài
dìtúshang zhǐshì gěi wǒ
ba [ching – dee-too-shahng
jur-shur gay wor bah]

it's just here jiù zài zhèr
[jyoh – jer]

see **way**

which: which bus? něilù chē?

[nay-loo chur]

哪路车？

dialogue

which one? nǎ yíge? [nah
yee-gur]

that one nèige [nay-gur]

this one? zhèige? [jay-gur]

no, that one búshì, nèige
[boo-shur]

while: while I'm here wǒ zài
zhèr de shíhou [wor dzai jer dur
shur-hoh]

我在这儿的时侯

whisky wēishìjì [way-shur-jee]

威士忌

white bái

白

white wine bái pútaojiǔ
[poo-tow-jyoh]

白葡萄酒

who? shéi? [shay]

谁

who is it? shéi? [shway]

谁

the man who ... ... de nèige
rén [dur nay-gur run]

... 的那个人

whole: the whole week
zhěngzheng yíge xīngqī
[jung-jung yee-gur hsing-chee]

整整一个星期

the whole lot quánbù

[choo-en-boo]

全部

whose: whose is this? zhèi shì shéide? [jay shur shay-dur]

这是谁的？

why? wèishénme?

[way-shun-mur]

为什么？

why not? wèishénme bù?

为什么不？

wide kuān de [kwahn dur]

宽的

wife qīzi [chee-dzur]

妻子

will*: will you do it for me? qǐng gěi wǒ zuò yíxià [ching gay wor dzwor yee-hsyah]

请给我作一下

wind (noun) fēng [fung]

风

window chuānghu [chwahng-hoo]

窗户

near the window kào chuānghu [kow]

靠窗户

in the window (of shop) zài chúchuāngli [dzai choo-chwahng-lee]

在橱窗里

window seat kào chuāng de zuòwei [kow chwahng dur dzwor-way]

靠窗的座位

windy: it's windy yǒufēng

[yoh-fung]

有风

wine pútaojiǔ [poo-tow-jyoh]

葡萄酒

can we have some more wine? qǐng zài lái diǎnr pútaojiǔ, hǎo ma? [ching dzai lai dyenr – how mah]

请再来点儿葡萄酒好吗？

see **spirits**

wine list jiǔdān [jyoh-dahn]

酒单

winter dōngtian [doong-tyen]

冬天

in the winter dōngtian

冬天

with* hé ... yìqǐ [hur ... yee-chee]

和 ... 一起

I'm staying with ... wǒ gēn ... zhù zài yìqǐ [wor gun ... joo dzai yee-chee]

我跟 ... 住在一起

without méiyǒu [may-yoh]

没有

witness zhèngren [jung-run]

证人

wok guō [gwor]

锅

woman fùnǚ [foo-nyew]

妇女

women

Women travellers usually find incidences of sexual

harassment much less of a problem than in other Asian countries. You may get some hassles, however, in Dongbei, where Chinese men may take you for a Russian prostitute (much embarrassment ensues when they realize their mistake) and in Muslim Xinjiang. As ever, it pays to be aware of how local women are dressing and follow their lead.

wonderful hǎojíle [how-jee-lur]
好极了

won't*: it won't start bù dáhuǒ
[dah-hwor]
不打火

wood (material) mùtou
[moo-toh]
木头
(forest) shùlín [shoo-lin]
树林

wool yángmáo [yang-mow]
羊毛

word cí [tsur]
词

work (noun) gōngzuò
[goong-dzwor]
工作
it's not working huàile [lur]
坏了

world shìjiè [shur-jyeh]
世界

worry: I'm worried wǒ bù ān
[wor bwahn]
我不安

worse: it's worse huàile
[hway-lur]
坏了

worst zuì huài [dzway hwai]
最坏

would: would you give this to ...? qǐng nín bǎ zhèige gěi ..., hǎo ma? [ching nin bah jay gay ... how mah]
请您把这个给 ... 好吗？

wrap: could you wrap it up? qǐng nín bāng wǒ bāo yíxia, hǎo ma? [ching nin bahng wor bow yee-hsyah how mah]
请您帮我包一下好吗？

wrapping paper bāozhuāngzhǐ [bow-jwahng-jur]
包装纸

wrist shǒuwànr [shoh-wahnr]
手腕儿

write xiě [hsyeh]
写

writing paper xìnzhǐ [hsin-jur]
信纸

wrong: this is the wrong train wǒmen shàngcuò huǒchēle [wor-mun chung-tswor-lur hwor-chur-lur]
我们上错火车了
the bill's wrong zhàngdānr cuòle [jahng-dahnr tswor-lur]
帐单儿错了
sorry, wrong number duìbuqǐ, dǎcuòle

[dway-boo-chee dah–]

对不起打错了

sorry, wrong room duìbuqǐ,
zhàocuò fángjiān le

[jow-fahng-jyen]

对不起找错房间了

**there's something wrong
with ...** ... yǒu máobìng [yoh

mow-bing]

... 有毛病

what's wrong? zěnmele?

[dzun-mur-lur]

怎么了？

Y

yacht fānchuán [fahn-chwahn]

帆船

Yangtze Gorge Chángjiāng

sānxiá [chahng-jyang sahn-syah]

长江三峡

Yangtze River Chángjiāng

长江

year nián [nyen]

年

yellow huángsè [hwahng-sur]

黄色

Yellow River Huáng Hé

[hwahng hur]

黄河

Yellow Sea Huánghǎi

黄海

yes* shìde [shur-dur]

是的

yesterday zuótiān [dzwor-tyen]

昨天

yesterday morning zuótiān

zǎoshang [dzow-shahng]

昨天早上

the day before yesterday

qiántiān [chyen-tyen]

前天

yet hái

还

dialogue

is it here yet? hái láile

méiyou? [lai-lur may-yoh]

no, not yet hái méilái

[may-lai]

**you'll have to wait a little

longer yet** nǐ hái yào děng

yídiǎnr [yow dung yee-dyenr]

yoghurt suānnǎi [swahn-nai]

酸奶

you* (sing) nǐ

你

(sing, pol) nín

您

(pl) nǐmen [nee-mun]

你们

this is for you zhèi shì géi nǐ

de [jay shur gay nee dur]

这是给你的

with you gēn nǐ yìqǐ [gun nee

yee-chee]

跟你一起

young niánqīng [nyen-ching]
年轻
your/yours* (sing) nǐde
[nee-dur]
你的
(sing, pol) nínde [nin-dur]
您的

Z

zero líng
零
zip lāliàn [lah-lyen]
拉链
could you put a new zip on?
qíng nǐn bāng wǒ huànge
xīn lāliànr, hǎo ma? [ching nin
bahng wor hwahn-gur hsin – how
mah]
请您帮我换个新拉链
好吗？
zoo dòngwùyuán
[doong-woo-yew-ahn]
动物园

Chinese

→

English

Colloquialisms

You might well hear the following expressions, but on no account should you use any of the stronger ones — they will cause great offence if used by a foreigner.

bèndàn! [bun-dahn] idiot!
chǔnhuò! [chun-hwor] idiot!
dàbízi! [dah-bee-dzur] big nose!
dà tuánjié [dah twahn-jyeh] ten-yuán note
fèihuà! [fay-hwah] rubbish!
gàile màorle [gai-lur mow-lur] absolutely the best
gǔn! [goon] go away!, get lost!
gǔnchūqù! [goon-choo-chyew] get out!
húndàn! [hoon-dahn] bastard!
juéle [jweh-lur] wonderful, unique
lǎowài! [low-wai] foreigner!
liǎobude [lyow-boo-dur] terrific, extraordinary
méizhìle [may-jur-lur] excellent
nǎli, nǎli [nah-lee] oh, it was nothing, you're welcome
suànle [swahn-lur] forget it
suíbiàn [sway-byen] as you wish
tāmāde! [tah-mah-dur] hell!, damn!
tài bàngle [bahng-lur] that's great
tài zāogāole [dzow-gow-lur] that's terrible
tài zāotòule [dzow-toh-lur] that's awful
xīpíshì [hshee-pee-shur] hippy
yángguǐzi! [yang-gway-dzur] foreign devil!
yāpíshì [yah-pee-shur] yuppie
yílù píng'ān [yee-loo ping-ahn] safe journey, bon voyage
yuánmù qiúyú [yew-ahn-moo choh-yoo] a waste of time (literally: climbing a tree to catch fish)
zāole! [dzow-lur] damn!, shit!
zhù zuǐ! [joo dzway] shut up!
zǒu kāi! [dzoh] go away!

A

ǎi short
Àiěrlán [ai-ur-lahn] Ireland; Irish
àizībìng [ai-dzur-bing] AIDS
àn [ahn] dark; shore
ānjìng [ahn-jing] quiet
ānquán [ahn-choo-en] safe
ānzuò [ahn-dzwor] saddle
Àodàlìyà [or-dah-lee-yah] Australia; Australian (adj)

B

ba [bah] particle at the end of a sentence to indicate a suggestion, piece of advice etc
bā eight
bǎ measure word* used for chairs, knives, teapots, tools or implements with handles, stems and bunches of flowers
bàba [bah-bah] father
bābǎi eight hundred
bái white
báidù ferry
báisè [bai-sur] white
bái tiān [tyen] day, daytime
bǎiwàn [bai-wahn] one million
bàn [bahn] half
bàndá [bahn-dah] half a dozen
bàngjíle [bahng-jee-lur] terrific
bàngōngshì [bahn-goong-shur] office

bāngzhù [bahng-joo] help
bànr [bahnr] partner, boyfriend; girlfriend
bànyè [bahn-yur] midnight; at midnight
báo [bow] thin
bàofēngyǔ [bow-fung-yew] storm
bàozhǐ [bow-jur] newspaper
bāoguǒ [bow-gwor] package, parcel
bāokuò [bow-kwor] include
bǎole [bow-lur] full
bǎozhèng [bow-jung] promise; guarantee
báozhǐ [bow-jur] tissue, Kleenex®
bāshí [bah-shur] eighty
bāyuè [bah-yew-eh] August
bēi [bay] cup, glass
běi north
Běi Ài'ěrlán [ai-er-lahn] Northern Ireland
bēizi [bay-dzur] cup
bèn [bun] stupid
běn measure word* used for books, magazines etc
bēngdài [bung-dai] bandage
bǐ [bee] than
bǐ ... gèng [gung] even more than ...
bǐ nèi duō diǎnr [nay dwor dyenr] more than that
biānjiè [byen-jyeh] border
biānjìng [byen-jing] border
biānr [byenr] side
biǎo [byow] form
biǎodì [byow-dee] cousin (male, younger than speaker)

biǎogē [byow-gur] cousin (male, older than speaker)

biáojiě [byow-jyeh] cousin (female, older than speaker)

biǎomèi [byow-may] cousin (female, younger than speaker)

biéde dìfang [byeh-dur dee-fahng] somewhere else

biéde dōngxi [byeh-dur doong-hshee] something else

bīng ice

bīngdòngde [–doong-dur] frozen

bìngfáng [–fahng] ward

bīnguǎn [–wahn] hotel

bīngxiāng [–hsyang] fridge

bǐsài game; match; race

bìxū [bee-hsyew] must

bìyào(de) [bee-yow(-dur)] necessary

bíyǒu [bee-yoh] penfriend

bízi [bee-dzur] nose

bōhào [bor-how] dial

bōli [bor-lee] glass (material)

bōli bēi [bay] glass (for drinking)

bówùguǎn [bor-woo-gwahn] museum

bózi [boh-dzur] neck

bù [boo] no; not; material, fabric

  bù duō [dwor] not much

  bù chángjiàn(de) [chahng-jyen(-dur)] unusual

bú kèqi [kur-chee] you're welcome, don't mention it

bùfen [boo-fun] part

bùhǎo [boo-how] bad

bù jiǔ [jyoh] soon

bù kěnéng [kur-nung] impossible

bùliào [boo-lyow] cloth, fabric

bù lǐmào [lee-mow] rude

búshì [boo-shur] no, it is not the case

búshì ... jiùshì ... [jyoh-shur] either ... or ...

bùtóng [boo-toong] different; difference

bùxíng [boo-sing] on foot

búyào! [boo-yow] don't!

búyàole [–lur] that's all; nothing else

búyòng xiè [hsyeh] you're welcome, don't mention it

C

cài [tsai] dish; meal

cái only

cānchē [tsahn-chur] buffet car

cánfèi [tsahn-fay] disabled

cáng [tsahng] hide

cāngbái [–bai] pale

cānguān [–wahn] visit

cāngying fly (noun)

cānjīn [tsahn-jin] napkin

cāntīng [tsahn-ting] restaurant; dining room

cǎo [tsow] grass

cǎoyào [tsow-yow] herbs (medicinal)

céng [tsung] floor (in hotel etc)

cèsuǒ [tsur-swor] toilet, rest room

chá [chah] tea (drink)

chà to (the hour)

chàbuduō [chah-boo-dwor]

almost, nearly

cháchí [chah-chur] teaspoon

cháhàotái [chah-how-tai] directory enquiries

chán [chahn] greedy

cháng [chahng] long

chànggē [–gur] sing

chàngpiàn [–pyen] record (music)

chángtú chēzhàn [–too chur-jahn] long-distance bus station

chángtú diànhuà [dyen-hwah] long-distance call

chángtú qìchē [chee-chur] long-distance bus

chángtú qūhào [chew-how] dialling code

chāojí shìchǎng [chow-jee shur-chahng] supermarket

chǎole [chow-lur] noisy

chāopiào [chow-pyow] banknote, (US) bill

cháoshī [chow-shur] damp; humid

cháozhe [chow-jur] towards

chápán [chah-pahn] tray

chāzi [chah-dzur] fork

chē [chur] city bus

chēfèi [chur-fay] fare

chēlún [chur-lun] wheel

chéngbǎo [chung-bow] castle

chéngjiā [–jyah] married

chéngkè [–kur] passenger

chéngli [–lee] in town, in the city

chéngshì [–shur] city, town

chéngshí honest

chéngzhèn [–jun] town

chènyī [chun-yee] shirt

chētāi [chur-tai] tyre

chēzhàn [chur-jahn] bus station; bus stop

chī [chur] eat

chí late

chǐcùn [chur-tsun] size

chīde [chur-dur] food

chīsùde [chur-soo-dur] vegetarian

chóngfù [choong-foo] repeat

chuán [chwahn] ship, boat

chuáncāng [–tsahng] cabin

chuáng [chwahng] bed

chuángdān [–dahn] sheet

chuángdiàn [–dyen] mattress

chuānghu [–hoo] window

chuānkǒng [chwahn-koong] puncture

chuánrǎn [–rahn] infectious

chuántǒng [–toong] traditional

chuánzhēn [–jun] fax

chúfáng [choo-fahng] kitchen

chūkǒu [choo-koh] exit

chúle ... yǐwài [choo-lur ... yee-wai] except ..., apart from ...

chǔn silly

chūnjié [chun-jyeh] Chinese New Year

chūntian [chun-tyen] spring; in the spring

chúxī [choo-hshee] New Year's Eve

chǔxù [choo-hsyew] deposit

chūzū [choo-dzoo] hire, rent

chūzūchē diǎnr [–chur dyenr] taxi rank

chūzū qìchē [chee-chur] taxi

cí [tsur] word

cídài [tsur-dai] tape, cassette

cóng [tsoong] from

cōngcong hurriedly

cónglái bù never (referring to the past or present)

cōngming clever, intelligent

cūnzhuāng [tsun-jwahng] village

cuò(wù) [tswor(-woo)] mistake, error; fault

D

dà [dah] big, large

dǎ hit

dàbó [dah-bor] brother-in-law (husband's elder brother)

dà bùfen shíjian [dah boo-fun shur-jyen] most of the time

dǎcuòle [dah-tswor-lur] wrong number

dǎ diànhuà [dyen-hwah] phone, call

dàgài probably

dàhuì [dah-hway] conference

dáhuǒjī [dah-hwor-jee] cigarette lighter

dài take (something somewhere)

dàilái bring

dàilǐng yóujiàn [yoh-jyen] poste restante

dàitì instead

dàjíle [dah-jee-lur] enormous

dàlù main road

dàmǐ uncooked rice

dàn [dahn] weak; pale

dānchéngpiào [dahn-chung-pyow] single ticket, one-way ticket

dāndú alone

dāngrán [dahng-grahn] of course, certainly

dànián sānshí [dah-nyen sahn-shur] Chinese New Year's Eve

dānrén jiān [dahn-run jyen] single room

dānshēn [dahn-shun] single, unmarried

dànshì [dahn-shur] but

dānyuán [dahn-yew-ahn] flat, apartment

dǎo [dow] island

dāo knife

dào to; arrive

dào ... wéizhǐ [way-jur] until ...

dàodá [dow-dah] arrive

dàodá shíjiān [shur-jyen] arrival

dàotián [dow-tyen] paddy field, rice field

dǎoyóu [dow-yoh] tour guide

dāozi [dow-dzur] knife

dàrén [dah-run] adult

dàshēng de [dah-shung dur] loud

dàshíguǎn [dah-shur-gwahn] embassy

dàxióngmāo [hsyoong–mow] panda

dàxué [dah-hsyew-eh] university

dàyī [dah-yee] coat, overcoat

dàyuē [dah-yew-eh] roughly, approximately

dǎzhàng [dah-jahng] fight

de [dur] of (particle inserted

between adjective and noun to
denote possession)

dé get, obtain

de duō: ... de duō [dwor]
much more ...

Déguó [dur-gwor] Germany;
German (adj)

dēng [dung] light; lamp

děng wait

dēngjì [dung-jee] check-in

dēngjīkŏu [–koh] gate (at
airport)

dēngjī pái boarding pass

dēngpào [dung-pow] lightbulb

dì [dee] floor

dì èr tiān [tyen] the day after

dī low

diàn [dyen] electric; electricity

-diǎn hour; o'clock

diànchí [dyen-chur] battery

diànchuīfēng [dyen-chway-fung]
hairdryer

diàndòng tìxú dāo [dyen-doong
tee-hsyew dow] shaver

diàngōng [dyen-goong]
electrician

diànhuà [dyen-hwah] phone

diànhuà hàomă bù [how-mah]
phone book

diànhuàtíng phone box

diànnăo [dyen-now] computer

diǎnr [dyenr] a little bit

... diǎnr more ...

diànshì [dyen-shur] television

diàntī lift, elevator

diàntìdāo [dyen-tee-dow]
electric shaver

diànxiàn [dyen-hsyen] wire;
lead

diănxíng [dyen-hsing] typical

diànyā [dyen-yah] voltage

diànyĭng [dyen-ying] film,
movie

diànyĭng yuàn [yew-ahn]
cinema, movie theater

diànyuán chāzuò [dyen-yew-ahn
chah-dzwor] power point

diànzi [dyen-dzur] cushion

diàochuáng [dyow-chwahng] cot

dìbā [dee-bah] eighth

dìdi younger brother

dì'èr(ge) [–gur] second

diézi [dyeh-dzur] dish, bowl;
saucer

dìfāng [dee-fahng] place

dìjiŭ [dee-jyoh] ninth

dìliăng [dee-lyang] second

dìliù [dee-lyoh] sixth

dìnghūnle [–hun-lur] engaged
(to be married)

dĭngshang: zài dĭngshang [dzai
ding-shahng] at the top

dìngzuò [–dzwor] reserve

dìqī [dee-chee] seventh

dìqū [dee-chew] region

dĭr [deer] bottom

dìsān [dee-sahn] third

dìshang [dee-shahng] on the
ground

dìshí [dee-shur] tenth

dìsì [dee-sur] fourth

dísīkē [–kur] disco

dìtăn [dee-tahn] carpet

dìtiĕ [dee-tyeh] underground,
(US) subway

dìtiĕ zhàn [jahn] underground
station, subway station

dìtú [dee-too] map

diū [dyoh] lose

dìwǔ [dee-woo] fifth

dìyī first

dìzhǐ [dee-jur] address

dǒng: nǐ dǒngle? [doong-lur] do you understand?

wǒ bù dǒng [wor] I don't understand

dōng [doong] east

dòng hole; puncture

dōngběi [–bay] northeast

dōngbiān [–byen] in the east

dōngnán [–nahn] southeast

dǒngshì [–shur] director

dōngtian [–tyen] winter; in the winter

dòngwù [–woo] animal

dòngwùyuán [–yew-ahn] zoo

dōngxi [–hshee] thing (object)

dōu [doh] both, all

dǒu steep

dú [doo] read

duǎn [dwahn] short

duǎnkù shorts

duànle [–lur] broken

duǎnwà [–wah] sock

duì [dway] right, correct; towards; with regard to; queue; side

duìbuqǐ [dway-boo-chee] sorry, excuse me

duìfāng fùkuǎn [–fahng foo-kwahn] collect call

duìhuàn [dway-hwahn] change (verb: money)

duìhuànlǜ [–lyew] exchange rate

duìjíle! [–jee-lur] exactly!

duìle yes, that's it, that's right

duō [dwor] much; more than

duōde duō [–dur] a lot more

duōle: ... duōle [–lur] far more ...

duōshao? [dwor-show] how much?, how many? (if answer is likely to be more than ten)

duōxiè [–hsyeh] thank you very much

duō yíbèi [yee-bay] twice as much

duō yìdiǎnr [yee-dyenr] a bit more

duōyòng chātóu [–yoong chah-toh] adapter

dúpǐn [doo-pin] drugs, narcotics

dǔzhùle [doo-joo-lur] blocked

E

è [ur] hungry

Éguó [ur-gwor] Russia; Russian (adj)

èr two

èrbǎi two hundred

èr děng [dung] second class

ěrduo [er-dwor] ear

ěrhuán [er-hwahn] earring

ěr lóng [loong] deaf

èrlóu [er-loh] first floor, (US) second floor

èrshí [er-shur] twenty

értóng [er-toong] children

èrwàn [er-wahn] twenty thousand

érxí [er-hshee] daughter-in-law

èryuè [er-yew-eh] February

érzi [er-dzur] son

ěxīn [ur-hsin] disgusting; nausea

F

Fǎguó [fah-gwor] France; French (adj)

fán [fahn] bored

fàn meal

fàndiàn [fahn-dyen] large restaurant; luxury hotel

fǎng [fahng] imitation

fàng put

fāngbiàn [–byen] convenient

fángdǐng roof; ceiling

fángfǔjì [–foo-jee] antiseptic

fángjiān [–jyen] room

fànguǎnr [fahn-gwahnr] small restaurant

fāngxiàng [–hsyang] direction

fángzi [–dzur] building; house

fángzū [–dzoo] rent (noun)

fànwǎn [fahn-wahn] rice bowl

fānyì translate; translation; translator

fāshēng [fah-shung] happen

fēi [fay] fly (verb)

fēicháng [fay-chahng] very, extremely

fēijī [fay-jee] plane

  zuò fēijī [dzwor] by air

fēijīchǎng [–chahng] airport

fèixū [fay-hsyew] ruins

féizào [fay-dzow] soap

fēi zhèngshì [jung-shur] informal

fēn [fun] minute

fēng [fung] mad, insane; wind; measure word* used for letters

fēngjǐng [fung-jing] scenery; sights

fēngshàn [fung-shahn] fan (electrical)

fēngsú [fung-soo] custom

fěnhóng [fun-hoong] pink

fēnjī [fun-jee] extension

fēnkāi separate

fēnzhōng [fun-joong] minute

Fó [for] Buddha

Fójiào [for-jyow] Buddhism; Buddhist

fù(qián) [foo(-chyen)] pay

fūfù couple (two people)

fùjiāfèi [foo-jyah-fay] supplement, extra charge

fùjìn [foo-jin] nearby; near

fùmǔ parents

fùnǚ [foo-nyew] woman

fùqin [foo-chin] father

fūren [foo-run] Mrs

fúshǒu [foo-shoh] handle

fúwùtái reception

fúwùyuán [–yew-ahn] receptionist

fùzá [foo-zah] complicated

G

gàir [gai-r] lid

gālí [gah-lee] curry

gān [gahn] dry; liver

gǎn catch up

gānbēi! [gahn-bay] cheers!

gāngbǐ [gahng-bee] pen

gángkǒu [–koh] port, harbour

gānjìng [gahn-jing] clean

gǎnjué [gahn-jyew-eh] feel

gǎnmào [gahn-mow] cold (illness)

gánrǎn [gahn-rahn] infection

gāo [gow] high; tall

gāodiǎndiàn [–dyen] cake shop

gāomíng [gow-ming] brilliant

gāoxìng [gow-hsing] pleased, glad

  hěn gāoxìng jiàndào nǐ [hun – jyen dow] pleased to meet you

ge [gur] general all-purpose measure word*

gē song

gēbo [gur-bor] arm

gēbozhǒu [–joh] elbow

gēchàngjiā [gur-chahng-jyah] singer

gēge [gur-gur] elder brother

gěi [gay] give; for

gējù [gur-jyew] opera

gēn [gun] with

gèng: ... gèng [gung] even more ...

  gèng hǎo [how] better; even better

Gòngchándǎng [goong-chahn-dahng] Communist Party

Gòngchándǎngyuán [–yew-ahn] Communist Party member

gōngchǎng [–chahng] factory

gòngchánzhǔyì [–chahn-joo-yee] communism

gōngchǐ [–chur] metre

gōngdiàn [–dyen] palace

gōnggòng cèsuǒ [tsur-swor] public convenience

gōnggong pópo [por-por] wife's parents-in-law

gōnggòng qìchē [chee-chur] city bus

gōnggòng qìchē zhàn [jahn] bus stop

gōnggòng qìchē zǒngzhàn [dzoong-jahn] bus station

gōngjià [–jyah] public holiday

gōngjīn [–jin] kilogram

gōngli kilometre

gōnglù motorway, (US) highway, (US) freeway

gōngsī [–sur] company, business, firm

gōngxǐ! gōngxǐ! [–hshee] congratulations!

gōngyuán [–yew-ahn] park

gōngzuò [–dzwor] job; work

gǒu [goh] dog

gòu(le) [–lur] enough

guài [gwai] peculiar

guān [gwahn] close, shut

guàn jug

guángchǎng [gwahng-chahng] square

Guǎngdōng [–doong] Cantonese (adj)

Guǎngdōnghuà [–hwah] Cantonese (language)

Guǎngdōng rén [run] Cantonese (person)

guānkǒu [gwahn-koh] pass (in mountains)
guānle [–lur] closed
guānménle [–mun-lur] closed
guānshang le [shahng] off, switched off
guàntou [–toh] can, tin
guānyú [–yew] about, concerning
gúdǒng [goo-doong] antique
gūgu aunt (father's sister)
guì(le) [gway(-lur)] expensive
guìzi [gway-dzur] cupboard
-guo [gwor] verb suffix indicating a past experience
guóhuà [–hwah] Chinese painting
guójí [–jee] nationality
guójì [–jee] international
guójiā [–jyah] country, nation; national, state
guòle [–lur] beyond
guòmǐn allergic
guòqu [–chew] in the past
guòshí(de) [–shur(-dur)] old-fashioned
guówài abroad
guòyè [–yur] overnight
gútou [goo-toh] bone
gùyì deliberately
gǔzhé [gyew-jur] fracture

H

hǎi sea
hái still
hái hǎo ma? [how mah] are you OK?
hǎibiānr [hai-byenr] sea; seaside
hǎibīn coast
hǎiguān [hai-gwahn] Customs
háishi [hai-shur] or
hǎitān [hai-tahn] beach
hǎiwān [hai-wahn] bay
háizi [hai-dzur] child
hǎn [hahn] shout
hángbān [hahng-bahn] flight
hángbān hào [how] flight number
hángkōng [–koong] by airmail
hángkōng xìnfēng [hsin-fung] airmail envelope
Hànyǔ [hahn-yew] Chinese (spoken language)
hǎo [how] good; nice; all right, OK
hǎo, xièxie [hsyeh-hsyeh] yes, please
hǎochī [how-chur] delicious
háohuá [how-hwah] luxurious; posh
hǎojíle [how-jee-lur] great, wonderful, excellent
hǎokàn [how-kahn] attractive
hàomǎ [how-mah] number
hǎo yìdiǎnr [yee-dyenr] better
hé [hur] and; river
hé ... yìqǐ [yee-chee] together with ...
... hé ... dōu bù ... [doh boo] neither ... nor ...
hē drink (verb)
hēi [hay] black
hēi àn [ahn] dark
hélǐ [hur-lee] reasonable
hěn [hun] very

hěnduō [hun-dwor] a lot, lots; many

hěnkuài di [kwai] quickly

hézi [hur-dzur] box

hēzuìle [hur-dzway-lur] drunk

hóngsède [hoong-sur-dur] red

hóngshuǐ [–shway] flood

hòu [hoh] thick

hòulái later; later on

hóulóng [hoh-loong] throat

hòumian [hoh-myen] behind

　zài hòumian [dzai] at the back

　zài ... hòumian behind ...

hòutiān [hoh-tyen] the day after tomorrow

hú lake

huā [hwah] flower

huà picture, painting

huāfèi [hwah-fay] spend

huài [hwai] bad

huàile [hwai-lur] broken

huáiyùn [hwai-yewn] pregnant

huáji [hwah-jee] funny

huàjù [hwah-jew] play (in theatre)

huáng [hwahng] yellow

huángdì emperor

huángfēng [–fung] wasp

huángjīn gold

huángsè [–sur] yellow

huānyíng dào ... [hwahn-ying dow] welcome to ...

huāpíng [hwah-ping] vase

huàr [hwar] painting, picture

huàxiàng [hwah-hsyang] portrait

huāyuán [hwah-yew-ahn] garden

huì [hway] meeting,

conference

huílai come back

huīsède [hway-sur-dur] grey

huítóujiàn [hway-toh-jyen] see you later

huìyì [hway-yee] meeting, conference

hūnlǐ [hun-lee] wedding

huǒ [hwor] fire

huǒchái [hwor-chai] matches

huòchē [hwor-chur] van

huǒchē train

　zuò huǒchē [dzwor] by train

huǒchēzhàn [–jahn] railway station

huǒzāi [hwor-dzai] fire

huòzhe ... huòzhe ... [hwor-jur] either ... or ...

huòzhě or

hùshi [hoo-shur] nurse

hútòng [hoo-toong] lane; side street

hùzhào [hoo-jow] passport

húzi [hoo-dzur] beard

J

jì [jee] post, mail (verb)

jǐ few

jiā [jyah] home

　zài jiā [dzai] at home

jiàgé [jyah-gur] price

jiǎn [jyen] cut

jiàn measure word* used for things, affairs etc

Jiānádà [jyah-nah-dah] Canada; Canadian (adj)

jiānbǎng [jyen-bahng] shoulder

jiǎndān [jyen-dahn] simple, easy

jiāng [jyang] river

jiǎng speak

jiānglái future; in future

jiànkāng [jyen-kahng] healthy

jiànzhù [jyen-joo] building

jiǎnzi [jyen-dzur] scissors

jiǎo [jyow] foot (of person)

jiào call, greet

jiāochākǒu [jyow-chah-koh] junction

jiáodǐ sole (of foot)

jiǎo gēn [gun] heel (of foot)

jiāojuǎnr [jyow-jew-ahnr] film (for camera)

jiāoqū [jyow-chew] suburb

jiāoqūchē [–chur] bus (in suburbs)

jiàotáng [jyow-tahng] church

jiāotōng tú [jyow-toong] streetmap

jiāoyì huì [jyow-yee hway] exhibition, trade fair

jiáozhǐtou [jyow-jur-toh] toe

jiàqī [jyah-chee] holiday, vacation

jiàqián [jyah-chyen] cost (noun)

jiātíng family

jiǎyá [jyah-yah] dentures

jiāyóu zhàn [jyah-yoh jahn] petrol station, gas station

jiàzhí [jyah-jur] value

jiàzi [jyah-dzur] shelf

jíbìng illness, disease

jīchǎng bānchē [jee-chahng bahn-chur] airport bus

jiē(dào) [jyeh(-dow)] avenue; street

jiè [jyeh] borrow

jiěfū [jyeh-foo] brother-in-law (elder sister's husband)

jiéhūn [jyeh-hun] married

nǐ jiéhūnle ma? [jyeh-hun-lur mah] are you married?

jiějie [jyeh-jyeh] elder sister

jiémùdānr [jyeh-moo-dahnr] programme

jiérì [jyeh-rur] festival; holiday

jiēshi [jyeh-shur] strong

jièzhi [jyeh-jur] ring (on finger)

jīfèi diànhuà [jee-fay dyen-hwah] payphone

jǐge [jee-gur] several

jǐge? how much?, how many? (if answer is likely to be ten or fewer)

jíjiù [jee-jyoh] first aid

jíjiùxiāng [–hsyang] first-aid kit

jìn [jin] near

jǐngchá [jing-chah] police; policeman

jīngcháng [jing-chahng] often, frequent

jīngguò [jing-gwor] through; via

jīnglǐ manager

jǐngr view

jīngrén de [jing-run dur] astonishing

jìngzi [jing-dzur] mirror

jīnhuángsè [jin-hwahng-sur] blond

jìniànbēi [jee-nyen-bay] monument

jìniànpǐn [jee-nyen-pin] souvenir

jǐnjí(de) [–dur] urgent

jǐnjin just, only

jīnshǔ metal

jīntian [jin-tyen] today

jīntiān wǎnshang
[wahn-shahng] tonight
jìntóu [jin-toh] end (of street etc)
jīnwǎn [jin-wahn] tonight
jīnzi [jin-dzur] gold
jīqì [jee-chee] machine
jìshi ... yě [jee-shur ... yur] even
if ...
jìsuànjī [jee-swahn-jee]
computer
jiǔ [jyoh] nine; alcohol;
alcoholic drink
jiù just; then; secondhand
jiù yìdiǎnr [yee-dyenr] just a
little
jiù yíhuǐr [yee-hwayr] just a
minute
jiúbǎi nine hundred
jiǔbājiān [jyoh-bah-jyen] bar
jiùde [jyoh-dur] secondhand
jiùhùchē [jyoh-hoo-chur]
ambulance
jiùjiu uncle (mother's brother)
jiǔshí [jyoh-shur] ninety
jiǔyuè [jyoh-yew-eh]
September
juǎnqūde [jwahn-chew-dur]
curly
jué búhuì [jew-eh boo-hway]
never (referring to the future)
juéde [–dur] feel
juédìng decide; decision
juéduì bàng [–dway bahng]
perfect
juéduìde! [–dur] absolutely!
júhuángsè [jyew-hwahng-sur]
orange (colour)
jùlí [joo-lee] distance
jùyuàn [jyew-yew-ahn] theatre

K

kǎchē [kah-chur] lorry, truck
kāfēi diàn [kah-fay dyen] café
kāfēiguǎnr [–gwahnr] café
kāi open (adj)
kāichē [kai-chur] drive
kāide [kai-dur] open (adj)
kāile [kai-lur] open (adj)
kāishǐ [kai-shur] begin; start;
beginning
yì kāishǐ at the beginning
kāishuǐ [kai-shway] boiled
water
kànbào [kahn-bow] read
(newspaper)
kàngjūnsù [kahng-jyewn-soo]
antibiotics
kànjian [kahn-jyen] see
kànshū [kahn-shoo] read (book)
kànyikàn [kahn-yee-kahn] have a
look
kào [kow] near
kǎoshì [kow-shur] exam
kǎoxiāng [kow-hsyang] oven
kè [kur] lesson; gram(me)
kē measure word* used for
trees etc
kěài lovely
kěnéng [kur-nung] maybe,
perhaps; possible
kěpà [kur-pah] horrible
kèqi [kur-chee] polite
kèrén [kur-run] guest
kěshì [kur-shur] but
késou [kur-soh] cough
kètīng lounge
kěyǐ [kur-yee] be able

kéyi qǐng [ching] yes please
nín kéyi ... ma? [mah] could you ...?
kōng [koong] empty
kōngjiān [–jyen] room, space
kōngqì [–chee] air
kōngtiáo [–tyow] air-conditioning
kóukě [koh-kur] thirsty
kǔ [koo] bitter
kū cry
kuài [kwai] quick, fast; sharp; soon; measure word* used for lumps or pieces
kuài chē [chur] express (train)
kuàidì express (mail)
kuài diǎnr! [dyenr] hurry up!
kuàilè [kwai-lur] happy
kuàir [kwai-r] piece
kuàizi [kwai-dzur] chopsticks
kuān de [kwahn dur] wide
kuāng [kwahng] basket
kuánghuānjié [–hwahn-jyeh] carnival
kùchǎ [koo-chah] underpants, men's underwear
kūnchóng [kun-choong] insect
kùnle [kun-lur] sleepy
kùnnan [kun-nahn] difficult; difficulty
kùzi [koo-dzur] trousers, (US) pants

L

là [lah] hot, spicy
lā pull
lái come, arrive

láide: nǐ shì cóng nǎr láide? [shur tsoong nar lai-dur] where do you come from?
láihuí piào [lai-hway pyow] return/round-trip ticket
lājī [lah-jee] rubbish, trash
lājīxiāng [–hsyang] dustbin, trashcan
lán [lahn] blue
lǎn lazy
lánzi [lahn-dzur] basket
lǎo [low] old
lǎolao grandmother (maternal)
lǎoniánren [low-nyen-run] senior citizen
lǎoshī [low-shur] teacher
lǎoshǔ [low-shoo] rat; mouse
Lǎowō [low-wor] Laos
lǎoye [low-yeh] grandfather (maternal)
làzhú [lah-joo] candle
le [lur] sentence particle indicating something in the past which is still relevant to the present or a change of circumstances in the present or future
-le [-lur] verb suffix indicating completion of action
lèi [lay] tired
léiyǔ [lay-yew] thunderstorm
lěng [lung] cold
li: zài ... li [dzai ... lee] inside ...
lí [lee] from; to; pear
-lǐ inside
liǎn [lyen] face
liǎng [lyang] two
liàng measure word* used for vehicles

liǎngcì [–tsur] twice

liǎngge dānrénchuáng [–gur dahn-run-chwahng] twin beds

liǎngge dōu [dow] both

liǎngge dōu bù [doh] neither (one) of them

liǎngge xīngqī [hsing-chee] fortnight

liángkuai [–kwai] cool

liángxié [–hsyeh] sandal

liánkùwà [lyen-koo-wah] tights, pantyhose

liánxi [lyen-hshee] contact

liányīqún [lyen-yee-chewn] dress

liányùn [lyen-yewn] connection

liǎobuqǐ [lyow-boo-chee] incredible, amazing

lièchē shíkè biǎo [lyeh-chur shur-kur byow] timetable, (US) schedule

lièzhì [lyeh-jur] poor

lǐfà [lee-fah] haircut

lǐfàdiàn [–dyen] hairdresser's; barber's

lǐfàshī [–shur] hairdresser's

líhūn [lee-hun] divorced

límǐ centimetre

límíng dawn

líng zero

lǐng take (someone somewhere)

lǐng tie, necktie

língqián [ling-chyen] change (noun: money)

lìngrén yúkuài [ling-run yew-kwai] pleasant

lǐngshìguǎn [ling-shur-gwahn] consulate

lìngwài another, different

lǐng yánglǎojīn de rén [–low-jin dur run] pensioner

lìng yíge [yee-gur] another, different; the other one

línyù [lin-yew] shower

dài línyù with shower

lìrú for example

liù [lyoh] six

liùbǎi six hundred

liúgǎn [lyoh-gahn] flu

liúlì fluent

liùshí [lyoh-shur] sixty

liúxíng [lyoh-hsing] popular, fashionable

liúxíngxìng gǎnmào [gahn-mow] flu

liúxíng yīnyuè [yin-yew-eh] pop music

liùyuè [lyoh-yew-eh] June

lǐwù [lee-woo] present, gift

lìzi [lee-dzur] example; chestnut

lóng [loong] dragon

lóu [loh] floor, storey; building (with more than one storey)

lóushàng [loh-shahng] upstairs

lóutī [loh-tee] stairs

lóuxià [loh-hsyah] downstairs

lǚxíng [lyew-hsing] travel; tour; journey

lǚxíngshè [–shur] travel agent's

lǚxíngzhě [–jur] tourist

lǚxíng zhīpiào [jur-pyow] traveller's cheque

lǚyóuchē [lyew-yoh-chur] tourist bus, coach

lǚyóuzhě [lyew-joh-jur] tourist

lǚguǎn [lyew-gwahn] small hotel

lǜsède [lyew-sur-dur] green
lù road; way
lúntāi tyre
lúnzi [lun-dzur] wheel
lùtiān [loo-tyen] outdoors
lùxiàn [loo-hsyen] route
lùxiàngdài [loo-hsyang-dai]
 video tape
lúzào [loo-dzow] cooker

M

ma? [mah] question particle
mā mother
mǎ horse
mà scold
máfan [mah-fahn] trouble
mǎi buy
mài sell
mǎimài business deal
mǎn [mahn] full
màn slow; slowly
 hěn màn [hun] very slowly
 màn diǎnr! [dyenr] slow
 down!
mángmang [mahng–] busy
māo [mow] cat
máobèixīn [mow-bay-hsin]
 pullover
máojīn towel
màopáirhuò [mow-pai-r-hwor]
 fake
máotǎn [mow-tahn] blanket
máoyī sweater
 màozi [mow-dzur] hat, cap
mǎshàng [mah-shahng] at once,
 immediately
mǎtóu [mah-toh] jetty

Máo zhǔxí [mow jyew-hshee]
 Chairman Mao
měi [may] each, every;
 beautiful
méi not; does not; no; have
 not
mèifū [may-foo]
 brother-in-law (younger sister's
 husband)
méi ...-guò [-gwor] has never;
 have never
měige [may-gur] every
měige dìfāng [dee-fahng]
 everywhere
měige rén [run] everyone
méi guānxi [gwahn-hshee]
 never mind, it doesn't matter
Měiguó [may-gwor] America;
 American (adj)
měijiàn shìqíng [may-jyen
 shur-ching] everything
měijiàn shìr [shur] everything
méi jìnr boring
měilì beautiful
mèimei younger sister
méiqì [may-chee] gas
měirén [may-run] everybody
méishìr le [may-shur lur] safe
měishùguǎn [may-shoo-gwahn]
 art gallery
měitiān [may-tyen] every day
méi wǎnshang [wahn-shahng]
 per night
méi wèntí! [wun-tee] no
 problem!
méixiǎngdào [may-hsyang-dow]
 amazing, surprising
měiyíge [may-yee-gur] each,
 every

měiyíge rén [run] everyone

méiyǒu [may-yoh] did not; has not, have not; without

méi ...-zhe [-zhur] was not ...-ing; is not ...-ing

-men suffix indicating the plural

mén [mun] door

Ménggǔ [mung-goo] Mongolia; Mongolian (adj)

mǐ metre; uncooked rice

Miǎndiàn [myen-dyen] Burma; Burmese (adj)

miǎn fèi [fay] free (no charge)

miánhuā [myen-hwah] cotton

miǎnshuì [myen-shway] duty-free goods

miǎo [myow] second (of time)

míngbai: wǒ míngba le [wor – lur] I see, I understand

míngpiàn [ming-pyen] card

míngtian [ming-tyen] tomorrow

míngtian zǎoshang [dzow-shahng] tomorrow morning

míngxìnpiàn [ming-hsin-pyen] postcard

míngzi [ming-dzur] name; first name

mòduān [mor-dwahn] end

mótuōchē [mor-twor-chur] motorbike

mǒudì [moh-dee] somewhere

mùdì cemetery

mùdìdì destination

mùjiān xiūxi [moo-jyen hsyoh-hshee] interval

mǔqīn [moo-chin] mother

mùtou [moo-toh] wood

N

ná [nah] carry; take

nà that; that one; the

nǎinai grandmother (paternal)

nǎiniú [nai-nyoh] cow

nǎli? [nah-lee] where?

nán [nahn] south; hard, difficult; man

nán cèsuǒ [tsur-swor] gents' toilet, men's room

nánfāng [nahn-fahng] in the south

Nánfēi [nahn-fay] South Africa; South African (adj)

nán fúwùyuán [foo-woo-yew-ahn] waiter; steward

nánguò [nahn-gwor] sad

nánhái boy

nánkàn [nahn-kahn] ugly

nán péngyou [pung-yoh] boyfriend

nánrén [nahn-run] man

nǎr? where?

zài nǎr? [dzai] where is it?

nǐ qù nǎr? [chew] where are you going?

nàr there

nà shí [nah shur] then, at that time

nà shì ... ma? [mah] is that ...?

nà shì shénme? [shun-mur]

what's that?

názhe [nah-jur] keep

ne [nur] sentence particle which adds emphasis or conveys the idea 'and what about ...?'

nèi [nay] that; that one

nèi? [nay] which?

nèidì brother-in-law (wife's younger brother)

nèige [nay-gur] that; that one

nèige shíhou [shur-hoh] then, at that time

nèixiōng [nay-hsyoong] brother-in-law (wife's elder brother)

nèi yíge [yee-gur] that one

néng: nǐ néng ... ma? [nung ... mah] can you ...?

wǒ bù néng ... [wor] I can't ...

nǐ you (sing)

niàn [nyen] read (aloud)

nián year

niánji [nyen-jee] age

nín duō dà niánji le? [dwor dah nyen-jee lur] how old are you?

niánlíng: nín duō dà niánlíng? [nyen-ling] how old are you?

niánqīng [nyen-ching] young

niǎo [nyow] bird

niàobù [nyow-boo] nappy, diaper

Níbóěr [nee-bor-er] Nepal; Nepali (adj)

nǐde [nee-dur] your; yours (sing)

nǐ hǎo [nee how] hello; hi; how do you do?

nǐ hǎo ma? [mah] how are you?

nǐmen [nee-mun] you (pl)

nǐmende [–dur] your; yours (pl)

nín you (sing, pol)

nínde [nin-dur] your; yours (sing, pol)

niúzǎikù [nyoh-dzai-koo] jeans

nóng [noong] strong

nóngchǎng [–chahng] farm

nóngcūn [–tsun] countryside

nǚ'ér [nyew-er] daughter

nǚ cèsuǒ [tsur-swor] ladies' room, ladies' toilets

nǚ chènshān [nyew-chun-shahn] blouse

nǚ fúwùyuán [foo-woo-yew-ahn] waitress; maid; stewardess

nǚ háir [hai-r] girl

nǚpéngyou [nyew-pung-yoh] girlfriend

nǚshì [nyew-shur] Ms; lady

nǚzhāodài [nyew-jow-dai] waitress

nuǎnhuo [nwahn-hwor] warm; mild

nuǎnqì [nwahn-chee] heating; central heating; radiator

O

Ōuzhōu [oh-joh] Europe; European (adj)

P

pàichūsuǒ [pai-choo-swor] police station

pán [pahn] measure word★

used for round objects

pàng [pahng] fat

páng side

pángbiān: zài ... pángbiān
[dzai ... pahng-byen] beside
the ..., next to ...

pánzi [pahn-dzur] plate

păo [pow] run

péngchē [pung-chur] van

pèngtóu dìdiăn [pung-toh
dee-dyen] meeting place

péngyou [pung-yoh] friend

pēnquán [pun-choo-en]
fountain

piányi [pyen-yee] be
inexpensive; inexpensive

piào [pyow] ticket; single
ticket, one-way ticket

piàoliang [pyow-lyang]
beautiful; pretty

pífu skin

pígé [pee-gur] leather

píng'ān [ping-ahn] safe

píngcháng [ping-chahng] usual,
normal

pīngpāngqiú [ping-pahng-chyoh]
table tennis

píngtăn [ping-tahn] flat (adj)

píngzi [ping-dzur] bottle

pŭtōng [poo-toong] ordinary

Pŭtōnghuà [–hwah] Mandarin

Q

qī [chee] seven

qián [chyen] money

qiánbāo [–bow] wallet; purse

qiānbĭ pencil

qiánbianr: zài qiánbianr [dzai
chyen-byenr] in front; at the
front

qiáng [chyang] wall

qiángjiān [–jyen] rape

qiăngle [–lur] robbed

qiánmiàn [chyen-myen] front

qiántiān [–tyen] the day before
yesterday

qiántīng lobby

qiānwàn [–wahn] ten million

qiánxiōng [–hsyoong] breast;
bust; chest

qián yì tiān [tyen] the day
before

qiānzhèng [–jung] visa

qiānzì [–dzur] signature

qiáo [chyow] bridge

qiăokèlì [–kur-lee] chocolate

qiāozhúgàng [–joo-gahng]
rip-off

qībăi [chee-bai] seven hundred

qìchē [chee-chur] car

zuò qìchē [dzwor] by car

qìchē chūzū [choo-dzoo] car
rental

qìchē zŏngzhàn [dzoong-jahn]
bus station (for city buses)

qìchē xiūlíchăng [hsyoh-
lur-chahng] garage (for repairs)

qĭchuáng [chee-chwahng] get
up (in the morning)

qiè [chyeh] cut

qĭfēi shíjiān [chee-fay shee-jyen]
departure

qíguài(de) [chee-gwai(-dur)]
weird, strange, odd

qí mă [chee mah] horse riding

qīng [ching] light (not heavy)

qǐng please; ask, request
qīngdàn [–dahn] mild
qǐng jìn come in
qīngshàonián [–show-nyen] teenager
qīngxīn [–hsin] fresh
qióng [chyoong] poor
qīshí [chee-shur] seventy
qítā [chee-tah] other
qìtǐng [chee-ting] motorboat
qiú [chyoh] ball
qiúmí sports fan
qiúpāi racket (tennis, squash)
qiūtiān [chyoh-tyen] autumn, (US) fall; in the autumn/fall
qìxiè [chee-hsyeh] equipment
qìyóu [chee-yoh] petrol, (US) gas
qīyuè [chee-yew-eh] July
qīzi [chee-dzur] wife
qí zìxíngchē de rén [chee dzur-sing-chur dur run] cyclist
qù [chew] go; to
qǔ get, fetch
quánbù [choo-en-boo] all; all of it, the whole lot
quánguó [–gwor] national, nationwide
qùnián [chew-nyen] last year
qúnzi [chewn-dzur] skirt

R

ránhòu [rahn-hoh] then, after that
rè [rur] hot; heat
rèdù [rur-doo] temperature; fever
rèle [rur-lur] hot
rén [run] person
  wǒ shì ... rén [wor shur] I come from ...
rènao [rur-now] busy, lively
rēng [rung] throw
rènhé [run-hur] any
rènhé rén anybody
rènhé shénme [shun-mur] anything
rénkǒu [run-koh] population
rénmín people
rénqún [run-chewn] crowd
rènshi [run-shur] know; recognize
rénxíng dào [run-hsing dow] pavement, sidewalk
rénxíng héngdào [hung-dow] pedestrian crossing
rèshuǐpíng [rur-shway-ping] Thermos® flask
Rìběn [ree-bun] Japan
rìjì [rur-jee] diary
róngyì [roong-yee] easy
ròu [roh] meat
ruǎn [rwahn] soft
ruǎnpán [–pahn] disk
ruǎnwò [–wor] soft sleeper, first class sleeper
ruǎnzuò [–dzwor] soft seat, first class seat
rúguǒ [roo-gwor] if
Ruìdiǎn [rway-dyen] Sweden
rùkǒu [roo-koh] entrance
ruò [rwor] weak

RU

235

S

sāi cheek
sāizi [sai-dzur] plug (in sink)
sān [sahn] three
sānbǎi three hundred
sānděng [sahn-dung] third class
sāngzi [sahng-dzur] Thursday
sānjiǎokù [sahn-jyow-koo] pants, panties
sānshí [sahn-shur] thirty
sānyuè [sahn-yew-eh] March
sēnlín [sun-lin] forest
shā [shah] sand; kill
shāfā [shah-fah] sofa
shǎguā [shah-gwah] idiot
shàiyīshéng [shai-yee-shung] clothes line
shān [shahn] mountain, hill
shāndòng [–doong] cave
shàng [shahng] up; above
zài ...-shàng [dzai] above ...
shàngdì God
shāngdiàn [–dyen] shop
shàngmian: zài ... shàngmian [dzai –myen] on ...
shàngtou: zài ... shàngtou [–toh] on top of ...
shāngǔ [shahn-goo] valley
shǎnguāngdēng [shahn-gwahng-dung] flash (for camera)
shàngwǔ a.m. (from 9 a.m. to noon)
shāngxīn [–hsin] sad
shàng xīngqī [hsing-chee] last week
shàngyī jacket

shàng yícì [yee-tsur] last time
shànzi [shahn-dzur] fan (hand-held)
shǎo [show] less
shāoshāng [show-shahng] burn (noun)
shǎoshù mínzú [show-shoo mind-zoo] nationality (for Chinese minorities)
shǎoyú [show-yew] under, less than
sháozi [show-dzur] spoon
shēchǐ [shur-chur] luxury
shéi? [shay] who?
shéide? [shay-dur] whose?
shēn [shun] deep
shēng [shung] be born; litre
shēng bìngle [shung bing-lur] ill
shèngdàn jié [–dahn jyeh] Christmas
shēngqì [–chee] angry
shēngrén [–run] stranger
shēngrì [–rur] birthday
shēngyi business
shēngyīn voice
shéngzi [–dzur] string; rope
shénjīngbìng [shun-jing-bing] crazy
shénkān [shun-kahn] shrine
shénme [shun-mur] anything; something
shénme? what?
shénme shíhòu? [shur-hoh] when?
shénme yàng de ...? [dur] what sort of ...?
nǐ shuō shénme? [shwor] sorry?, pardon (me)?

shénme yě méiyǒu [yur may-yoh] none

shēntǐ [shun-tee] body

shèshì [shur-shur] centigrade

shì [shur] to be; is; are; was; were; will be; it is; it was; yes, it is the case

  shì ... ma? [mah] is it ...?

shí ten

shī wet

shíbā [shur-bah] eighteen

shìchǎng [shur-chahng] market

shìde [shur-dur] yes, it is the case

shíèr [shur-er] twelve

shíèr yuè [yew-eh] December

shìgù [shur-goo] accident

shíhou: zài ... de shíhou [dzai ... dur shur-hoh] during ...

shíjiān [shur-jyen] time

shíjiānbiǎo [–byow] timetable, (US) schedule

shìjiè [shur-jyeh] world

shíjiǔ [shur-jyoh] nineteen

shíliù [shur-lyoh] sixteen

shímáo [shur-mow] fashionable

shìnèi [shur-nay] indoors; indoor

shípǐn diàn [shur-pin dyen] food store

shíqī [shur-chee] seventeen; period (of time)

shìqūchē [shur-chew-chur] city bus

shìr [shur] thing, matter

shísān [shur-sahn] thirteen

shísì [shur-sur] fourteen

shíwàn [shur-wahn] hundred thousand

shíwù [shur-woo] food

shíwǔ fifteen

shíwù zhòngdú [joong-doo] food poisoning

shíyī [shur-yee] eleven

shíyīyuè [shur-yee-yew-eh] November

shíyuè [shur-yew-eh] October

shìzhèngfǔ dàlóu [shur-jung-foo dah-loh] town hall

shì zhōngxīn [shur joong-sin] city centre

shízì lùkǒu [shur-dzur loo-koh] crossroads, intersection

shǒu [shoh] hand

shòu thin

shòu huānyíng [hwahn-ying] popular

shòuhuòtíng [shoh-hwor-ting] kiosk

shōujù [shoh-jyew] receipt

shǒujuànr [shoh-jwahnr] handkerchief

shòupiàochù [shoh-pyow-choo] ticket office; box office

shòushāng [shoh-shahng] injured

shǒushi [shoh-shur] jewellery

shǒushù operation

shǒutào [shoh-tow] glove

shǒutíbāo [shoh-tee-bow] handbag, (US) purse

shǒutíxiāng [shoh-tee-hsyang] suitcase

shǒutí xíngli [shoh-tee hsing-lee] hand luggage

shǒuwànr [shoh-wahnr] wrist

shǒuxiān [shoh-hsyen] at first

shōuyīnjī [shoh-yin-jee] radio

shóuzhǐ [shoh-jur] toilet paper;
  finger
shǒu zhítou [jur-toh] finger
shǒuzhuó [shoh-jwor] bracelet
shū [shoo] book
shú ripe
shù tree
shuāng [shwahng] double
shuāngrén chuáng [–run
  chwahng] double bed
shuāngrén fángjiān [fahng-jyen]
  double room
shūdiàn [shoo-dyen] bookshop,
  bookstore
shūfu well; comfortable
shuǐ [shway] water
shuǐchí [–chur] sink;
  swimming pool
shuǐguǎnr [–gwahnr] pipe
shuǐguǒ [–gwor] fruit
shuìjiào [–jyow] sleep; asleep
shuǐlóng tóu [–loong toh] tap,
  faucet
shuìqún [–chewn] nightdress
shuìyī pyjamas
shùlín woods, forest
shuō [shwor] say
shuōhuà [–hwah] talk
shuōmíngshū leaflet; brochure
shūshu uncle (father's younger
  brother)
shùzì [shoo-dzur] number
sǐ [sur] die; dead
sì four; Buddhist temple
sìbǎi four hundred
sīchóu [sur-choh] silk
sì fēn zhī yī [fun jur] quarter
sījī [sur-jee] driver
sǐle [sur-lur] dead

sīrén(de) [sur-run(-dur)] private
sìshí [sur-shur] forty
sǐwáng [sur-wahng] death
sìyuàn [sur-yew-ahn] Buddhist
  monastery
sìyuè [sur-yew-eh] April
sòng [soong] deliver; send
sòng fàn fúwù [fahn foo-woo]
  room service
sòngxìn delivery (of mail)
suān [swahn] be sour; sour
suānténg [–tung] ache
Sūgélán [soo-gur-lahn]
  Scotland; Scottish
suíbiàn [sway-byen] informal
suídào [sway-dow] tunnel
suīrán [sway-rahn] although
sùliào [soo-lyow] plastic
sùliàodài plastic bag
sūnnǚr [sun-nyewr]
  granddaughter (son's daughter)
sūnzi [sun-dzur] grandson (son's
  son)
suǒ [swor] lock; locked;
  measure word* used for
  buildings
suóyǒu de dōngxi [swor-yoh dur
  doong-hshee] everything
sùshǎir de [soo-shai-r dur] plain,
  not patterned
sùxiàng [soo-hsyang] statue

T

tā [tah] he; she; it; him;
  her
tǎ pagoda
tāde [tah-dur] his; her; hers; its

tài too (excessively)
  tài duō [dwor] too much
Tàiguó [tai-gwor] Thailand
tàihǎole [tai-how-lur] fantastic;
  well done
tài shòu [tai shoh] skinny
tàiyáng sun
tàiyángjìng sunglasses
tāmen [tah-mun] they; them
  tāmen quánbù [choo-en-boo]
  all of them
tāmende [tah-mun-dur] their;
  theirs
tān [tahn] greedy
tángdì [tahng-dee] cousin (son
  of father's brother)
tángjiě [–jyeh] cousin (daughter
  of father's brother)
tángkuàir [–kwai-r] sweets,
  candies
tángmèi [–may] cousin
  (daughter of father's brother)
tángniàobìng [–nyow-bing]
  diabetic
tángxiōng [–hsyoong] cousin
  (son of father's brother)
tǎnzi [tahn-dzur] blanket
táoqì [tow-chee] pottery
tàoshān [tow-shahn] jumper
tàozhuāng [tow-jwahng] suit
tèbié [tur-byeh] especially
téng [tung] pain, ache; painful
tiān [tyen] day; sky
tián sweet (taste)
tiándì field
tiānqi [tyen-chee] weather
tiáo [tyow] measure word★
  used for fish and long
  narrow objects

tiàowǔ [tyow-woo] dance
tiàozǎo [tyow-dzow] flea
tiělù [tyeh-loo] railway
tíng stop
tíngchē [–chur] park
tíngchēchǎng [–chahng] car
  park, parking lot; garage
tíngdiàn [–dyen] power cut
tíngzi [–dzur] pavilion
tíqián [tee-chyen] in advance
tìxūdāo [tee-hsyew-dow] razor
tǐyùguǎn [tee-yoo-gwahn] gym
tǒng [tonng] bucket
tóngyì agree
tóu [toh] head
tōu steal
tóufa [toh-fah] hair
tóujīn headscarf
tòumíng jiāobù [jyow-boo]
  Sellotape®, Scotch tape®
tóuténg [toh-tung] headache
tóuyūn [toh-yewn] dizzy, faint
tú'àn [too-ahn] pattern
tuán [twahn] group
tuántǐ [twahn-tee] party, group
tuì [tway] cancel
tuǐ leg
tuī push
tuìkuǎn [tway-kwahn] refund
túpiàn [too-pyen] picture
tūrán [too-rahn] suddenly

W

-wài outside
wàigōng [wai-goong]
  grandfather (maternal)
wàiguó [wai-gwor] foreign

wàiguó rén [run] foreigner

wàimian [wai-myen] outside

wàipó [wai-por] grandmother (maternal)

wàisūn [wai-sun] grandson (daughter's son)

wàisūnnǚr [–nyewr] granddaughter (daughter's daughter)

wài sūnzi [sun-dzur] grandson (daughter's son)

wàitào [wai-tow] jacket

wàiyī jacket; coat

wǎn'ān [wahn-ahn] good night

wǎn [wahn] late (at night)

wàn ten thousand

wǎncān [wahn-tsahn] dinner

wǎndiǎn [wahn-dyen] delay

wǎnfàn [wahn-fahn] evening meal; supper

wàng [wahng] forget

wǎng towards; net (in sport)

wǎnhuì [wahn-hway] party (celebration)

wánjù [wahn-jyew] toy

wánquándi [wahn-choo-en-dee] completely

wánr [wahnr] play (verb)

wǎnshang [wahn-shahng] evening; in the evening

jīntiān wǎnshang [jin-tyen] this evening

wánxiào [wahn-hsyow] joke

Wēi'ěrshì [way-er-shur] Welsh

wéi [way] hello

wèi because of; stomach; measure word* used politely to refer to ladies, gentlemen, guests etc

wèidao [way-dow] flavour

Wēiěrshì [way-er-shur] Wales

wèihūnfū fiancé

wèihūnqī [–chee] fiancée

wéijīn [way-jin] scarf

wèir [wayr] taste; smell

wèishēngjīn [way-shung-jin] sanitary napkin/towel

wèishēngzhǐ [way-shung-jur] toilet paper

wèishénme? [way-shun-mur] why?

wèishénme bù? why not?

wēixiǎn [way-hsyen] dangerous

wèn [wun] ask (a question)

wénhuà dà gémìng [wun-hwah dah gur-ming] Cultural Revolution

wénjiàn [wun-jyen] document

wèntí [wun-tee] problem, question

wènxùnchù [wun-hsyewn-choo] information desk

wénzhàng [wun-jahng] mosquito net

wénzi [wun-dzur] mosquito

wǒ [wor] I; me

wǒde [wor-dur] my; mine

wǒmen [wor-mun] we; us

wǒmende [–dur] our; ours

wòpù [wor-poo] couchette; sleeper; berth

wòpù chēxiāng [chur-hsyang] sleeping car

wòshì [wor-shur] bedroom

wǔ [woo] five

wù mist; fog

wǔbǎi five hundred

wǔfàn [woo-fahn] lunch

wùhuì [woo-hway]
misunderstanding
wūjiǎor [woo-jyowr] in the
corner of a room
wǔshí [woo-shur] fifty
wǔshù [woo-shoo] martial arts
wǔyuè [woo-yew-eh] May

X

xǐ [hshee] wash
xī west
xiā [hsyah] blind
xià down; below
  xià yícì [yee-tsur] next time
  xià yíge [yee-gur] next
  xià xīngqī [hsing-chee] next
  week
  zài ...-xià [dzai] under ...
xiàba [–bah] jaw, chin
xià chē [–chur] get out
xiàge [–gur] next
xiàmian: zài ... xiàmian
  [dzai –myen] below ...
xiàn [hsyen] line; thread
xiān: nǐ xiān qǐng [ching] after
  you
xiàndài modern
xiǎng want; think
xiāngdāng [–dahng] quite,
  fairly
  xiāngdāng duō [dwor] quite a
  lot
xiàngdǎo [–dow] guide
Xiānggǎng [–gahng] Hong
  Kong
xiàngjiāo [–jyow] rubber
xiāngjìn de [dur] similar

xiàngliàn [–lyen] necklace
xiàngpí rubber, eraser
xiàngqí [–chee] chess
xiāngshuǐr [–shwayr] perfume
xiāngxìn [–hsin] believe
xiāngyān [–yahn] cigarette
xiànqián [hsyen-chyen] cash
xiānsheng [hsyen-shung] Mr
xiānyàn [–yen] bright
xiànzài [–dzai] now
xiào [hsyow] laugh; smile
xiǎo little, small; tight
xiǎofángduì [–fahng-dway] fire
  brigade
xiǎofèi [–fay] service charge;
  tip
xiǎo húzi [hoo-dzur] moustache
xiáojiě [–jyeh] Miss
xiǎolù path
xiǎo qìchē [chee-chur] car
xiǎo sānjiǎokù [sahn-jyow-koo]
  pants, panties
xiǎoshān [–shahn] hill
xiǎosháor [–showr] spoon
xiǎoshí [–shur] hour
xiǎoshū brother-in-law
  (husband's younger brother)
xiāoxi [–hshee] information
xiǎoxī stream
xiǎoxīn! [–hsin] look out!
xiáozǔ [–dzyew] group
xiàshuǐdào [hsyah-shway-dow]
  drain
xiàtiān [–tyen] summer; in the
  summer
xiàwǔ afternoon; in the
  afternoon; p.m.
jīntiān xiàwǔ [jin-tyen] this
  afternoon

xià yíge [yee-gur] next

Xībānyá [hshee-bahn-yah] Spain; Spanish (adj)

xīběi [hshee-bay] northwest

xībiānr [–byenr] in the west

xīcān [–tsahn] Western-style food

xīcāntīng [–tsahn-ting] Western-style restaurant

xiě [hsyeh] blood; write

xié shoe

xiē a little bit

... xiē a bit more ...

xiédǐ [–dee] sole (of shoe)

xié hòugēn [hoh-gun] heel (of shoe)

xièxie [hsyeh-hsyeh] thank you

xièxie, wǒ bú yào [wor boo yow] no thanks

Xīfāng [hshee-fahng] West; in the West; Western

Xīfāng de [dur] Western (adj)

xīgài knee

xíhǎo de yīfu [–how dur yee-foo] washing (clean)

xǐhuan [–hwahn] like

xìn [hsin] letter, message

xīn new

xī'nán [hshee-ahn] southwest

xìnfēng [hsin-fung] envelope

xíng [hsing] all right

xìng surname

xìnggǎn [–gahn] sexy

xìngkuī [–kway] fortunately

xíngle [–lur] that's OK

xíngle awake

xíngli luggage, baggage

xīngqī [–chee] week

xīngqī'èr [–chee-er] Tuesday

xīngqīliù [–lyoh] Saturday

xīngqīsān [–chee-sahn] Wednesday

xīngqītiān [–tyen] Sunday

xīngqīwǔ [–woo] Friday

xīngqīyī Monday

xìngqu [–chew] interest

xīngxing star

xìnhào [hsin-how] signal

xìnshǐ [hsin-shur] courier

xīnwén [hsin-wun] news (radio, TV etc)

xīnxiān [hsin-hsyen] fresh

xìnxiāng [hsin-hsyang] postbox, mailbox

Xīnxīlán [hsin-hshee-lahn] New Zealand

xìnyòng kǎ [hsin-yoong kah] credit card

xīnzàng [hsin-dzahng] heart

xiōng [hsyoong] chest

xiōngdì brother

xiōngkǒu [–koh] chest

xiōngzhào [–jow] bra

xiōngzhēn [–jun] brooch

xìshéng [hshee-shung] string

xīshì [hshee-shur] Western-style

xiūlǐ [hsyoh-lee] repair

xiūxiéjiàng [–hsyeh-jyang] shoe repairer

xiūxiépù shoe repairer

xiūxishì [–hshee-shur] lounge

xiūxītīng foyer

xiùzhēn fàngyīnjī [–jun fahng-yin-jee] personal stereo

xiùzi [–dzur] sleeve

xīwàng [hshee-wahng] hope

xǐyīdiàn [–dyen] laundry (place)

xǐyījī washing machine

xīyǐnrén [–run] attractive
xīyǒu [–yoh] rare, uncommon
Xīzàng [–dzahng] Tibet
xǐzǎo [–dzow] bathe
xǐzǎojiān [–jyen] bathroom
xuǎn [hsyew-ahn] choose
xuányá [–yah] cliff
xǔduō [–dwor] a lot, lots, plenty of
xuě [hsyew-eh] snow
xuějiā [–jyah] cigar
xuéqī [–chur] term
xuésheng [–shung] student
xuéxí [–hshee] learn
xuéxiào [–hsyow] school
xuéyuàn [–yew-ahn] college
xuēzi [–dzur] boot (footwear)
xúkě zhèng [hsyew-kur jung] permit (noun)
xūyào [hsyew-yow] need

Y

yá [yah] tooth
yágāo [yah-gow] toothpaste
yājīn [yah-jin] deposit
yákē dàifu [yah-kur] dentist
yákē yīshēng [yee-shung] dentist
yān [yen] smoke
  nǐ chōu yān ma? [choh yen mah] do you smoke?
yāndǒu [yen-doh] pipe
yǎng itch
yángguāng [yang-gwahng] sunshine
yángmáo [yang-mow] wool
yángsǎn [yang-sahn] sunshade

yángtái balcony
yángwáwa [yang-wah-wah] doll
yànhuì [yen-hway] banquet
yǎnjing [yen-jing] eye
yǎnjìng glasses, eyeglasses
yǎnjìngdiàn [–dyen] optician
yǎnkē yīshēng [yen-kur yee-shung] optician
yánsè [yen-sur] colour
yǎo [yow] bite (by insect)
yāo waist; one
yào want; drug; Chinese medicine
  nǐ yào shénme? [shun-mur] what do you want?
yàobùrán [yow-boor-ahn] otherwise
yāodài [yow-dai] belt
yàodiàn [yow-dyen] pharmacy
yáodòng [yow-doong] cave (dwelling)
yàofāng [yow-fahng] prescription
yàogāo [yow-gow] ointment
yàomián [yow-myen] cotton wool, absorbent cotton
yāoqǐng [yow-ching] invitation; invite
yǎoshāng [yow-shahng] bite
yàoshi [yow-shur] key
yáshuā [yah-shwah] toothbrush
yáténg [yah-tung] toothache
yě [yur] also, too
yè night; page
yèlì at night; p.m.
yéye [yur-yur] grandfather (paternal)
yèzǒnghuì [yur-dzoong-hway] nightclub

yi [yee] one
yìbǎi one hundred
yíbàn [yee-bahn] half
yìbāo [yee-bow] packet
yìbēi [yee-bay] cup
yìcéng [yee-tsung] ground floor, (US) first floor
yícì [yee-tsur] once
xià yícì [hsyah] next time
yìdá [yee-dah] dozen
yídàkuàir [–kwai-r] a big bit
yìděng [yee-dung] first class
yìdiǎnr [yee-dyenr] a little bit
... yìdiǎnr a bit more ...
yìdiánrdiánr tiny
yídìng definitely
yīfu dress; clothes
yíge [yee-gur] one
nǎ yíge? [nah yee-gur] which one?
yígerén [yee-gur-run] alone
yígòng [yee-goong] altogether
yí guànr [gwahnr] can; jug
yǐhòu [yee-hoh] after; afterwards
yíhuìr [yee-hwayr] soon
yǐjīng already
yíkè [yee-kur] quarter past
yíkuàir [yee-kwai-r] piece
yīlǐng collar
yī lóu [loh] ground floor, (US) first floor
yílù shùnfēng! [yee-loo shun-fung] have a good journey!
yímā [yee-mah] aunt (mother's sister)
yīmàojiān [yee-mow-jyen] cloakroom

yímǔ [yee-moo] aunt (mother's sister)
yín(zi) [yin(-dzur)] silver
Yìndu [yin-doo] India; Indian (adj)
yìng hard
yìngbàng [ying-bahng] pound sterling
yìngbì coin
yīng'ér [ying-er] baby
Yīngguó [ying-gwor] England; Britain; English; British
Yīngguóde [–dur] English; British
yìngwò [ying-wor] hard sleeper, second class sleeper
Yīngyǔ [ying-yew] English (language)
yìngzuò [ying-dzwor] hard seat, third class seat
yínháng [yin-hahng] bank
yínshuǐ lóngtóu [yin-shway loong-toh] fountain (for drinking)
yīnwèi [yin-way] because
yǐnyòngshuǐ [yin-yoong-shway] drinking water
yīnyuè [yin-yew-eh] music
yīnyuèhuì [–way] concert
yìqǐ [yee-chee] together
yǐqián: ... yǐqián [yee-chyen] before ...
yìqiān one thousand
yírìyóu [yee-rur-yoh] day trip
yīsheng [yee-shung] doctor
yìshù [yee-shoo] art
yíwàn [yee-wahn] ten thousand
yǐxià: zài ... yǐxià [dzai ... yee-hsyah] below, less than
yìxiē [yee-hsyeh] a few

yí yì [yur yee] a hundred million

yīyuàn [yee-yew-ahn] hospital

yīyuè [yee-yew-eh] January

yìzhí cháoqián [yee-jur chow-chyen] straight ahead

yǐzi [yee-dzur] chair

yòng [yoong] with; by means of; use; in

yōngjǐ [–jee] crowded

yǒu [yoh] have; there is; there are

yǒu ... ma? [mah] is there ...?; are there ...?

yòu right (not left)

yòubiānr [yoh-byenr] right

yǒubìng [yoh-bing] ill, sick

yǒudúde [yoh-doo-dur] poisonous

yóuguǐ diànchē [yoh-gway dyen-chur] tram

yóuhǎo [yoh-how] friendly

yóujì [yoh-jee] post, mail (verb)

yóujiàn [yoh-jyen] post, mail

yóujú [yoh-jew] post office

yóulǎn [yoh-lahn] tour, visit

yǒu lǐmào [yoh lee-mow] polite

yǒu máobìng [yoh mow-bing] faulty

yǒumíng famous

yóunì greasy, oily (food)

yóupiào [yoh-pyow] stamp

yǒuqián [yoh-chyen] rich

yǒurén [yoh-run] somebody, someone; engaged, occupied

yǒushíhòu [yoh-shur-hoh] sometimes

Yóutàiren de [yoh-tai-run dur] Jewish

yóuxì [yoh-hshee] game

yǒuxiào [yoh-hsyow] valid

yòu yíge [yee-gur] another, one more

yǒu yìsi [yee-sur] interesting; funny, amusing

yóuyǒng [yoh-yoong] swim

yǒuyòng useful

yóuyǒngchí [–chur] swimming pool

yóuzhèng biānmǎ [yoh-jung byen-mah] postcode, zip code

yú [yow] fish

yù jade

yǔ rain

yuǎn [yew-ahn] far; far away

yuǎnchù: zài yuǎnchù [dzai yew-ahn-choo] in the distance

yuánlái de [dur] usual

yuánzhūbǐ [–joo-bee] ballpoint pen

yúchǔn [yew-chun] stupid

yùdìng [yew-ding] reservation; reserve

yuè [yew-eh] month

yuèfù father-in-law

yuèfù yuèmǔ [yew-eh-moo] husband's parents-in-law

yuèliang [yew-eh-lyang] moon

Yuènán [yew-eh-nahn] Vietnam

yúkuài [yew-kwai] lovely

yúkuàide [yew-kwai-dur] enjoyable

yùndòng [yewn-doong] sport

yùndǒu [yewn-doh] iron

yùnqi [yewn-chee] luck

yúsǎn [yew-sahn] umbrella

yùshì [yew-shur] bathroom

yǔyán [yew-yahn] language

yǔyán kè [yew-yahn kur] language course

yǔyī [yew-yee] raincoat

yùyuē [yew-yew-eh] appointment

Z

záhuòdiàn [dzah-hwor-dyen] grocer's

zài [dzai] in; at; on; be in/at a place; again

zài nǎr? where is it?

zài ... de shíhou [dur shur-hoh] during ...

zài ... hòumian [hoh-myen] behind ...

zàijiàn [dzai-jyen] goodbye

zài nàr over there; up there

zájì acrobatics

zài ...-li inside ...

zài ...-pángbiān [pahng-byen] beside the ..., next to ...

zài ...-shàng [shahng] above ...

zài ...-shàngmian [shahng-myen] on ...

zài ...-xià [hsyah] under ...

zài ...-xiàmian [hsyah-myen] below ...

zài ...-yǐxià [yee-hsyah] below ..., less than ...

zài ...-zhījiān [jur-jyen] between ...

zài ...-zhōng [joong] among ...

zāng [dzahng] dirty, filthy

zànglǐ funeral

zǎo [dzow] good morning; early

yì zǎo early in the morning

zǎofàn [dzow-fahn] breakfast

zǎopén [dzow-pun] bathtub

zǎoshang [dzow-shahng] morning; in the morning; a.m. (up to 9 a.m.)

jīntiān zǎoshang [jin-tyen] this morning

zàoyīn [dzow-yin] noise

zázhì [dzah-jur] magazine

zéi [dzay] thief

zěnme? [dzun-mur] how?

zěnme huí shìr? [hway shur] what's happening?; what's up?, what's wrong?

zěnme le? [lur] what's happening?

zěnmele? what's wrong?, what's the matter?

zhǎi [jai] narrow

zhāng [jahng] measure word* used for tables, beds, tickets and sheets of paper

zhàngdānr [–dahnr] bill, (US) check

zhàngfu husband

zhāngláng [–lahng] cockroach

zhàntái [jahn-tai] platform, (US) track

zhànxiàn [jahn-hsyen] engaged

zhànzhù [jahn-joo] stop

zhǎodào [jow-dow] find

zhàopiàn [jow-pyen] photo

zhāotiē [jow-tyeh] poster

zhàoxiàngjī [jow-hsyang-jee] camera

zhá tǔdòupiànr [jah too-doh-pyenr] crisps, (US) potato chips zhè [jur] this; the

-zhe verb suffix indicating continuous action or two actions taking place at the same time

zhèi [jay] this; this one
   zhèi? whose?

zhèicì [jay-tsur] this time

zhèige [jay-gur] this; this one

zhēn [jun] really

zhēnde [jun-dur] true; genuine, real; sure

zhèngcháng(de) [jung-chahng(-dur)] normal

zhèngfǔ [jung-foo] government

zhèngshì [jung-shur] formal

zhēngui(de) [jung-way(-dur)] valuable

zhéngzhěng whole, full

zhēnjiǔ [jun-jyoh] acupuncture

zhēn láijìn exciting

zhénsuǒ [jun-swor] clinic

zhèntou [jun-toh] pillow

zhènyǔ [jun-yew] shower

zhēnzhèng [jun-jung] genuine

zhèr [jer] here
   zài zhèr [dzai] over here

zhī [jur] measure word* used for hands, birds, suitcases and boats

zhīdao [jur-dow] know
   wǒ bù zhīdao [wor] I don't know

zhífēi [jur-fay] direct flight

zhījiān: zài ... zhījiān [dzai ... jur-jyen] between ...

zhíjiē [jur-jyeh] direct

zhījīn [jur-jin] tissue, Kleenex®

zhìliàng [jur-lyang] quality

zhínǚ [jin-yew] niece

zhǐshi [jur-shur] only

zhǐténgyào [jur-tung-yow] painkiller

zhíwù [jur-woo] plant

zhíxuě gāobù [jur-hsyew-eh gow-boo] plaster, Bandaid®

zhíyǒu [jur-yoh] only

zhìzào [jur-dzow] make (verb)

zhízi [jur-dzur] nephew

zhì [jur] cure (verb)

zhǐ just, only; paper

zhōng [joong] clock

-zhōng in the middle; between
   zài ...-zhōng [dzai] among ...

zhòng heavy

zhǒng type; swollen

zhōngdiǎnzhàn [–dyen-jahn] rail terminus

Zhōngguó [joong-gwor] China; Chinese (adj)
   Zhōngguó rén [run] Chinese (person)
   Zhōngguó rénmín [run-min] the Chinese

Zhōnghuá Rénmín Gònghéguó [–hwah run-min goong-hur-gwor] People's Republic of China

zhōngjiān: zài zhōngjiān [dzai joong-jyen] in the middle

zhòngliàng [–lyang] weight

Zhōngshì [–shur] Chinese-style

Zhōngwén [–wun] Chinese (written language)

zhōngwǔ noon; at noon

zhōngxīn [–hsin] central; centre

zhòngyào [–yow] important

zhōngzhuǎn [–jwahn] connection

zhōumò [joh-mor] weekend

zhù [joo] live (verb)
nín zhù nǎr? what's your address?

zhuǎnxìn dìzhǐ [–hsin dee-jur] forwarding address

zhújiàn de [joo-jyen dur] gradually

zhǔnbèi hǎo le [jun-bay how lur] ready

zhù nǐ shùnlì! [joo nee shun-lee] good luck!

zhuōzi [jwor-dzur] table

zhǔyào de [joo-yow dur] main

zhǔyì [joo-yee] idea

zhúzi [joo-dzur] bamboo

zǐ [dzur] purple

zìdòng [dzur-doong] automatic

zìdòng qǔkuǎnjī [chew-kwahn-jee] cash dispenser, ATM

zìjǐ [dzur-jee] oneself

zìrán [dzur-rahn] natural

zìxíngchē [dzur-hsing-chur] bicycle

zìyóu [dzur-yoh] free

zìzhù [dzur-joo] self-service

zǒng [dzoong] always

zǒng fúwùtái reception desk

zǒnggòng [–goong] total

zǒngjī operator

zōngjiào [–jyow] religion

zōngsè [–sur] brown

zǒngshì [–shur] always

zǒu [dzoh] leave, depart, go

zǒuláng [dzoh-lahng] corridor

zǒuzou go for a walk

zū [dzoo] hire, rent

zuǐ [dzway] mouth

zuì drunk
zuì ... ...-est, the most ...

zuǐba [-bah] mouth

zuì hǎo [how] best

zuìhòu [–hoh] eventually; last

zuì huài [hwai] worst

zuìjìn recently; last, latest

zuò [dzwor] by; do
zuò fēijī [fay-jee] by air
zuò huǒchē [hwor-chur] by rail

zuǒ left

zuǒbiānr [–byenr] left

zuò fānyì [fahn-yee] interpret

zuótiān [–tyen] yesterday
zuótiān wǎnshang [wahn-shahng] last night

zuótian zǎoshang [dzow-shahng] yesterday morning

zuòwei [–way] seat

zuòxià [–hsyah] sit down

zuǒyòu [–yoh] about

zúqiúsài football

Chinese

→

English
Signs and Notices

Contents

General Signs

危险 wēixiǎn danger
请勿乱踏草地 qǐng wù luàntà cǎodì keep off the grass
军事要地请勿靠近 jūnshì yàodì, qǐng wù kàojìn military zone, keep out
禁止入内 jìnzhǐ rù nèi no entry
外国人未经许可禁止超越 wàiguórén wèi jīng xúkě, jìnzhǐ chāoyuè no foreigners beyond this point without permission
请勿随地乱扔果皮纸屑 qǐng wù suídì luànrēng guǒpí zhǐxiè no litter
请勿大声喧哗 qǐng wù dàshēng xuānhuá no noise, please
禁止拍照 jìnzhǐ pāizhào no photographs
请勿吸烟 qǐng wù xī yān no smoking
请勿随地吐痰 qǐng wù suídì tǔtán no spitting
人行横道 rénxíng héngdào pedestrian crossing
肃静 sùjìng quiet
一慢二看三通过 yī màn, èr kàn, sān tōngguò slow down, look and then cross
闲人免进 xiánrén miǎn jìn

staff only
楼下 lóuxià downstairs
楼上 lóushàng upstairs

Airport, Planes

机场 jīchǎng airport
机场班车 jīchǎng bānchē airport bus
来自 láizì arriving from
前往 qiánwǎng departing to
起飞时间 qǐfēi shíjiān departure time
终点站 zhōngdiǎnzhàn destination
预计到达时间 yùjì dàodá shíjiān estimated time of arrival
航班号 hángbānhào flight number
预计时间 yùjì shíjiān scheduled time
延误 yánwù delayed
经停站 jīngtíngzhàn via
国内航班进站 guónèi hángbān jìnzhàn domestic arrivals
国内航班出站 guónèi hángbān chūzhàn domestic departures
国际航班进站 guójì hángbān jìnzhàn international arrivals
国际航班出站 guójì

hángbān chūzhàn
international departures

登记牌 dēngjìpái boarding
pass

日期 rìqī date

行李牌儿 xínglipáir baggage
check

行李领取处 xíngli língqǔchù
baggage claim

办理登机手续 bànlǐ dēngjī
shǒuxù check-in

问讯处 wènxùnchù
information desk

登机口 dēngjīkǒu gate

安全检查 ānquán jiǎnchá
security control

中转旅客 zhōngzhuǎn lǚkè
transfer passengers

中转 zhōngzhuǎn transfers

过境旅客 guòjìng lǚkè transit
passengers

侯机室 hòujīshì departure
lounge

免税商店 miǎnshuì
shāngdiàn duty-free shop

系好安全带 jìhǎo ānquándài
fasten seat belts

救生衣 jiùshēngyī life jacket

请勿吸烟 qǐng wù xīyān no
smoking

座位号 zuòwèihào seat
number

Banks, Money

帐户 zhànghù account

帐号 zhànghào account no.

银行 yínháng bank

中国银行 Zhōngguó Yínháng
Bank of China

分行 fēnháng branch

营业时间 yíngyè shíjiān
business hours

买价 mǎijià buying rate

交款处 jiāokuǎnchù cashier

信用卡 xìnyòng kǎ credit
card

外币兑换 wàibì duìhuàn
foreign exchange

中国人民银行 Zhōngguó
Rénmín Yínháng People's
Bank of China

卖价 màijià selling rate

今日牌价 jīnrì páijià today's
exchange rate

旅行支票 lǚxíng zhīpiào
traveller's cheque

元 yuán unit of currency

澳元 Àoyuán Australian
dollar

加拿大元 Jiānádà yuán
Canadian dollar

人民币 Rénmínbì Chinese
currency

港币 Gǎngbì Hong Kong
dollar

英镑 Yīngbàng pound sterling

美元 Měiyuán US dollar

Bus and Taxi Travel

长途汽车站 chángtú qìchē zhàn long-distance bus station

夜班车 yèbān chē all-night bus

公共汽车 gōnggòng qìchē bus

快车 kuàichē express bus

小公共汽车 xiǎo gōnggòng qìchē minibus

区间车 qūjiānchē part-route shuttle bus

无轨电车 wúguǐ diànchē trolley bus

游览车 yóulǎnchē tourist bus

售票处 shòupiàokǒu booking office

长途汽车时刻表 chángtú qìchē shíkèbiǎo long-distance bus timetable/schedule

城市交通图 chéngshì jiāotōngtú city transport map

始发站 shǐfāzhàn departure point

票价 piàojià fare

问讯处 wènxùnchù information office

月票 yuèpiào monthly ticket

一日游 yí rì yóu one-day tour

就近下车 jiùjìn xiàchē alight on request

先下后上 xiān xià hòu shàng allow passengers to alight before boarding

保持车内清洁 bǎochí chēnèi qīngjié keep the bus tidy

请勿与司机谈话 qǐng wù yǔ sījī tánhuà please do not speak to the driver

老弱病残孕专座 lǎoruò bìngcānyùn zhuānzuò seats for the elderly or disabled and for pregnant women

招手上车 zhāoshǒu shàngchē stop on request

小卖部 xiǎomàibù kiosk

小吃店 xiǎochīdiàn snack bar

候车室 hòuchēshì waiting room

出租汽车 chūzū qìchē taxis

Chinese Culture

寺 sì Buddhist temple

文化大革命 Wénhuà Dàgémìng Cultural Revolution (1966-1976)

天安门 Tiān'ānmén Gate of Heavenly Peace

长城 Chángchéng the Great Wall

五四运动 Wǔsì Yùndòng May 4th Movement (1919)

明 Míng Ming Dynasty (1368-1644)

十三陵 **Shísānlíng** Ming Tombs

年画 **niánhuà** New Year prints

塔 **tǎ** pagoda

故宫 **Gùgōng** Forbidden City

八达岭 **Bādálǐng** pass at Great Wall

京剧 **Jīngjù** Peking opera

木偶戏 **mù'ǒuxì** puppet show

清 **Qīng** Qing Dynasty (1644-1911)

宋 **Sòng** Song Dynasty (960-1279)

颐和园 **Yíhéyuán** Summer Palace

唐 **Táng** Tang Dynasty (618-907)

宫 **gōng** Taoist temple

观 **guàn** Taoist temple

庙 **miào** temple

天坛 **Tiāntán** Temple of Heaven

兵马俑 **Bīngmǎyǒng** Terracotta Army

辛亥革命 **Xīnhài Gémìng** Xinhai Revolution (1911)

Countries, Nationalities

美国 **Měiguó** America; American

澳大利亚 **Àodàlìyà** Australia; Australian

缅甸 **Miǎndiàn** Burma; Burmese

加拿大 **Jiānádà** Canada; Canadian

中国 **Zhōngguó** China; Chinese

英国 **Yīngguó** England; English; UK; British

法国 **Fǎguó** France; French

德国 **Déguó** Germany; German

香港 **Xiānggǎng** Hong Kong

印度尼西亚 **Yìndùníxīyà** Indonesia; Indonesian

爱尔兰 **Ài'ěrlán** Ireland; Irish

日本 **Rìběn** Japan; Japanese

朝鲜 **Cháoxiǎn** Korea; Korean

老挝 **Lǎowō** Laos; Laotian

马来西亚 **Mǎláixīyà** Malaysia; Malaysian

满 **Mǎn** minority people from North-East China

维吾尔 **Wéiwú'ěr** minority people from North-West China

傣 **Dǎi** minority people from South-West China

苗 **Miáo** minority people from South-West China

彝 **Yí** minority people from South-West China

僮 **Zhuàng** minority people

from South-West China

蒙 **Měng** Mongol

蒙古 **Ménggǔ** Mongolia

回 **Huí** Muslim minority people

尼泊尔 **Níbó'ěr** Nepal; Nepali

中华人民共和国 **Zhōnghuá Rénmín Gònghéguó** People's Republic of China

菲律宾 **Fēilǜbīn** Philippines; Filipino

俄国 **Éguó** Russia; Russian

苏格兰 **Sūgélán** Scotland; Scottish

新加坡 **Xīnjiāpō** Singapore; Singaporean

西藏 **Xīzàng** Tibet

藏 **Zàng** Tibetan

台湾 **Táiwān** Taiwan; Taiwanese

泰国 **Tàiguó** Thailand; Thai

威尔士 **Wēi'ěrshì** Wales; Welsh

Customs

中国海关 **Zhōngguó hǎiguān** Chinese Customs

海关 **hǎiguān** Customs

边防检查站 **biānfáng jiǎncházhàn** frontier checkpoint

免疫检查 **miǎnyì jiǎnchá** health inspection

护照检查 **hùzhào jiǎnchá** passport control

报关 **bàoguān** goods to declare

不用报关 **búyòng bàoguān** nothing to declare

绿色通道 **lǜsè tōngdào** green channel, nothing to declare

红色通道 **hóngsè tōngdào** red channel, goods to declare

入境签证 **rùjìng qiānzhèng** entry visa

出境签证 **chūjìng qiānzhèng** exit visa

护照 **hùzhào** passport

过境签证 **guòjìng qiānzhèng** transit visa

旅行证 **lǚxíngzhèng** travel permit

免税物品 **miǎnshuì wùpǐn** duty-free goods

Emergencies

救护车 **jiùhùchē** ambulance

太平门 **tàipíngmén** emergency exit

火警匪警 **huǒjǐng, féijǐng** emergency telephone number: fire, robbery

消防队 **xiāofángduì** fire brigade, fire department

急诊室 **jízhěnshì** first-aid room

派出所 Pàichūsuǒ local police station

警察 jǐngchá police

公安局 gōng'ānjú Public Security Bureau

Entertainment

售票处 shòupiàochù box office

入场券 rùchǎngquàn cinema ticket

电影院 diànyǐngyuàn cinema

迪斯科 dísīkē disco

夜场 yèchǎng evening performance

全满 quánmǎn house full

休息 xiūxi interval

京剧 Jīngjù Peking Opera

节目单 jiémùdān programme

排 ... pái row ...

号 ... hào seat number ...

票已售完 piào yǐ shòu wán sold out

剧场 jùchǎng theatre

剧院 jùyuàn theatre

戏院 xìyuàn theatre

表演时间 biáoyǎn shíjiān times of performance

Forms

从何处来 cóng héchù lái arriving from

出生年月 chūshēng niányuè date of birth

籍贯 jíguàn father's place of birth

到何处去 dào héchù qù heading for

拟住天数 nǐ zhù tiānshù length of stay

姓名 xìngmíng full name

国籍 guójí nationality

性别 xìngbié (nán/nǚ) sex (male/female)

护照号码 hùzhào hàomǎ passport number

永久地址 yóngjiǔ dìzhǐ permanent address

旅客登记表 lǚkè dēngjìbiǎo registration form

签名 qiānmíng signature

Geographical Terms

自治区 zìzhìqū autonomous region

运河 yùnhé canal

市 shì city

国家 guójiā country

县 xiàn county

森林 sēnlín forest

岛 dǎo island

湖 hú lake

江 jiāng large river

地图 dìtú map

山 shān mountain, hill

山脉 shānmài mountains

海洋 **hǎiyáng** ocean
省 **shěng** province
河 **hé** river
海 **hǎi** sea
镇 **zhèn** town
山谷 **shāngǔ** valley
村 **cūn** village
树林 **shùlín** woods

Health

中医科 **zhōngyīkē** Chinese medicine department
中药房 **zhōngyàofáng** Chinese medicine dispensary
牙科 **yákē** dental department
急诊室 **jízhěnshì** emergency
外宾门诊部 **wàibīn ménzhěnbù** foreign outpatients
医院 **yīyuàn** hospital
住院处 **zhùyuànchù** hospital admissions office
内科 **nèikē** medical department
门诊部 **ménzhěnbù** outpatients
挂号 **guàhào** registration
西药房 **xīyàofáng** Western medicine dispensary

Hiring, Renting

出租自行车 **chūzū zìxíngchē** bikes to rent

租船 **zū chuán** boats to rent
出租 **chūzū** for hire, to rent

Hotels

中国国际旅行社 **Zhōngguó Guójì Lǚxíngshè** China International Travel Service
中国旅行社 **Zhōngguó Lǚxíngshè** China Travel Service
宾馆 **bīnguǎn** hotel
饭店 **fàndiàn** hotel
小卖部 **xiǎomàibù** kiosk
总服务台 **zǒng fúwùtái** reception
游艺室 **yóuyìshì** recreation room
电传室 **diànchuánshì** telex office

Lifts (Elevators)

关 **guān** close
下 **xià** down
电梯 **diàntī** lifts, elevators
开 **kāi** open
上 **shàng** up

Medicines

抗菌素 **kàngjùnsù** antibiotics
阿斯匹林 **āsīpǐlín** aspirin
咳鼻清 **kébìqīng** cough lozenges

259

棕色合剂 zōngsè héjì cough mixture

止咳糖浆 zhǐké tángjiāng cough syrup

止疼片儿 zhǐténgpiànr painkillers

青霉素 qīngméisù penicillin

含碘片 hándiǎnpiàn throat pastilles

剂量 jìliàng dosage

失效期 shīxiàoqī expiry date

初诊 chūzhěn first treatment

外用 wàiyòng for external use

一日三次 yírì sān cì three times a day

胃炎 wèiyán gastritis

饭前／后温开水送服 fàn qián/hòu wēnkāishuǐ sòngfú to be taken with warm water before/after food

每四／六小时服一次 měi sì/liù xiǎoshí fú yícì one dose every four/six hours

一日四次 yírì sìcì four times a day

内服 nèifú to be taken orally

每次一个 měi cì yì gé one measure at a time

每次一丸 měicì yì wán one pill at a time

每次一片儿 měicì yí piànr one tablet at a time

必要时服 bìyào shí fú when necessary

Notices on Doors

太平门 tàipíngmén emergency exit

入口 rùkǒu entrance

出口 chūkǒu exit

顾客止步 gùkè zhǐ bù no entry for customers

未经许可禁止入内 wèi jīng xúkě, jìnzhǐ rù nèi no entry without permission

拉 lā pull

推 tuī push

闲人免进 xiánrén miǎn jìn staff only

Phones

长途区号 chángtú qūhào area code

用卡电话亭 yòng kǎ diànhuà tíng cardphone

查号台 cháhàotái directory enquiries

分机 fēnjī extension

国际长途 guójì chángtú international call

长途电话 chángtú diànhuà long-distance call

电话卡 diànhuàkǎ phonecard

公用电话 gōngyòng diànhuà public telephone

总机 zǒngjī switchboard

电话簿 diànhuàbù telephone directory

一次一角(毛) yícì yìjiǎo (máo) ten fen per call
磁卡电话 cíkǎ diànhuà cardphone

Place Names

北京 Běijīng Beijing
成都 Chéngdū Chengdu
敦煌 Dūnhuáng Dunhuang
峨嵋山 Éméishān Emei Mountains
广州 Guǎngzhōu Canton
长城 Chángchéng the Great Wall
桂林 Guìlín Guilin
杭州 Hángzhōu Hangzhou
昆明 Kūnmíng Kunming
拉萨 Lāsā Lhasa
洛阳 Luòyáng Luoyang
南京 Nánjīng Nanjing
深圳 Shēnzhèn Shenzhen
天津 Tiānjīn Tientsin
西湖 Xīhú West Lake
西安 Xī'ān Xi'an
长江三峡 Chángjiāng Sānxiá Yangtze Gorges

Post Office

邮局 yóujú post office
开箱时间 kāixiāng shíjiān collection times
信封 xìnfēng envelope
邮筒 yóutǒng letterbox, mailbox
信函 xìnhán letters
杂志报刊 zázhì bàokān magazines and newspapers
包裹单 bāoguǒdān parcel form
包裹, 印刷品 bāoguǒ, yìnshuāpǐn parcels, printed matter
邮电局 yóudiànjú post and telecommunications office
信箱电报 xìnxiāng postbox
邮政编码 yóuzhèng biānmǎ postcode, zip code
邮票, 挂号 yóupiào, guàhào stamps, registered mail
电报纸 diànbàozhì telegram form
电报 diànbào telegram
电报大楼 diànbào dàlóu telegraph building

Public Buildings

浴池 yùchí baths
学院 xuéyuàn college
领事馆 lǐngshìguǎn consulate
大使馆 dàshǐguǎn embassy
工厂 gōngchǎng factory
游泳馆 yóuyǒngguǎn indoor swimming pool
图书馆 túshūguǎn library
博物馆 bówùguǎn museum
中学 zhōngxué secondary school

体育馆 tǐyùguǎn sports hall, indoor stadium

体育场 tǐyùchǎng stadium

大学 dàxué university

Restaurants, Cafés, Bars

酒吧 jiǔbā bar

咖啡店 kāfēidiàn café, coffee house

茶楼 chálóu café, teahouse

茶馆 cháguǎn café, teahouse

茶室 cháshì café, teahouse

收款台 shōukuǎntái cashier

冷饮店 lěngyǐndiàn cold drinks bar

中餐厅 Zhōng cāntīng Chinese dining room

清真饭店 qīngzhēn fàndiàn Muslim restaurant

面馆 miànguǎn noodle shop

菜馆 càiguǎn large restaurant

饭店 fàndiàn large restaurant

酒家 jiǔjiā large restaurant

酒楼 jiǔlóu large restaurant

餐厅 cāntīng restaurant; dining room

快餐 kuàicān snack bar

小吃店 xiǎochīdiàn snack bar

今日供应 jīnrì gòngyìng today's menu

素菜馆 sùcàiguǎn vegetarian restaurant

西餐厅 xī cāntīng Western dining room

西菜馆 xīcàiguǎn Western restaurant

Shopping

文物商店 wénwù shāngdiàn antique shop

工艺美术商店 gōngyì měishù shāngdiàn arts and crafts shop

自行车 zìxíngchē bicycles

收款台 shōukuǎntái cashier

烟酒糖茶 yān jiǔ táng chá cigarettes, wine, confectionery, tea

服装店 fúzhuāngdiàn clothes shop

男女服装 nánnǚ fúzhuāng clothing

化妆用品 huàzhuāng yòngpǐn cosmetics

百货商店 bǎihuò shāngdiàn department store

家用电器 jiāyòng diànqì domestic appliances

食品商店 shípǐn shāngdiàn food shop

食品糕点 shípǐn gāodiǎn food and confectionery

自由市场 zìyóu shìchǎng free market

友谊商店 yǒuyí shāngdiàn Friendship store

菜市场 càishìchǎng

greengrocer

副食品商店 **fùshípǐn shāngdiàn** grocery store

五金交电 **wǔjīn jiāodiàn** hardware and electrical goods

袜了鞋帽 **wàzi xiémào** hosiery, shoes, hats

日用杂品 **rìyòng zápǐn** household goods

橱房用品 **chúfáng yòngpǐn** kitchenware

妇女用品 **fùnǚ yòngpǐn** ladies' accessories

女装 **nǚzhuāng** ladies' wear

洗衣店 **xǐyīdiàn** laundry

皮革制品 **pígé zhìpǐn** leather goods

市场 **shìchǎng** market

男装 **nán zhuāng** menswear

乐器行 **yuèqì háng** musical instruments section

新华书店 **xīnhuá shūdiàn** New China bookshop

夜市 **yèshì** night market

眼镜店 **yǎnjìngdiàn** optician

复印 **fùyìn** photocopying

照相器材 **zhàoxiàng qìcái** photographic equipment

钱票当面点清过后该不负责 **qián piào dāngmiàn diǎnqīng, guòhòu gāi bù fùzé** please check your change before leaving as mistakes cannot be rectified

雨伞雨具 **yúsǎn yǔjù** rainwear

大减价 **dàjiǎnjià** sale

古旧书店 **gǔjiù shūdiàn** secondhand bookshop

购物中心 **gòuwù zhōngxīn** shopping centre

体育用品 **tǐyù yòngpǐn** sports goods

文具商店 **wénjù shāngdiàn** stationery

文具用品 **wénjù yòngpǐn** stationery

牙膏牙刷 **yágāo yáshuā** toothpaste and toothbrushes

儿童玩具 **értóng wánjù** toys

针织用品 **zhēnzhī yòngpǐn** underwear

Streets and Roads

大街 **dàjiē** avenue

胡同 **hútòng** lane

巷 **xiàng** lane

路 **lù** road

广场 **guángchǎng** square

街 **jiē** street

Toilets

有人 **yǒurén** engaged, occupied

男厕所 **náncèsuǒ** gents' toilet, men's room

男厕 **náncè** gents' toilet, men's room

女厕所 **nǔcèsuǒ** ladies' toilet, ladies' room

女厕 **nǔcè** ladies' toilet, ladies' room

公厕 **gōngcè** public toilets, rest rooms

盥洗室 **guànxǐshì** toilet, rest room

无人 **wúrén** vacant, free

Train and Underground Travel

火车站 **huǒchēzhàn** station

火车 **huǒchē** train

列车到站时刻表 **lièchē dàozhàn shíkèbiǎo** arrival times

列车离站时刻表 **lièchē lízhàn shíkèbiǎo** departure times

开往 ... 方向 ... **kāiwǎng ... fāngxiàng** to ...

车次 **chēcì** train number

检票处 **jiǎnpiàochù** barrier

站台 **zhàntái** platform, (US) track

站台票 **zhàntáipiào** platform ticket

问讯处 **wènxùnchù** information desk

火车时刻表 **huǒchē**

shíkèbiǎo timetable, (US) schedule

天 **tiān** day

特快 **tèkuài** express

直快 **zhíkuài** through train

快车 **kuàichē** fast train

客车 **kèchē** ordinary passenger train

站名 **zhànmíng** station name

开往 ... **kāiwǎng ...** to ...

旅游车 **lǚyóuchē** tourist train

车次 **chēcì** train number

星期 **xīngqī** week

行李寄存处 **xíngli jìcúnchù** left luggage, baggage checkroom

乘警 **chéngjǐng** railway police

售票处 **shòupiàochù** ticket office

候车室 **hòuchēshì** waiting room

餐车 **cānchē** dining car

硬席 **yìngxí** hard seat

硬席车 **yìngxíchē** hard seat carriage

硬卧 **yìngwò** hard sleeper

硬卧车 **yìngwòchē** hard sleeper carriage

软席 **ruǎnxí** soft seat

软席车 **ruǎnxíchē** soft seat carriage

软卧 **ruǎnwò** soft sleeper

软卧车 **ruǎnwòchē** soft sleeper carriage

紧急制动闸 **jǐnjí zhìdòngzhá**

emergency brake

乘务员 **chéngwùyuán** train attendant

地铁 **dìtiě** underground, (US) subway

Menu Reader:
Food

Contents

Essential Terms

碟子 **bowl** diézi 〖dyeh-dzur〗
筷子 **chopsticks** kuàizi 〖kwai-dzur〗
杯子 **cup** bēizi 〖bay-dzur〗
甜品 **dessert** tiánpǐn 〖tyen-pin〗
叉 **fork** (for eating) chā 〖chah〗
炒面 **fried noodles** chǎomiàn 〖chow-myen〗
炒饭 **fried rice** chǎofàn 〖chow-fahn〗
玻璃杯 **glass** bōli bēi 〖bor-lee bay〗
刀子 **knife** dāozi 〖dow-dzur〗
菜单儿 **menu** càidānr 〖tsai-dahnr〗
面条 **noodles** miàntiáo 〖myen-tyow〗
盘子 **plate** pánzi 〖pahn-dzur〗
米饭 **rice** mǐfàn 〖mee-fahn〗
汤 **soup** tāng 〖tahng〗
酱油 **soy sauce** jiàngyóu 〖jyahn-gyoh〗
勺子 **spoon** sháozi 〖show-dzur〗
桌子 **table** zhuōzi 〖jwor-dzur〗

劳驾 **excuse me** láojià 〖low-jyah〗
请帮我结帐好吗？ **could I have the bill, please?** qǐng bāng
wǒ jiézhàng, hǎo ma? 〖ching bahng wor jyeh-jahng how mah〗

Basic Foods

黄油 huángyóu [hwahng-yoh]
butter
奶酪 nǎilào [nai-low] cheese
辣椒油 làjiāo yóu [lah-jyow
yoh] chilli oil
辣椒酱 làjiāo jiàng [jyang]
chilli paste
椰子油 yēzi yóu [yur-dzur yoh]
coconut milk
奶油 nǎiyóu [nai-yoh] cream
豆腐干儿 dòufu gānr [doh-foo
gahnr] dried bean curd
大蒜 dàsuàn [dah-swahn]
garlic
黄米 huángmǐ [hwahng-mee]
glutinous millet
豆瓣儿辣酱儿 dòubànr
làjiàngr [doh-bahnr lah-jyengr]
hot soya bean paste
玉米 yùmǐ [yoo-mee] maize
小米 xiáomǐ [hsyah-mee]
millet
蚝油 háoyóu [how-yoh] oyster
sauce
花生油 huāshēng yóu [hwah-
shung yoh] peanut oil
咸菜 xiáncài [hsyen-tsai]
pickles
松花蛋 sōnghuādàn [soong-
hwah-dahn] preserved eggs
菜籽油 càizi yóu [tsai-dzur
yoh] rape oil
大米 dàmǐ [dah-mee] rice

盐 yán [yahn] salt
芝麻油 zhīma yóu [jur-mah
yoh] sesame oil
高粱 gāoliáng [gow-lyang]
sorghum (similar to corn)
豆油 dòuyóu [doh-yoh] soya
bean oil
酱油 jiàngyóu [jyang-yoh] soy
sauce
糖 táng [tahng] sugar
番茄酱 fānqié jiàng [fahn-
chyeh jyang] tomato paste
素鸡 sùjī [soo-jee] 'vegetarian
chicken' (made from soya
beans)
小麦 xiǎomài [hsyow-mai]
wheat
面粉 miànfěn [myen-fun]
wheat flour

Basic Preparation and Cooking Methods

什锦 . . . shíjǐn . . . [shur-jin]
assorted . . .
. . . 丸 . . . wán [wahn] . . . balls
. . . 圆 . . . yuán [yew-ahn] . . .
balls
叉烧 . . . chāshāo . . . [chah-
show] barbecued . . .
煮 . . . zhǔ . . . [joo] boiled . . .
烧 . . . shāo . . . [show]
braised . . .
. . . 块儿 . . . kuàir [kwair] . . .

chunks, pieces

香酥 ... xiāngsū ... [hsyang-soo] crispy deep-fried ...

咖喱 ... gālí ... [gah-lee] curried ...

炸 ... zhá ... [jah] deep-fried ...

... 丁 ... dīng diced ...

家常 ... jiācháng ... [jyah-chahng] home-style ... (plain)

火锅 ... huǒguō ... [hwor-gwor] ... in hot pot, i.e. served with a pot of boiling water in which the meat or fish is cooked, also creating a soup

烤 ... kǎo ... [kow] roasted, baked

... 片儿 ... piànr [pyenr] ... slices

蒸 ... zhēng ... [jung] steamed ...

清蒸 ... qīngzhēng ... [ching-jung] steamed ...

烩 ... huì ... [hway] stewed ...

炒 ... chǎo ... [chow] stir-fried ...

糖醋 ... tángcù ... [tahng-tsoo] sweet and sour ...

三鲜 ... sānxiān ... [sahn-hsyen] 'three-fresh' ... (with three ingredients which vary)

Bean Curd Dishes

麻婆豆腐 mápó dòufu [mah-por doh-foo] bean curd with minced beef in spicy sauce

三鲜豆腐 sānxiān dòufu [sahn-hsyen] 'three-fresh' bean curd (made with three ingredients)

沙锅豆腐 shāguō dòufu [shah-gwor] bean curd served with a pot of boiling water in which the bean curd is cooked, also creating a soup

麻辣豆腐 málà dòufu [mah-lah] bean curd with chilli and wild pepper

虾仁豆腐 xiārén dòufu [hsyah-run] bean curd with shrimps

家常豆腐 jiācháng dòufu [jyah-chahng] home-style bean curd

Beef Dishes

红烧牛肉 hóngshāo niúròu [hoong-show nyoh-roh] beef braised in brown sauce

麻酱牛肉 májiàng niúròu [mah-jyang] beef quick-fried in sesame paste

酱爆牛肉 jiàngbào niúròu

[jyang-bow] beef quick-fried with black bean sauce

葱爆牛肉 cōngbào niúròu [tsoong-bow] beef quick-fried with spring onions

咖喱牛肉 gālí niúròu [gah-lee] curried beef

时菜牛肉片儿 shícài niúròupiànr [shur-tsai nyoh-roh-pyenr] shredded beef with seasonal vegetables

鱼香牛肉 yúxiāng niúròu [yoo-hsyang nyoh-roh] stir-fried beef in hot spicy sauce

笋炒牛肉 súnchǎo niúròu [sun-chow] stir-fried beef with bamboo shoots

麻辣牛肉 málà niúròu [mah-lah] stir-fried beef with chilli and wild pepper

蚝油牛肉 háoyóu niúròu [how-yoh] stir-fried beef with oyster sauce

宫保牛肉 gōngbǎo niúròu [goong-bow] stir-fried beef with peanuts and chilli

茄汁牛肉 qiézhī niúròu [chyeh-jur] stir-fried sliced beef with tomato sauce

Bread, Dumplings etc

葱油饼 cōngyóubǐng [tsoong-yoh-bing] spring onion

pancake

水饺 shuǐjiǎo [shway-jyow] Chinese ravioli

饺子 jiǎozi [jyow-dzur] dumplings

锅贴 guōtiē [gwor-tyeh] fried Chinese ravioli

馄饨 húntun small Chinese ravioli in soup

馒头 mántou [mahn-toh] steamed bread containing various fillings

蒸饺 zhēngjiǎo [jung-jyow] steamed Chinese ravioli

烧卖 shāomài [show-mai] steamed dumplings open at the top

包子 bāozi [bow-dzur] steamed dumplings with various fillings, usually minced pork

花卷儿 huājuǎnr [hwah-jwahnr] steamed rolls

三鲜水饺 sānxiān shuǐjiǎo [sahn-hsyen shoo-jyow] 'three-fresh' Chinese ravioli (pork, shrimps and chives)

面包 miànbāo [myen-bow] white bread

Cold Platters

什锦冷盘儿 shíjǐn lěngpánr [shur-jin lung-pahnr] assorted cold platter

273

海杂拌儿 **hǎi zábànr** 〖hai zah-bahnr〗 seafood cold platter

七彩冷拼盘儿 **qīcǎi lěng pīnpánr** 〖chee-tsai lung pin-pahnr〗 'seven colours' cold platter

Desserts

西瓜盅 **xīgua zhōng** 〖hshee-gwah joong〗 assorted fruit and water melon

什锦水果羹 **shíjǐn shuíguo gēng** 〖shur-jin shway-gwor gung〗 fruit salad

莲子羹 **liánzi gēng** 〖lyen-dzur〗 lotus-seed in syrup

酸奶 **suānnǎi** 〖swahn-nai〗 yoghurt

Fish and Seafood

鲈鱼 **lúyú** 〖loo-yoo〗 bass

螃蟹 **pángxiè** 〖pahng-hsyeh〗 crab

鱼 **yú** 〖yoo〗 fish

鲳鱼 **chāngyú** pomfret

虾 **xiā** 〖hsyah〗 prawns

加级鱼 **jiājí** 〖jyah-jee〗 red snapper

鱿鱼 **yóuyú** 〖yoh-yoo〗 squid

红烧鲤鱼 **hóngshāo lǐyú** 〖hoong-show lee-yoo〗 carp braised in brown sauce

干烧桂鱼 **gānshāo guìyú** 〖gahn-show gway-yoo〗 Chinese perch braised with chilli and black bean sauce

咖喱鱿鱼 **gālí yóuyú** 〖gah-lee yoh-yoo〗 curried squid

茄汁石斑块儿 **qiézhī shíbānkuàir** 〖chyeh-jur shur-bahn-kwair〗 deep-fried grouper with tomato sauce

火锅鱼虾 **huǒguō yúxiā** 〖hwor-gwor yoo-hsyah〗 fish and prawns served with a pot of boiling water in which they are cooked, creating a soup

家常鱼块儿 **jiācháng yúkuàir** 〖jyah-chahng yoo-kwair〗 home-style fish

干烧黄鳝 **gānshāo huángshàn** 〖gahn-show hwahng-shahn〗 paddyfield eel braised with chilli and black bean sauce

时菜虾球 **shícài xiāqiú** 〖shoo-tsai hsyah-chew〗 prawn balls with seasonal vegetables

虾仁干贝 **xiārén gānbèi** 〖hsyah-run gahn-bay〗 scallops with shrimps

葱爆海参 **cōngbào hǎishēn** 〖tsoong-bow hai-shun〗 sea cucumber quick-fried with spring onions

蚝油鲍鱼 **háoyóu bāoyú** 〖how-yoh bow-yoo〗 stir-fried

abalone with oyster sauce

滑溜鱼片儿 **huáliū yúpiànr** [hwah-lyoh yoo-pyenr] stir-fried fish slices with thick sauce

鱼香龙虾 **yúxiāng lóngxiā** [yoo-hsyang loong-hsyah] stir-fried lobster in hot spicy sauce

冬笋炒海参 **dōngsǔn cháo hǎishēn** [doong-sun chow hai-shun] stir-fried sea cucumber with bamboo shoots

糖醋鱼块儿 **tángcù yúkuàir** [tahng-tsoo yoo-kwair] sweet and sour fish

Fruit

苹果 **píngguǒ** [ping-gwor] apple

杏 **xìng** [hsing] apricot

香蕉 **xiāngjiāo** [hsyang-jyow] banana

椰子 **yēzi** [yur-dzur] coconut

海棠果 **hǎitángguǒ** [hai-tahng-gwor] crab apple

枣 **zǎo** [dzow] date

葡萄 **pútao** [poo-tow] grape

广柑 **guǎnggān** [gwahng-gahn] Guangdong orange

哈密瓜 **hāmìguā** [hah-mee-gwah] honeydew melon

龙眼 **lóngyǎn** [loong-yahn] longan (similar to lychee)

荔枝 **lìzhī** [lee-jur] lychee

柑子 **gānzi** [gahn-dzur] orange

桔子 **júzi** [joo-dzur] orange

桃子 **táozi** [tow-dzur] peach

梨 **lí** [lee] pear

柿子 **shìzi** [shur-dzur] persimmon, sharon fruit

菠萝 **bōluó** [bor-lwor] pineapple

李子 **lǐzi** [lee-dzur] plum

石榴 **shíliu** [shur-lyoh] pomegranate

沙田柚 **shātiányòu** [shah-tyen-yoh] pomelo

橘子 **júzi** [joo-dzur] tangerine

蜜桔 **mìjú** [mee-joo] tangerine

西瓜 **xīguā** [hshee-gwah] water melon

Lamb and Mutton Dishes

咖喱羊肉 **gāli yángròu** [gah-lee yahn-roh] curried mutton

烤羊肉串儿 **kǎo yángròuchuànr** [kow yahng-roh-chwahnr] lamb kebabs

涮羊肉 **shuàn yángròu** [shwahn yang-roh] Mongolian lamb served with a pot of boiling water in which the meat is cooked, also creating a soup

红烧羊肉 **hóngshāo yángròu** [hoong-show] mutton braised

in brown sauce

火锅羊肉 **huǒguō yángròu**
[hwor-gwor] mutton served
with a pot of boiling water
in which the meat is
cooked, also creating a
soup

酱爆羊肉 **jiàngbào yángròu**
[jyang-bow] mutton
quick-fried with black
bean sauce

葱爆羊肉 **cōngbào yángròu**
[tsoong-bow] mutton quick-
fried with spring onions

时菜羊肉片儿 **shícài
yángròupiànr** [shur-tsai yang-
roh-pyenr] shredded mutton
with seasonal vegetables

麻辣羊肉 **málà yángròu**
[mah-lah] stir-fried mutton
with chilli and wild pepper

蚝油羊肉 **háoyóu yángròu**
[how-yoh] stir-fried mutton
with oyster sauce

Meats

牛肉 **niúròu** [nyoh-roh] beef
鸡 **jī** [jee] chicken
鸭 **yā** [yah] duck
羊肉 **yángròu** [yahng-roh]
lamb; mutton
肉 **ròu** [roh] meat (usually pork)
猪肉 **zhūròu** [joo-roh] pork

Noodles

炒面 **chǎomiàn** [chow-myen]
fried noodles

鸡丝炒面 **jīsī chǎomiàn** [jee-
sur] fried noodles with
shredded chicken

肉丝炒面 **ròusī chǎomiàn**
[roh-sur] fried noodles with
shredded pork

虾仁炒面 **xiārén chǎomiàn**
[hsyah-run chow-myen] fried
noodles with shrimps

炒米粉 **cháomǐfěn** [chow-mee-
fun] fried rice noodles

面条 **miàntiáo** [myen-tyow]
noodles

Pork Dishes

叉烧肉 **chāshāo ròu** [chah-
show roh] barbecued pork

咖喱肉丸 **gālí ròuwán** [gah-
lee roh-wahn] curried
meatballs

狮子头 **shīzi tóu** [shur-dzur toh]
a large meatball stewed
with cabbage

火锅猪排 **huǒguō zhūpái**
[hwor-gwor joo-pai] pork
chop served with a pot of
boiling water in which the
meat is cooked, also
creating a soup

酱爆三样 **jiàngbào sānyàng**

[jyang-bow sahn-yang] pork,
pig's liver and kidney
quick-fried with black
bean sauce

烤乳猪 **káo rǔzhū** [kow roo-
joo] roast sucking pig

米粉蒸肉 **mǐfěn zhēngròu**
[mee-fun jung-roh] steamed
pork with rice

宫保肉丁 **gōngbǎo ròudīng**
[goong-bow roh-ding] stir-fried
diced pork with peanuts
and chilli

鱼香肉丝 **yúxiāng ròusī** [yoo-
hsyang roh-sur] stir-fried
shredded pork in hot sauce

冬笋肉丝 **dōngsǔn ròusī**
[doong-sun] stir-fried
shredded pork with
bamboo shoots

榨菜炒肉丝 **zhàcài chǎo
ròusī** [jah-tsai chow] stir-fried
shredded pork with pickled
mustard greens

笋炒肉片儿 **súnchǎo
ròupiànr** [sun-chow roh-pyenr]
stir-fried sliced pork with
bamboo shoots

芙蓉肉片儿 **fúróng ròupiànr**
[foo-roong] stir-fried sliced
pork with egg white

青椒炒肉片儿 **qīngjiāo
chǎo ròupiànr** [ching-jyow
chow] stir-fried sliced pork
with green pepper

时菜炒 肉片儿 **shícài chǎo
ròupiànr** [shur-tsai] stir-fried
sliced pork with seasonal
vegetables

滑溜肉片儿 **huáliū ròupiànr**
[hwah-lyoh] stir-fried sliced
pork with thick sauce

回锅肉 **huíguō ròu** [hway-gwor
roh] boiled then stir-fried
pork

Poultry and Poultry Dishes

时 菜扒鸭 **shícài páyā** [shur-
tsai pah-yah] braised duck
with seasonal vegetables

佛跳墙 **fó tiào qiáng** [for tyow
chyang] chicken with duck,
pig's trotters and seafood
stewed in rice wine (literally:
Buddha leaps the wall)

茄汁鸡脯 **qiézhī jīpú** [chyeh-
jur jee-poo] chicken breast
with tomato sauce

咖喱鸡块儿 **gāli jīkuàir** [gah-
lee jee-kwair] curried chicken
pieces

酱爆鸡丁 **jiàngbào jīdīng**
[jyang-bow jee-ding] diced
chicken quick-fried with
black bean sauce

冬笋鸡片儿 **dōngsǔn jīpiànr**
[doong-sun jee-pyenr] chicken
slices with bamboo shoots

冬菇鸡片儿 dōnggū jīpiànr [doong-goo] chicken slices with mushrooms

香酥鸡 xiāngsū jī [hsyang-soo jee] crispy deep-fried whole chicken

香酥鸭 xiāngsū yā [yah] crispy deep-fried whole duck

辣子鸡丁 làzi jīdīng [lah-dzur jee-ding] diced chicken with chilli

麻辣鸡丁 málà jīdīng [mah-lah] diced chicken with chilli and wild pepper

香菇鸭掌 xiānggū yāzhǎng [hsyang-goo yah-jahng] duck's foot with mushroom

茄汁煎软鸭 qiézhī jiān ruǎnyā [chyeh-jur jyen rwahn-yah] fried duck with tomato sauce

家常焖鸡 jiācháng mènjī [jyah-chahng mun-jee] home-style braised chicken

北京烤鸭 Běijīng kǎoyā [bay-jing kow-yah] Peking duck

酱爆鸭片儿菜心 jiàngbào yāpiànr càixīn [jyang-bow yah-pyenr tsai-hsin] sliced duck and green vegetables quick-fried with black bean sauce

葱爆烧鸭片儿 cōngbào shāoyāpiànr [tsoong-bow show-yah-pyenr] sliced duck quick-fried with spring onions

宫保鸡丁 gōngbǎo jīdīng [goong-bow jee-ding] stir-fried diced chicken with peanuts and chilli

怪味儿鸡 guàiwèirjī [gwai-wayr-jee] whole chicken with peanuts and pepper (literally: strange-tasting chicken)

汽锅蒸鸡 qìguō zhēngjī [chee-gwor jung-jee] whole chicken steamed in a pot

红烧全鸭 hóngshāo quányā [hoong-show choo-en-yah] whole duck braised in brown sauce

红烧全鸡 hóngshāo quánjī [choo-en-jee] whole chicken braised in brown sauce

Rice

炒饭 chǎofàn [chow-fahn] fried rice

蛋炒饭 dàn chǎofàn [dahn] fried rice with eggs

鸡丝炒饭 jīsī chǎofàn [jee-sur] fried rice with shredded chicken

肉丝炒饭 ròusī chǎofàn [roh-sur] fried rice with shredded pork

虾仁炒饭 xiārén chǎofàn

[hsyah-run] fried rice with shrimps

米饭 **mǐfàn** [mee-fahn] rice

稀饭 **xīfàn** [hshee-fahn] rice porridge

叉烧包 **chāshāobāo** [chah-show-bow] steamed dumplings with pork filling

Seasonings, Spices

桂皮 **guìpí** [gway-pee] Chinese cinnamon

丁香 **dīngxiāng** [ding-hsyang] cloves

茴香 **huíxiāng** [hway-hsyang] fennel seed

五香面儿 **wǔxiāng miànr** [woo-hsyang myenr] 'five spice' powder

生姜 **shēngjiāng** [shung-jyang] ginger

辣椒 **làjiāo** [lah-jyow] chilli, chilli peppers

辣椒粉 **làjiāo fěn** [fun] chilli powder

胡椒 **hújiāo** [hoo-jyow] pepper

盐 **yán** [yahn] salt

醋 **cù** [tsoo] vinegar

Snacks

豆沙酥饼 **dòushā sūbǐng** [doh-shah soo-bing] baked flaky

cake with sweet bean paste filling

火烧 **huǒshāo** [hwor-show] baked wheaten bun

糖火烧 **táng huǒshāo** [tahng] baked wheaten bun with sugar

油饼 **yóubǐng** [yoh-bing] deep-fried savoury pancake

油炸糕 **yóuzhágāo** [yoh-jah-gow] deep-fried sweet pancake

馅儿饼 **xiànrbǐng** [hsyenr-bing] savoury fritter

烧饼 **shāobǐng** [show-bing] sesame pancake

春卷儿 **chūnjuǎnr** [chun-jwahnr] spring rolls

豆沙包 **dòushābāo** [doh-shah-bow] steamed dumpling with sweet bean paste filling

油条 **yóutiáo** [yoh-tyow] unsweetened doughnut sticks

Soups

开水白菜 **kāishuǐ báicài** [kai-shway bai-tsai] Chinese cabbage in clear soup

酸辣汤 **suān là tāng** [swahn lah tahng] hot and sour soup

汤 **tāng** [tahng] soup

竹笋鲜蘑汤 **zhúsǔn xiānmó**

汤 [joo-sun hsyen-mor] soup with bamboo shoots and mushrooms

西红柿鸡蛋汤 xīhóngshì jīdan tāng [hshee-hoong-shur jee-dahn] soup with eggs and tomato

榨菜肉丝汤 zhàcài ròusī tāng [jah-tsai roh-sur] soup with shredded pork and pickled mustard greens

时菜肉片儿汤 shícài ròupiànr tāng [shur-tsai roh-pyenr] soup with sliced pork and seasonal vegetables

菠菜粉丝汤 bōcài fěnsī tāng [bor-tsai fun-sur] soup with spinach and vermicelli

三鲜汤 sānxiān tāng [sahn-hsyen] 'three-fresh' soup (prawns, meat and a vegetable)

圆汤素烩 yuántāng sùhuì [ywahn-tahng soo-hway] vegetable chowder

Typical Combinations

红烧 . . . hóngshāo . . . [hoong-show] . . . braised in soy sauce

干烧 . . . gānshāo . . . [gahn-show] . . . braised with chilli and black bean sauce

麻酱 . . . jiàngbào . . . [jyang-bow] . . . quick-fried with black bean sauce

葱爆 . . . cōngbào . . . [tsoong-bow] . . . quick-fried with spring onions

鱼香 . . . yúxiāng . . . [yoo-hsyang] stir-fried . . . in hot spicy sauce (literally: fish fragrance; not always with fish)

笋炒 . . . súnchǎo . . . [sun-chow] stir-fried . . . with bamboo shoots

宫保 . . . gōngbǎo . . . [goong-bow] stir-fried . . . with peanuts and chilli

滑溜 . . . huáliū . . . [hwah-lyoh] stir-fried . . . with sauce

冬笋 . . . dōngsǔn . . . [doong-sun] . . . with bamboo shoots

辣子 . . . làzi . . . [lah-dzur] . . . with chilli

麻辣 . . . málà . . . [mah-lah] . . . with chilli and wild pepper

蟹肉 . . . xièròu . . . [hsyeh-roh] . . . with crab

火腿 . . . huótuǐ . . . [hwor-tway] . . . with ham

冬菇 . . . dōnggū . . . [doong-goo] . . . with mushrooms

香菇 . . . xiānggū . . . [hsyang-goo] . . . with mushrooms

蚝油 . . . háoyóu . . . [how-yoh] . . . with oyster sauce

榨菜 . . . zhàcài . . . [jah-tsai] . . . with pickled mustard

greens
时菜 ... shícài ... [shur-tsai] ...
with seasonal vegetables
虾仁 ... xiārén ... [hsyah-run]
... with shrimps
茄汁 ... qiézhī ... [chyeh-jur]
... with tomato sauce
番茄 ... fānqié ... [fahn-chyeh]
... with tomato sauce

Vegetables

茄子 qiézi [chyeh-dzur]
aubergine, eggplant
竹笋 zhúsǔn [joo-sun]
bamboo shoots
豆芽 dòuyá [doh-yah] bean
sprouts
卷心菜 juǎnxīncài [jwahn-hsin-tsai] cabbage
胡萝卜 húluóbo [hoo-lwor-bor]
carrots
白菜 báicài [bai-tsai] Chinese
cabbage
青豆 qīngdòu [ching-doh]
green beans
蘑菇 mógu [mor-goo]
mushrooms
菠菜 bōcài [bor-tsai] spinach
红薯 hóngshǔ [hoong-shoo]
sweet potato
西红柿 xīhóngshì [hshee-hoong-shur] tomato
蔬菜 shūcài [shoo-tsai]
vegetables

Vegetable Dishes

烧茄子 shāo qiézi [show chyeh-dzur] stewed aubergine/eggplant
烧胡萝卜 shāo húluóbo [hoo-lwor-bor] stewed carrot
烧三鲜 shāo sānxiān [sahn-hsyen] stewed 'three-fresh' vegetables
炒玉兰片儿 chǎo yùlánpiànr [chow yoo-lahn-pyenr] stir-fried bamboo shoots
炒豆芽 chǎo dòuyá [doh-yah] stir-fried bean sprouts
炒白菜 chǎo báicài [bai-tsai] stir-fried Chinese cabbage
海米白菜 háimǐ báicài [hai-mee] stir-fried Chinese cabbage with dried shrimps
韭菜炒鸡蛋 jiǔcài chǎo jīdàn [jyoh-tsai-chow jee-dyen] stir-fried chives with eggs
黄瓜炒鸡蛋 huángguā chǎo jīdàn [hwahng-gwah chow jee-dahn] stir-fried cucumber with eggs
鱼香茄子 yúxiāng qiézi [yoo-hsyang chyeh-dzur] stir-fried aubergine in hot spicy sauce
冬笋扁豆 dōngsǔn biǎndòu [doong-sun byen-doh] stir-fried French beans with bamboo shoots

烧二冬 shāo èr dōng [show er doong] stir-fried mushrooms and bamboo shoots with vegetables

鲜蘑豌豆 xiānmó wāndòu [hsyen-mor wahn-doh] stir-fried peas with mushrooms

炒土豆丝 chǎo tǔdòusī [chow too-doh-sur] stir-fried shredded potato

炒萝卜丝 chǎo luóbosī [lwor-bor-sur] stir-fried shredded turnip

菠菜炒鸡蛋 bōcài chǎo jīdàn [bor-tsai — jee-dahn] stir-fried spinach with eggs

西红柿炒鸡蛋 xīhóngshì chǎo jīdàn [hshee-hoong-shur] stir-fried tomato with eggs

Menu Reader:
Reader:
Drink

Contents

Essential Terms

啤酒 beer píjiǔ [pee-jyoh]

瓶子 bottle píngzi [ping-dzur]

咖啡 coffee kāfēi [kah-fay]

杯子 cup bēizi [bay-dzee]

玻璃杯 glass bolibēi [bor-lee-bay]

牛奶 milk niúnǎi [nyoh-nai]

矿泉水儿 mineral water kuàngquánshuǐr [kwahng-choo-en-shwayr]

鲜橘汁 orange juice xiānjúzhī [hsyen-jyew-jur]

米酒 rice wine mǐjiǔ [mee-jyoh]

汽水儿 soft drink qìshuǐr [chee-shwayr]

糖 sugar táng [tahng]

茶 tea chá [chah]

水 water shuǐ [shway]

威士忌 whisky wēishìjì [way-shur-jee]

酒水在外 jiúshuǐ zài wài drinks not included

一杯茶／咖啡 a cup of tea/coffee, please yì bēi chá/kāfēi [bay]

请再来一杯啤酒 another beer, please qǐng zài lái yì bēi píjiǔ [ching dzai lai yee bay pee-jyoh]

（来）一杯茅台酒 a glass of Maotai (lái) yì bēi Máotáijiǔ [yee bay mow-tai-jyoh]

Beer

啤酒 píjiǔ [pee-jyoh] beer
冰镇啤酒 bīngzhèn píjiǔ [bing-jun] iced beer
青岛啤酒 Qīngdǎo píjiǔ [ching-dow] most famous type of Chinese beer

Coffee, Tea etc

红茶 hóngchá [hoong-chah] black tea
菊花茶 júhuāchá [joo-hwah-chah] chrysanthemum tea
咖啡 kāfēi [kah-fay] coffee
绿茶 lǜchá [lyew-chah] green tea
茉莉花茶 mòli huāchá [mor-lee hwah-chah] jasmine tea
乌龙茶 wūlóngchá [woo-loong-chah] oolong tea, famous semi-fermented tea, half green, half black
花茶 huāchá [hwah-chah] scented tea
牛奶咖啡 niúnǎi kāfēi [nyoh-nai kah-fay] white coffee, coffee with milk

Soft Drinks

可口可乐 kékou kělè [kur-koh kur-lur] Coke®
果子汁 guǒzizhī [gwor-dzur-jur] fruit juice
冰水 bīngshuǐ [bing-shway] iced water
崂山可乐 Láoshān kělè [low-shahn kur-lur] Chinese variety of cola made from Laoshan water
柠檬汽水儿 níngméng qìshuǐr [ning-mung chee-shwayr] lemonade
牛奶 niúnǎi [nyoh-nai] milk
矿泉水儿 kuàngquánshuǐr [kwahng-chwahn-shwayr] mineral water
橘子汽水儿 júzi qìshuǐr [joo-dzur chee-shwayr] orangeade
橘子汁 júzizhī [joo-dzur-jee] orange juice
菠萝汁 bōluozhī [bor-lwor-jur] pineapple juice
酸梅汤 suānméitāng [swahn-may-tahng] sweet-sour plum juice

Wine, Spirits etc

白兰地 báilándì [bai-lahn-dee] brandy
香槟酒 xiāngbīnjiǔ [hsyang-bin-jyoh] champagne
白干儿 báigānr [bai-gahnr] clear spirit, distilled from sorghum grain
白酒 báijiǔ [bai-jyoh] clear

spirit, distilled from sorghum grain

法国白兰地 **fǎguó báilándì** [fah-gwor bai-lahn-dee] cognac

干红葡萄酒 **gān hóng pútaojiǔ** [gahn hoong poo-tow-jyow] dry red wine

干白葡萄酒 **gān bái pútaojiǔ** dry white wine

金酒 **jīnjiǔ** [jin-jyoh] gin

果子酒 **guǒzijiǔ** [gwor-dzur-jyoh] liqueur

茅台酒 **Máotáijiǔ** [mow-tai-jyoh] Maotai spirit

红葡萄酒 **hóng pútaojiǔ** [hoong poo-tow-jyoh] red wine

黄酒 **huángjiǔ** [hwahng-jyoh] rice wine

老酒 **láojiǔ** [low-jyoh] rice wine

朗姆酒 **lángmújiǔ** [lahng-moo-jyoh] rum

苏格兰威士忌 **Sūgélán wēishìjì** [soo-gur-lahn] Scotch whisky

汽水儿 **qìshuǐr** [chee-shwayr] soda water

汽酒 **qìjiǔ** [chee-jyoh] sparkling wine

味美思 **wèiměisī** [way-may-sur] vermouth

俄得克酒 **édékèjiǔ** [ur-dur-kur-jyoh] vodka

威士忌 **wēishìjì** [way-shur-jur] whisky

白葡萄酒 **bái pútaojiǔ** [poo-tow-jyoh] white wine

葡萄酒 [poo-tow-jyoh] **pútaojiǔ** wine